Open and Distance Learning in the Developing World

2nd Edition

'... an absolute "must read" not only for those involved or contemplating involvement in open and distance learning but for anyone interested in general change ...'

P. S. Cookson, Choice

'... critical, bold, straightforward, informative, guiding, and facilitating ...'

Santosh Panda, Indira Gandhi National Open University

This extensively revised and updated edition of *Open and Distance Learning in the Developing World* sets distance education in the context of general educational change, and explores its use for basic and nonformal education, schooling, teacher training and higher education.

It provides a comprehensive overview and includes new material on:

- the rise and fall of nonformal education in Latin America and Africa
- new developments in open schooling in Africa and Asia
- crossborder enrolments, fuelled by the rise of e-learning
- recent developments driven by the new technologies, globalisation, funding policies and international agencies.

The book collects together and reviews the evidence on the effects, costs and process of open and distance learning in order to provide a unique, detached and informed appraisal of its strengths and weaknesses. It is aimed at policy makers and practitioners whether they are working in open and distance learning or in education more generally.

Hilary Perraton has worked in international education for more than 30 years. He is now a research associate at the von Hügel Institute, St Edmund's College, Cambridge.

Routledge Studies in Distance Education
Edited by Desmond Keegan and Alan Tait

Open and Distance Learning in the Developing World
2nd Edition

Hilary Perraton

Routledge
Taylor & Francis Group

LONDON AND NEW YORK

First published 2000 by Routledge
This edition published 2007 by Routledge
2 Park Square, Milton Park, Abingdon OX14 4RN

Simultaneously published in the USA and Canada
by Routledge
270 Madison Avenue, New York, NY 10016

*Routledge is an imprint of the Taylor & Francis Group,
an informa business*

Typeset in Sabon by Keyword Group Ltd
Printed and bound in Great Britain by MPG Books Ltd, Bodmin,
Cornwall

British Library Cataloguing in Publication Data
A Catalogue record for this book is available from the British
Library

Library of Congress Cataloging in Publication Data

Perraton, H.D.
Open and distance learning in the developing world / Hilary Perraton.
-- 2nd ed.
p. cm.
Includes bibliographical references and index.
1. Distance education--Developing countries. 2. Open learning--
Developing countries. I. Title.
LC5808.D48P47 2007
371.3′5091724--dc22
2006020720

ISBN10 0-415-39397-3 (hbk)
ISBN10 0-415-39398-1 (pbk)
ISBN10 0-203-96553-1 (ebk)

ISBN13 978-0-415-39397-3 (hbk)
ISBN13 978-0-415-39398-0 (pbk)
ISBN13 978-0-203-96553-5 (ebk)

Contents

PART III
Evaluation   197

Tables

Foreword

In the now distant year 1980, I was greatly stimulated to read one of the most fascinating books on distance learning that I had ever read. Hilary Perraton, author of this important new work, was one of the co-authors. I had been deeply involved in distance learning myself in the planning of the Open University, and two years earlier had become its Chancellor. The idea of carrying distance learning to the third world carried with it a sense of moral as well as organisational challenge. The key word for me as for others was access. *Distance Teaching for the Third World* was less about words, however, or ideas than about experience.

Michael Young, the first person to appreciate the potential of distance learning, was the first of the co-authors in 1980: he had extended internationally the work of the National Extension College which he founded – before the Open University – in 1963. The other two were Tony Dodds, who turned the International Extension College into an active force 'in the field', and Janet Jenkins, its Research and Planning Officer. From the start, great importance was attached to research. Michael Young ensured that. Planning was a necessity.

I had the pleasure of working with Hilary myself in the planning of the Commonwealth of Learning, an imaginative multilateral venture brought into life in Vancouver in 1988. For five years, as its first Chairman from 1988 to 1993, I learnt from my own experience about the problems as well as the opportunities of international educational action. For this reason alone, this new book by Hilary, this time writing alone, is for me, as it will be for all its readers, something more than an exciting, if sometimes frustrating, story.

Open and Distance Learning in the Developing World, a broader term than Commonwealth, is at the same time an analysis and a synthesis of experience or rather experiences, for as it ranges from continent to continent, never leaving out Europe, it charts vision, effort, opposition and sometimes failure, maintaining throughout a sense of shared commitment. The analysis is necessary. The synthesis has never before been forthcoming.

The book speaks for itself. Some readers will turn first to the chapter on technology. As many educational hopes are now placed on the internet as they were in the 1960s on television, so that a cool look from outside the United States at what is actually happening, and could happen in the next twenty years is valuable, indeed indispensable, at the end not of a century but of a millennium. Technology in all its phases of development has always had to be related to economics, as economics, which involves choices, has always had to be related to politics and society. We now also appreciate – and appreciate fully – that culture determines much in the story. It is as a historian, however, a future-orientated historian, that I have turned expectantly to this book, having participated in part of the history myself. I trust that there will be a sequel in the year 2020.

Asa Briggs
Lewes, Bastille Day 1999

Acknowledgments

For the first and second edition my deepest gratitude is, as ever, to Jean Perraton for her support, encouragement, help and advice during the book's repeated gestation, and long before.

Many friends and colleagues have contributed ideas and perceptions that have fed into the book. The list would be too long to record here. For both editions I benefited above all from the work and friendship of colleagues at the International Research Foundation for Open Learning: Honor Carter, Charlotte Creed, Palitha Edirisingha, Alicia Fentiman, Thomas Hülsmann and Reehana Raza.

For the first edition I was also particularly grateful for information, advice, ideas and practical help from Egino Chale, Raj Dhanarajan, Patrick Guiton, Keith Harry, Barbara Kanathigoda, Colin Latchem, Roger Mills, Ros Morpeth, Steve Packer, Jonathan Perraton, Bernadette Robinson, Greville Rumble, Richard Siaciwena, Alan Tait, Thai-quan Lieu, David Warr, Chris Yates and the late Michael Young. It is a pleasure to acknowledge this again.

For the second edition I have debts for further help to many of those named above and to others who include Jon Baggaley, Svava Bjarnason, Diki, Sandhya Kumar, Veronica McKay, Frances Mensah, Kris Murugan, C. Gajendra Naidu, Jan Nitschke, Ibrahim Ouedraogo, Santosh Panda, Geoff Peters, Cyrille Simard, Walter Sukati and Daniel Tau.

I am grateful for permission to reproduce copyright material from the International Extension College, for an account in chapter 2 of rural education in Pakistan, from David Warr's *Distance teaching in the village*, and from the Commonwealth Secretariat for material in chapter 4 from my own *Distance education for teacher training*.

Errors, omissions and opinions remain my responsibility.

1 Introduction: golden goose or ugly duckling

There is the familiar circle to be squared: a poor country cannot afford health and education, but without them it cannot even develop such economic resources as it has.

W. M. Macmillan 1938[1]

Distance education began in 1963. In that year Michael Young and Brian Jackson were establishing the National Extension College as a pilot for an open university; Harold Wilson, soon to become prime minister, was calling for one; UNESCO was planning to use distance education to train refugee Palestinian teachers, and the Ecole Normale Supérieure at St Cloud was beginning to experiment with what came to be called educational technology. The Robbins report on higher education noticed with approval and surprise that the Soviet Union was using correspondence education. A global flurry of activity has followed. The Open University was established in Britain to be followed by over forty more across four continents. Radio campaigns were used for public education in Africa, and open schools set up in Asia. Today, between 5 and 15 per cent of university students in industrialised countries are likely to be studying at a distance; in developing countries the figure is often between 10 and 20 per cent. The pace at which this has happened, and the scale it has now reached, make open and distance learning worth critical analysis. This book attempts that analysis, asking how well open and distance learning responded to the educational needs of the south in the late twentieth century and what are its achievements and prospects, in the twenty-first.

Open and distance learning has grown because of its perceived advantages.

First is its economy: school buildings are not required and teachers and administrators can be responsible for many times more students than they can accommodate in a school. Its second main advantage is its flexibility: people who have got jobs can study in their own time, in their own homes, without being removed from their work for long periods.

Its third advantage is its seven-league boots: it can operate over long distances and cater for widely scattered student bodies.

(Dodds *et al.* 1972: 10)

Responding to this kind of argument, educators in industrialised, developing and transition countries have used open and distance learning to help solve their problems of resources, access, quality and quantity: running education with too little money; opening doors to new groups of students; raising the quality and standard of education; expanding numbers.

Expansion and constraint

Open and distance learning has grown within a more general expansion of education. The world's schools, colleges and universities have grown more rapidly in the last half century than ever before. In 1960, as the European empires were fading away, only one child in four got to school in subsaharan Africa, one in two in Asia, and only just over one in two in Latin America. Today, though millions are still outside school, most children, throughout the world, at least begin at primary school. Some countries of the south are now sending to school and college nearly as many of their children and young people as the industrialised countries of the north; others have reached the levels that were the norm in OECD countries in the 1960s (UNESCO 1993: 30–1). And this huge improvement has been achieved alongside other dramatic social advances. The world has managed to get to 80 per cent immunisation of children and, just in the 1980s, to increase the 'proportion of families with access to safe drinking water from 38 to 66 per cent in South-East Asia, from 66 to 79 per cent in Latin America, and from 32 to 45 per cent in Africa' (Bellamy 1996: 62). Although it has been uneven, and inadequate, there has been progress, in an old-fashioned nineteenth-century sense, which can be measured in terms of the numbers of children and young people in school or college (table 1.1). We can acclaim that progress, noticing the colossal human achievement in filling the educational cup even half-full. But of course it is not the whole story.

The process of educational expansion has been neither smooth nor simple. There was a 'quantitative mismatch between the social demand for education and the means for meeting it' as the developing countries of the world faced an unprecedented set of demands (Coombs 1985: 34). They needed to expand education, in response both to political pressure and to the growing economic and social evidence of its benefits. They were doing so with dependency ratios much less favourable than those that had applied as industrialised countries moved to universal education. (When Britain attained universal primary education in 1880, 36 per cent of the population were below the age of 15; the figure had fallen to 22 per cent when Britain reached universal secondary education in 1947. The comparable figures for subsaharan Africa and south Asia in 1970 were 44 and 45 per cent.) And they were doing so at a time

Table 1.1 World educational expansion

			(figures in millions)	
	1970	*1980*	*1990*	*2000*
Total student numbers				
Developing countries total	404.4	625.5	742.6	967.2
Primary	312.8	449.2	505.9	570.4
Secondary	84.8	159.4	207.9	358.8
Tertiary	7.0	16.9	28.8	38.0
Countries in transition total			78.6	58.3
Primary			29.7	15.0
Secondary			38.2	31.3
Tertiary			10.7	12.0
Industrialised countries total	204.1	231.5	159.3	196.1
Primary	98.6	92.4	61.3	69.5
Secondary	84.5	105.0	68.9	89.6
Tertiary	21.1	34.2	29.1	37.0
Gross enrolment ratio				
Developing countries ratio				
Primary	81.2	94.9	98.9	101
Secondary	22.7	35.3	42.1	55
Tertiary	2.9	5.2	7.1	13
Countries in transition ratio				
Primary			96.5	105
Secondary			91.6	90
Tertiary			36.1	49
Industrialised countries ratio				
Primary	99.2	100.9	102.8	102
Secondary	75.7	89.4	94.5	105
Tertiary	26.1	36.2	48.0	56

Source:*UNESCO Statistical Yearbook* 1999 (1970–80); UNESCO 2000 (1990) UNESCO 2005 (2000, using figures for 2000/1).[2]

when rapid population growth meant that educational systems needed to run in order to stay still. Literacy figures illustrate the conundrum; while the proportion of illiterate people in the world has been falling since the 1960s, it was only some time in the 1980s that the actual number began to drop, to a figure of around 860 million; in three regions of the world – south and west Asia, subsaharan Africa and the Arab states and north Africa – numbers continued to rise through the 1990s (UNESCO 2002a: 61–2).

Ministries of education needed to resolve another paradox as they built more schools and enrolled more children. The shortage of qualified labour for the modern economy, and the need to localise employment in the highly visible public sector, together made the case for expanding secondary and tertiary education a priority. This view fitted with that of the major funding agencies. From its very first loans for education in the 1960s, the World

Bank was prepared to lend for secondary and vocational education (Jones 1992: 75) and in practice, over many years, has also funded higher education (*ibid*: 208). Expansion at these levels also responded to powerful political demands: the children of the urban elites, of those who were making the key educational decisions, were the ones who would suffer if investment in secondary and tertiary education was held back at the expense of primary schools, and especially of rural primary schools. The cost per student at these levels was higher, in some cases dramatically so, than the costs of primary education. At the most extreme, putting one child into university kept sixty out of primary school.[3] And yet the social, political and economic case for expanding primary education remained unassailable.

A series of checks have also constrained the expansion of schooling. In the 1970s one 'was the OPEC oil shock, which sent prices soaring and ended the era of cheap energy and cheap industrialization – and therefore of cheap development. The other was the global food shortage brought about by two disastrous world harvests in 1972 and 1974' (Bellamy 1996: 55). Developing countries found that they could not expand education at the same pace in the 1970s as in the 1960s. Worse was to come. Falling prices for primary products marked the downturn in world economies in the 1980s. Many countries were forced to turn to the World Bank and IMF who negotiated or imposed policies of structural adjustment designed to transform long-term economic prospects. One element of structural adjustment, which fitted well with the views of the new right, was to hold back government expenditure, on education as in other sectors. Public expenditure on education in developing countries, set out in table 1.2, fell from *$230 billion* in 1980 to *$180 billion* in 1985 (in constant 2005 currency);[4] expenditure per inhabitant fell by 30 per cent from *$73* to *$50*.

The effect was at its most severe in subsaharan Africa. Africa's total debt, as a proportion of GNP, soared between 1980 and 1995, so that it surpassed its GNP (*ibid.*); increases in Asia were more modest while indebtedness in Latin America and the Caribbean declined from the early 1980s. Less money meant fewer children in school. In fourteen countries, a smaller proportion

Table 1.2 Estimated world total public expenditure on education 1970–97

(currency: constant 2005 US$)

	1970	1975	1980	1985	1990	1995	1997
Total public expenditure in $ billion							
World	802	1 196	1 340	1 097	1 495	1 713	1 659
Developing country	72	148	233	181	206	261	294
Countries in transition	–	–	145	113	74	47	55
Industrialised country	729	1 047	963	803	1 215	1 406	1 331

Source: UNESCO *Statistical Yearbook 1986* (1970–75); UNESCO 2000(1980–97).

of primary-age children were going to school in 1992 than in 1980 (UNESCO 1995: 130–1). Sadly, a decade later, UNESCO reported that 'net enrolments appear to have either faltered or scarcely increased during the 1990s' (UNESCO 2002a: 47).

While educational progress has been faltering, at least in some parts of the south, it has done so under a new international spotlight. Two world conferences on Education for All, at Jomtien in Thailand in 1990 and Dakar in Senegal in 2000 drew world attention, and in particular the attention of the international funding agencies, to the needs of basic education. At Dakar the world's representatives pledged themselves to achieving gender parity in basic education by 2005 and basic education for all by 2015. During the course of the Dakar conference targets for adult education were added to those for children. The effects of the conferences are more difficult to assess. By 1995 it was clear that the targets agreed in Jomtien would not be achieved although basic education was 'now firmly established as a central objective of education aid by virtually all donors' (Bennell 1997: 27). By 2005 it was clear that the gender target would not be met. While entry to primary school has risen, the 2015 target still looks improbable, especially in south Asia and subsaharan Africa: large numbers of children, more of them girls than boys, remain outside school.

The shortage of resources has not just kept children out of school but has restricted the quality of education for those who do get there.

> Schools in developing countries often lack the most basic resources needed for education such as qualified teachers, facilities and textbooks. Double and triple shifts of a few hours are the norm in some regions; the number of days in the school year has been reduced; and teachers' salaries have declined so much that fully qualified teachers are often a luxury and teacher turnover and attendance are problematic. Even with low salaries, almost all of the school budgets are spent on personnel, so there is little left for school textbooks and other instructional materials – less than $1 in low-income countries at the primary level, versus $52 in industrialized countries
>
> (Levin and Lockheed 1993: 3)

The Dakar conference was, in its turn, warned that,

> the huge efforts and resources being deployed to make quantitative gains have yet to be matched in large parts of the world by equal attention to the quality of teaching, learning, facilities and resources. Many of the reports [from countries at the conference] speak with feeling about very basic requirements which are not being met in some countries and regions within them – South Asia and Sub-Saharan Africa, for example.
>
> (Skilbeck 2000: 56)

Recent accounts of higher education, in many countries of the south, tell a comparable story: of teaching without resources, of libraries without journals, of the desperate pursuit of research without equipment. Quality has inevitably suffered as education has been impoverished.

Numbers tell only part of the story. There has always been a golden age in education, just before the span of memory, when schools were enlightened, standards high, children hardworking, and teachers respected. Aristophanes saw it that way in the fourth century. Comparisons of the quality or of the standards of education across generations and across cultures are notoriously difficult; we cannot accept at face value populist criticisms that education is at fault in England today because children perform badly on mathematical tests of 1911 or in Barbados because coeducation has reduced the significance of cricket in school. (Raising quality is rarely simple: neither spending more money on schools nor improving the pupil:teacher ratio will automatically produce better results [UNESCO 2004: 60–5].) But, despite the difficulties, there is evidence enough that, even where the world is moving towards education for all, its quality is still far short of adequate.

While the assessment of quality is problematic, some measures are available. If education is interesting, affordable, and clearly relevant to children's adult life, then they are likely to stay in school and complete one, two or even three cycles. Measures of school dropout are one proxy for a measure of quality. On the face of it, we can expect schools in Botswana, where 85 per cent of pupils (and 89 per cent of girls) reach the last grade of primary school, to be doing a better job than Mozambique where the figure is only 52 per cent (*ibid*: table 7). Quality depends on teachers and we might therefore seek another indicator of quality by looking at the educational background of the teaching force. Although, as we shall see in chapter 4, it is not quite that simple, there should be some correlation between the training of the teaching force and the quality of education. Again, the figures are disturbing. In India, for example, in 1996 there were 240 000 untrained teachers (out of a total primary-school teaching force of 1.7 million) and the number of untrained and unqualified teachers was increasing (National Steering Committee 1996: 2).

Since 1960 the International Association for the Evaluation of Educational Achievement has been using similar tests to measure children's performance in language, mathematics and science. While international comparisons are crude, and beg questions about resources, language and culture, the one consistent result from the comparisons is that developing countries 'almost invariably come bottom of these "cognitive Olympics"' (UNESCO 1993: 87). In tests on reading by 14-year olds in 1990–1, Finland, Hong Kong, New Zealand and Sweden headed the table with Venezuela, Nigeria, Zimbabwe and Botswana at the foot. The results need to be treated with caution. They are notoriously not comparing like with like; learners in their mother tongue are being compared with learners in a second or third language and UNESCO make the point that they tell us nothing about the efficiency with which schools in developing countries are working, or about the added value of the education they provide. But, for all their limitations, the tests confirm the comparative intellectual poverty of the education offered by many schools of the south.

With more than 25 million teachers, and a billion students in the world, most of them in the developing countries of the south, any summary of educational progress over several decades is inevitably crude. The purpose of summarising is to ground the argument that follows about the role of open and distance learning. At the most general, the quantitative advances mean that, in much of the world, we are in sight of universal primary education and have some chance of attaining universal secondary education. The main exceptions are in subsaharan Africa and south Asia. The expansion of education, particularly at primary-school level, has itself driven a demand for more secondary education, more tertiary education, and more teachers. At the same time, budgetary constraints are holding back the expansion and improvement of education. There remain large numbers of adults who never went to school or dropped out early; their life chances are restricted and their potential contribution to their society and economy may also be reduced. The combination of budgetary restraint and rapid expansion means that much education is of limited quality and so of restricted effectiveness.

The use of distance education

Over the last twenty-five years developing countries have used open and distance learning, where they have, as part of a response to the critical educational problems of numbers, resources and quality. They have done so to offer education outside school, to widen access to schooling and raise its quality, to help train teachers, and to respond to the demand for higher education, usually within national frontiers but sometimes across them.

Educational techniques that do not demand school buildings seem to lend themselves to public or adult education, described in chapter 2. Both ministries and nongovernment organisations have long used mass media for public education about agriculture and health and for literacy and basic education. Radio continues to be used to guide farmers as a regular part of many programmes of agricultural extension. In Latin America, radio schools, with backing from the church, ran adult education classes for rural families for much of the late twentieth century.

Distance education has struggled to find an alternative to schools, with study centres in southern Africa running parallel to regular schools and with open schools being developed in Asia. If the right model could be found, the techniques of open and distance learning might be adapted to the needs of some of the millions who drop out of school, or who dropped out in a previous generation. But distance education has also been used within schools, either with the grand ambition of transforming them or the more modest one of strengthening some parts of their teaching, with television, with radio, and now sometimes with computers. These are the themes of chapter 3.

In the last twenty-five years teachers have received part of their education and training through distance education in every continent. The record is discussed in chapter 4. Distance education's attraction to the planner lies partly in its capacity to reach large numbers without taking them away from the classroom, and partly as a way of raising school quality. For, 'although some researchers, mainly in North America and Europe, have questioned whether teachers really make a difference in students' learning, the puzzle is to explain how the latter is going to be improved without them' (UNESCO 1991: 81).

Higher education always gets the most attention and demands the most resources; the one development in distance education that has caught the headlines is the creation of open universities in thirty or more developing countries. Where the national population makes it difficult to justify the establishment of a dedicated open university, a growing number of universities are introducing or expanding distance-education departments. Chapter 5 discusses these achievements.

Over the last few years changes in technology have encouraged universities to experiment with crossborder enrolment. The African Virtual University was set up as a multinational distance-teaching institution while universities in Europe, Australia and America have sought, with varying degrees of aggression and probity, to recruit off-campus students internationally. This story is in chapter 6.

In the second part of the book, chapters 7 to 10 distinguish between economics, technology, globalisation, and national politics as forces that have been driving these developments.

The promise that open and distance learning could extend educational opportunities at a lower cost than conventional education was a powerful motivator. If it could teach more, and reach more, at lower cost, this was reason enough for the educational planner to try it. Chapter 7 looks at the evidence on costs.

Technology, the theme of chapter 8, has spurred the development of open and distance learning. In the north and south alike there have been waves of projects that have responded to the availability of new technologies at least as much as they have tried to solve major educational problems. Television was once seen as a way of transforming education in the south, even of leapfrogging the north, with the same enthusiasm that the information and communication technologies provoke today. Computer and satellite technologies are both offering new ways of extending the range of education and so providing new opportunities to open and distance learning.

Of course these arguments, about economics and technology, spring from particular educational philosophies, justifying expansion and reform and operating internationally and nationally. Chapter 9 asks how far the rapid diffusion of the idea of open and distance learning can best be explained in terms of global pressures, exerted either through the market or through the deliberate policy of international actors.

National ideologies have also been at play. Ideological justifications for educational change, and so for the use of open and distance learning as a mechanism, can be distinguished from the economic arguments. In comparing the British and Chinese Open Universities, Wei (1997) noticed, for example, that while ideological arguments about access to higher education influenced decisions in Britain, distance education was used in China to expand the trained workforce as the education system recovered from the cultural revolution. Half a world away the University of the West Indies argued for the expansion of its work in distance education as a way of increasing the production of graduates where the region was lagging behind east Asia. All this is the theme of chapter 10.

In the light of this account of the various uses of open and distance learning, and examination of the ways in which economics, changing technologies, globalisation and national policies have shaped it, the final chapter moves from description and analysis to evaluation, attempting to answer questions about its quality and legitimacy.

Expansion and legitimacy

One consequence of the expansion of open and distance learning is that it has acquired a new legitimacy. Correspondence education developed in the nineteenth century but spent the first half of the twentieth at the educational margins, dominated by profit-making colleges, and used as a route to social mobility by the socially and educationally disadvantaged. Of course there were exceptions: land-grant universities ran correspondence programmes from the late nineteenth century and, in Britain, it was a staple of vocational training in the few professions with significant working-class entrants like accountancy and surveying. In the colonial world it was an important route to educational qualifications; discussions of distance education among ministers of education in Africa in the 1970s got a warm response because many of the ministers had done some of their education by correspondence. The Soviet Union used distance education to increase the stock of trained labour in the 1930s. For all the exceptions, it was an area of education that attracted neither government support nor regulation. It had little public esteem: 'she spoke in a strange, little girl's voice, with an accent that suggested she had taken a correspondence course in posh, but had failed to complete the curriculum' (Forbes 1996: 144).

All this has changed. Governments have invested heavily in open and distance learning, and a new academic literature has grown up as a protective thicket around it. The promise, or the glamour, of e-learning has boosted government interest. The main international agencies have generated policy statements: the European Commission in 1991 and UNESCO in 1997 and 2002 (Commission of the European Communities 1991; UNESCO 1997, 2002b). Open and distance learning was specifically referred to in the Maastricht treaty in 1993. The European Commission's policy statement was matched by money: 63 regional open and distance learning projects were funded in 1998 alone within the Socrates programme for educational cooperation. The World Bank and other regional development banks have provided support for distance education. Expenditure on open and distance learning, its volume of academic literature, its appearance in legislation, even the fact that distance-education students today read their Open University texts as they commute where they used to hide them in brown paper wrappers, all are markers of a new legitimacy.

The new legitimacy does not adequately explain why distance education has attracted public support and funding. This book is a third attempt at describing and explaining the process. With colleagues I looked in 1980 at the role distance education might play in responding to some of the educational problems of the south in both formal and nonformal education (Young *et al.* 1980).[5] We argued the case for a parallel, nonformal, curriculum and organisational structure in which Africa might build on the experience of the radio schools of Latin America. And of course we got things wrong. On the grand scale, we did not foresee the intellectual and economic domination of the neo-liberals. On our own patch we did not notice how the large open universities, then just getting under way in Asia, would become the dominant institutions in distance education at least in terms of enrolments. Our general conclusion was upbeat, that radio colleges of the kind we were advocating, had advantages which meant that they could 'offer a different kind of education – not an inadequate copy of traditional schooling but something qualitatively different' (*ibid*: 130). Our argument was buttressed by theory: the multistep theory of human communication argues that we learn most effectively from mass media when, as in the radio college model, we discuss their content with our peers (Rogers with Shoemaker 1971). In practice, while open and distance learning has expanded and changed since then, gaining a legitimacy we might not have expected, its main achievements have been in quite other areas from those for which we argued.

The first edition of this book told the story of the next twenty years; this edition takes things on into the present century – a period in which higher education has continued its dramatic expansion, globalisation has given a new impetus to crossborder enrolment, the theme of a new chapter, and technologies have continued to attract acclaim and criticism. All these are themes of this book. They are set against the counter arguments of the critics of distance education. (There are oddly few of them: perhaps a mark that, despite its claims, open and distance learning remains a much smaller enterprise than the huge human activity of teaching children in schools.)

Effectiveness, efficiency, quality

One line of criticism has questioned the evidence of the effectiveness, efficiency and quality of open and distance learning. Many evaluations have been carried out by researchers closely associated with the projects they were assessing. Their work has suffered from two biases:

> The first is called the 'benefit of the doubt' or BOD aspects of the analy-
> sis which led [researchers] to accept and utilize very deficient data when
> they favor the instructional technology over traditional alternatives ...
> The second bias is that which is reflected in the narrowing of the scope
> of the analysis to those items on the agenda of the sponsoring agency
> while ignoring other effects.
>
> (Carnoy and Levin 1975: 387)

Reflecting their caution, we need, for example, to view with some care the claims of parity between open and conventional universities where we have data on enrolment rates but not on graduation rates.

The evidence that open and distance learning can be effective is reasonably firm, and contrasts with that on efficiency and quality. Ample studies have shown that people studying at a distance and through open learning can pass examinations and gain qualifications that attract formal recognition and public esteem. Teacher trainees, studying at a distance, perform as well in the classroom as those trained more conventionally. Nonformal programmes have achieved results in terms of changes of practice in health and agriculture. Questions remain, however, about efficiency. The easiest measures of efficiency include examination pass rates and successful completion rates, or their inverse, dropout rates. Some forms of distance education are notoriously inefficient; correspondence colleges used to make their money by taking students' money in advance and providing such a poor service that they could spend the minimum on tuition. Profitability depended on inefficiency. Nor can we attribute this inefficiency just to the conflict between educational values and those of the market place: successful completion rates tend to be lower for open and distance learning than for conventional education, where it has been possible to make direct comparisons between them.

In asking questions about the quality of open and distance learning we move on to more difficult ground. If we are to avoid the naturalistic fallacy then we are likely to sympathise with Pirsig's hero:

> Even the name 'Quality', was a kind of definition since it tended to asso-
> ciate mystic reality with certain fixed and limited understandings. Already
> he was in trouble. Was the mystic reality of the universe really more imma-
> nent in the higher-priced cuts of meat in the butcher's shop? These were
> 'Quality' meats, weren't they? Was the butcher using the term incorrectly?
>
> (Pirsig 1991: 131–2)

Nor can we avoid the difficulty by equating 'quality' with 'fitness for purpose': if the purpose of an educational programme is to contain educational demand (as has been asserted of nonformal education) or to prevent students meeting and threatening the state (as was asserted of the Free University of Iran under the Shah) or to educate Christian gentlemen to rule the empire (as was asserted by some English schools when there was an empire), then some educators will be uncomfortable with the equation. Whose fitness, whose purpose? Without seeking to answer those questions at this point, we can rephrase them to ask whether the methods of open and distance learning are inherently at odds with widely accepted educational values. A fuller answer will be attempted in the last chapter after reviewing the evidence for various sectors of education. It is easy enough to argue that open and distance learning lends itself to rote learning, or that it enables people to pass their examinations without following a worthwhile programme of study. But these are not of the essence: there are bound to be low-quality programmes of distance education just as there are poor schools. We need also to ask broader questions about the process and the social and economic consequences of open and distance learning.

The believers and sceptics have chosen higher education as the ground on which to argue their case. Klees drew evidence from higher education in arguing that, 'distance education systems ... have thus usually been seen as giving a second-class inferior education to ... the most disadvantaged' (Klees 1995: 403). From the slightly more restricted standpoint of the large open universities, Daniel reached an upbeat conclusion that, 'these mega-universities are revolutionary in two respects: they have brought down the cost of higher education dramatically and they have made lifelong learning a reality for adults wherever they live and work' (Daniel 1996: 86). The contrast between the two views, especially if we were to generalise from them to the use of open and distance learning at other levels of formal and nonformal education, justifies the analysis that follows.

Definitions

Alongside the alarming growth of literature about open and distance learning there is even a meta-literature about its terminology. (Those who want to follow it can start with Rumble 1989 and Lewis 1990 but should remember Robert Browning's warning against pedantry that, 'There's a great text in Galatians, Once you trip on it entails Twenty-nine distinct damnations, One sure if another fails'.) I proposed in 1982 a definition for distance education as 'an educational process in which a significant proportion of the teaching is conducted by someone removed in space and/or time from the learner' (Perraton 1982: 4) This was good enough for the World Bank, and has been used as the basis of legislation, so I will stick with it. The term 'open learning', with its ambiguities about the meanings of the term 'open' has led some of its protagonists to shy away from defining it, labelling it a philosophy rather than a method, as if that were an excuse for vagueness. Here it is used for 'an organised educational activity, based on the use of teaching materials, in which constraints on study are minimised either in terms of access, or of time and place, pace, methods of study, or any combination of these' (Perraton 1997). The European Commission has adopted the term 'open and distance learning' to cover work that would fall within either of these definitions. Language follows funding and I have generally followed European usage in this chapter. But language also reflects geography and, in much of the developing world, the term 'open learning' is hardly used, perhaps because it suggests openness to entry requirements, seldom a popular idea. 'Distance education' remains the more usual term. In this book therefore, while genuflecting towards the term 'open and distance learning', the term 'distance education' will be used to embrace both distance education and open learning – as defined more narrowly above.

In much the same way I have used the terms 'south' and 'developing countries' and 'third world' almost as synonyms, with no ideological intent, accepting that New Zealand is in the south, that industrialised countries are also developing, and that the destruction of the Berlin wall ended the actual and symbolic division between the first and second worlds. There is a real difficulty, unavoidable in an overview, in bringing together evidence from the whole variety of the south. The linguistic problems matter less. Purists can object. The meaning should be clear.

Part I
Evidence

2 Nonformal education: the light that never shone

Read book, and learn to be rogue as well as white man.

Early nineteenth-century proverb from Sierra Leone

Suppose you have a completely successful scheme of mass education – everybody eating fruit and vegetables as well as carbohydrates, composting and contour ridging, preventing hookworm with shoes and latrines and malaria with mosquito nets and DDT ... with dances and folksong, puppet plays and embroidery and everything that mass educators have ever thought of. I cannot see that this is going to increase the country's wealth at all.

Colonial Office Deputy Educational Adviser 1948

Education is for adults as well as children. In the 1960s and 1970s there was a new enthusiasm for adult education, stimulated by political, economic and religious ideas. Newly independent states wanted an educated electorate. From Ghana in the 1950s to Nicaragua in the 1980s and Namibia in the 1990s reforming governments saw adult education as part of a virtuous circle of political change. There is an apparently obvious economic case for adult education. Programmes of agricultural education and extension, or of health and nutrition, have with good reason been based on the assumption that better education will directly improve people's livelihoods. Nyerere carried the argument further, pressing that, 'we must educate the adults of Tanzania ... we cannot wait until our educated children are grown up before we get economic and social development; it is the task of those who are already full-grown citizens of our country to begin this work' (Nyerere 1973: 137). Liberation theology, too, gave an impetus for adult education. Popular education in Latin America can trace its origins back to Simón Rodríguez, Bolivar's teacher, but gained increased support from the priesthood after Vatican II and the church's commitment to building a new social order of which improved education was part (La Belle 1986: 184).

The euphoria about the potential of nonformal education is captured in a 1968 chapter heading: 'Nonformal education: to catch up, keep up, and get ahead' (Coombs 1968: 138). It, at least temporarily, interested the World Bank which, in the 1970s commissioned a review of nonformal education

(Coombs with Ahmed 1974),[1] seen as possibly offering 'less costly education through nonformal training' and 'alternatives to formal primary education' (Romain and Armstrong 1987: 2). Money, though briefly, followed the words so that, 'of the 92 [World Bank] education projects with nonformal education and training components between 1963 and 1985, 63 were funded between 1973 and 1979' (King 1991: 168).

While much of this work used conventional methods of education, the new support for adult education was linked with an interest in using mass media for education. There were good theoretical reasons for arguing both that education was relevant to the fight against poverty and that the mass media offered weapons to be used for it.

> On the one hand, influential development theorists argued that poor rates of development might be explained, in part, by deficits in knowledge and skills among people in developing countries. On the other hand, it was readily understood that programmes for repairing those deficits with face-to-face instruction were implausible. This led many to argue for using the mass media with their potential for reaching audiences otherwise beyond the reach of government resources ... Enthusiasm for the power of mass media led to the creation of hundreds of mass-media-based projects worldwide during the 1950s, 1960s, and 1970s.
>
> (Hornik 1988: ix–x)

Governments and nongovernment organisations were both at work here. Governments used mass media to set up alternative schools, the theme of chapter 3, and deployed a variety of media, from radio to mobile cinema vans, to buttress their work in agriculture, health, nutrition, family planning and political education, often in support of the work of regular extension services. Some nongovernment organisations, notably the radio schools of Latin America, had broad programmes of adult education, offering something like an equivalence to schooling. Others, like INADES-formation and the African Medical and Research Foundation, had more focused programmes, mainly in agriculture and health. Some examples are set out in table 2.1.

Many of these programmes tried to combine the use of mass media with opportunities for learners to meet as a group. One influential model here was the Canadian farm radio forum, that ran in the 1940s with the motto 'Read, listen, discuss, act'. The Canadian experience was copied initially in India and then in Ghana. It was quoted, too, in planning radio campaigns in Tanzania in the early 1970s. All these approaches respected the multistep theory of human communication (p. 10) in linking radio programmes with opportunities for group learning.

When we reviewed this experience twenty-five years ago we ended on a hopeful note. We concluded that the radio schools had 'both catered for the immediate needs of members of rural societies and gradually made available to them a comprehensive education comparable to that provided in schools'.

Table 2.1 Some mass-media educational programmes

	Programme with broad educational aims	Programmes with narrower aims
Government	Alternative schools Air Correspondence High School, Korea Study centres, Zambia, Telesecundaria, Mexico	Support for extension e.g. Extension aids service, Malawi Farm forums India, Senegal, Zambia Radio campaigns Campaigns for nutrition, political education, agriculture, cooperative movement in Tanzania, Botswana and Zambia
Non-government	Radiophonic schools ACPO Colombia, ACPH Honduras Capability through literacy ABET South Africa	Mass media for health education AMREF East Africa Materials-based education for rural development and agriculture INADES-formation in Africa

Radio campaigns had stimulated self-help latrine building in Tanzania. Farm forums had improved agricultural practice in Mali and marketing in Ghana. Senegal and Botswana had used radio groups to tackle political education (Young *et al.* 1980: 102). And we went on to argue that the record was encouraging enough to suggest that one might 'create a whole system of non-formal education' which would complement the formal' (*ibid*: 103).

But it has not happened like that. There has been less demand for nonformal and out-of-school education than was anticipated, the communication sector has not developed in the way that had been expected, and research findings have not buttressed the claims for adult education.

Where has all the euphoria gone?

In its heyday there was an expectation that nonformal education would respond to public demand for an alternative to the formal system. There were at least two different ideas here. One was curricular: that nonformal education, free from the irrelevant constraints of the school syllabus, could offer a curriculum that was more appropriate for adults, addressing their needs and interests as citizens. The other was that it would be impossible to expand formal schooling in pace with demand, or to reach the most remote children, and a nonformal route to education should be created. Both arguments have since been challenged.

Research, in that most influential of institutions the World Bank, has weakened the curricular argument for an alternative. Jamison and Lau (1982) found, on the basis of thirty-seven studies, that there were correlations between length of education and agricultural productivity: farmers who had been to school grew more. These effects were the result not of a specifically agricultural curriculum, but of regular schooling. The finding is counterintuitive that the much-derided formal curriculum yields benefits even in an area like conventional peasant agriculture (King 1991: 124). Along with findings about the effect of schooling on fertility, and on child health in the next generation, this work gave a new reassurance that economic benefits would flow from entirely conventional, formal, primary education.

Over the years, too, it is formal education that has flourished, attracting support from learners, parents, governments and funding agencies alike. With partial exceptions, considered in the next chapter, formal education has expanded at a pace not far, if at all, short of demand. It seems a workable hypothesis that the expansion of formal education, at a rate faster than had been predicted, has been rapid enough to restrain demand for an alternative.

While formal education has expanded, the early assumptions, that governments would want to mobilise their communication systems in the interest of education and development, began to fall away. UNESCO found, in 1980, that while governments paid lip service to 'the importance of communications for development', this was not 'reflected in assistance to communication projects (MacBride *et al.* 1980: 221). More recently privatisation has made it more difficult or more costly for educators to get access to mass media: the former school broadcasting service in Jamaica, for example, is now a successful production company, priced out of the public education market while out-of-school programmes in Thailand no longer have the access to satellite broadcasting that they could once expect.

The economics of nonformal education did not encourage investment. With the possible exception of Acción Cultural Popular in Colombia, nonformal education does not appear to have been able to provide basic education at a cost that compares with that of primary schooling (Perraton 1984: 170–1).[2] If it was not a cheaper alternative to regular schools, it was difficult to see why governments should invest in something that attracted less public support. Even if the educational and economic arguments for investment in nonformal education had been stronger, they would probably have had little effect, in much of the south, in the 1980s. The effects of the international recession in the 1980s on Latin American economies were worse than that of the 1930s (Kay 1989: 202) and resulted in a shrinking of state activity in education, and of public willingness to take part in adult education. In subsaharan Africa educational expenditure fell from $15.8 billion (*$37.3 billion*) in 1980 to $11.3 billion (*$20.4 billion*) in 1985: in at least two subcontinents there was neither the capacity nor the will to expand nonformal education when formal was struggling to survive.[3]

Politics along with economics has frustrated nonformal education. One of the success stories was that of Acción Cultural Popular (ACPO) in Colombia, founded by a priest in 1947 who worked out a structure for a radiophonic school and set up a radio station, Radio Sutantenza, to support it. Small groups of learners met to learn from radio broadcasts and printed lessons. A national network of monitors and supervisors, backed by the priesthood offered support. By 1972 it had a budget of $4.2 million (*$19.5 million*) and in its heyday was enrolling 230 000 students a year. The radiophonic school model was copied throughout much of Latin America with different schools struggling to provide an education that was relevant and helpful to their *campesino* students while remaining within the bounds of what was politically acceptable. ACPO itself was attacked from the left for lacking ideological fervour and from the right for threatening the status quo (Bernal cited in Fraser and Restrepo-Estrada 1998: 160). While ACPO was more cautious than some radio schools it nevertheless fell foul of both church and state. Tensions between ACPO and the church hierarchy led to a reduction in support from Catholic charities; in due course the ministry of education, too, cut all contractual and financial links. Amid accusations of the misuse of funds, staff numbers were cut, Radio Sutatenza was sold to one of the two most popular commercial networks, and the whole organisation was closed down in 1987 (Fraser and Restrepo-Estrada 1998: 156–60). A model of nonformal education that had looked robust, and had been copied across Latin America and admired even more widely, proved to have an unforeseen fragility.

The result of these varied challenges to the idea of media-based adult education is that there is less to report than we might have expected. Several early models looked promising. Radio farm forums brought together farmers to listen to radio extension broadcasts and discuss their relevance. Many of these have fallen away, though some have continued, surviving on the periphery of the attention of ministries of agriculture. In Zambia, for example, while the number of forums was reported to have declined in the 1970s, a more recent evaluation found that about 1440 were still in existence and found useful by members, with some evidence of their changing their agricultural practice as a result of forum activities (Sibalwa 2000: 120–40). Another early model that looked promising was that of the radio campaign, which mobilised a group of national agencies to run intensive, short-term, educational projects for major developmental ends. The collapse of this model illustrates the way support for nonformal programmes fell away in the 1980s. Tanzania ran four national campaigns, two political, one on health and one on nutrition between 1970 and 1975. A regional campaign on forestry followed soon after; nothing since. Botswana used the same techniques with a campaign to raise awareness of the national development plan in 1973, one on a new policy for cattle on tribally owned land in 1976, and then one on good health practice; nothing since. The Zambian cooperative movement ran a campaign to stimulate interest in the cooperative movement in 1982: nothing since.

And yet the wealth of experience means that we can prescribe as well as describe. In 1988 Hornik concluded, from a review of agricultural and nutrition programmes using communication technology, that, 'most efforts to use communication technology for development do not do what they are meant to' (1988: ix). This was principally not because information was 'no solution for lack of resources' nor that audiences were unresponsive but simply that 'information programs have not worked because they have not been done appropriately' (*ibid*: 155). His prescription was to integrate programmes with the regular work of the relevant ministry, rather than making them a function of a communication service that spans ministries, and argued that:

> In sum, an information service with the most promise depends on a mass medium as its central delivery mechanism, incorporates field agents as passive channels, is linked with a substantive ministry, and spends much of its energy and budget gathering and analyzing information in order to respond systematically to the heterogeneous needs of its audience ... It addresses important targets that justify the expense of slow and intense materials production process and require patience toward the pace of consequential change.
>
> (*ibid*: 163)

But this is a prescription, not a record of recent practice and we seem to have reached a strange position. Nonformal education has been in decline, as has the use of distance-education methods within it, while we have gathered the experience that means we know how to do it better and more effectively.

Of course there is a danger of underestimating the scale and achievements of nonformal education. Its varied and uncoordinated nature means that the work of farm radio and extension services and much health education goes unnoticed in the educational literature or statistics. But, even with that caution, it seems that government-sponsored activity in nonformal education has remained of marginal and probably declining importance. And the extensive literature for education about HIV-AIDS seems to describe individual, one-off, projects that have not generally attempted to build on the earlier experience of combining mass media with local support.

Before writing it off, it is worth looking at a handful of examples that show how, given the opportunity, one might again practise what Hornik and others have taught us how to preach. Universities and nongovernment organisations, with a freedom to act outside the mainstream of national policy, provide four examples from west Africa, Pakistan, Kenya and South Africa that illustrate the past and may guide the future.

The African Institute for Economic and Social Development

INADES-formation (the training arm of the African Institute for Economic and Social Development) was founded by Jesuits in west Africa in 1962 to promote African development. From its original base in Côte d'Ivoire, where its headquarters remain, it has established semi-independent branches in seven other francophone states and in Kenya and Tanzania. One of its major activities has been to provide education for farmers. It does so through a variety of means, including distance education. It also works with farmers' organisations, trains agricultural extension agents and has developed programmes on women's participation in development, soil conservation, water supply and civic education.

Over the years INADES-formation has evolved. Pictures of its staff now have more west Africans and fewer expatriate priests. In 1984 INADES-formation began moving towards programmes of integrated rural development and in 1995 redefined its aims in these terms:

> We want a world in which peasants have a real power through their organisations to:
>
> be an influence for social peace and build up their solidarity;
> contribute to the establishment of a state based on the rule of law;
> have the power to negotiate in order to influence national developmental policies;
> control natural resources and the channels through which agricultural products are marketed;
> increase their autonomy in relation to external agencies;
> be recognised and respected by reason of their status as peasants.
>
> (INADES-formation 1997: 8 [author's translation])

The adoption of this new set of aims, designed to put the peasant at the centre of policy and practice, has led to a movement away from the association's historic concern to raise the capacity of individual farmers – the main focus of its distance-education courses – and towards education to strengthen groups within society. Group activities in areas such as self-management of the water supply in Rwanda, local democracy in Chad, or cashew-nut marketing in Côte d'Ivoire now dominate its annual report.

Since the 1970s INADES-formation has used correspondence lessons and assignments as one of its main ways of teaching, alongside the organisation of seminars for peasant farmers, the production of educational materials, and a continuing programme of research to inform these activities. In Cameroon, for example, its students could follow four cycles of courses, over four years, on general agriculture, the farmer's products, the farmer's trade, and agricultural extension and the rural economy (Jenkins and Perraton 1982: 9). The course material is simply presented and, in contrast to the prescriptive traditions of agricultural extension, seeks to give reasoned explanation for its recommendations, starting from the principle that good science can always be simply explained. Students are recruited by INADES-formation field staff and do written assignments on which they get detailed responses from their tutors. INADES-formation supplements this work with programmes of seminars, generally run over three days and including both discussion and practical work (*ibid*: 15).

The idea of using correspondence courses to teach better farming practice to peasant farmers, often with modest levels of literacy, seems old-fashioned and bizarre, a mismatch between educational technology and audience. And yet, in Cameroon, 'it was quite startling to arrive with INADES-formation staff, in village after village, often miles from a main road and often with no warning, to be met by students coming from their houses carrying their correspondence assignments ready to be marked' (*ibid*: 13). There is some evidence of knowledge gain and changes in behaviour by those who follow courses, and completion rates compare favourably with those of other programmes of out-of-school education (Perraton 1984: 243–6).

Despite a long record of achievement, the future of this correspondence work looks uncertain. By the mid–1990s, influenced by a shift towards cash crops, its students were showing a greater interest in marketing than in agricultural techniques (INADES-formation 1997: 13). Enrolments, as high as 24 244 in 1991, had tended to fall even before the 1995 policy changes; new enrolments fell to 2987 in 1995–6 though later increased again (see table 2.2). By 2004 INADES-formation was devoting decreasing resources to its correspondence courses and was concerned that only 634 people completed their study that year; it recognised the need either to abandon the courses or to find a way of reinvigorating them (INADES-formation 2004: 9).

INADES-formation's influence is limited. In 2004 it had 164 staff spread across ten countries and a total annual budget of 2298 million CFA francs (*$4.48 million*), both figures down on those reported in the mid 1990s. Between them they contacted 58 386 learners with a total of 310 400 participant days, a significant increase in the figure for the previous year (*ibid*: 6). Leaving out of account its multiplier effects, when working with groups or extension agents, INADES-formation's costs per farmer have been higher than those of much extension or adult education, partly because of the relatively small number on its courses. An early study suggested that the cost of following a year's correspondence lessons, and attending three seminars associated with them, was then (1977) US$365 (*$1172*) with a cost per learning hour of $3.17 (*$10.18*). The cost per learning day at a seminar was $59.14 (*$190*)

Table 2.2 Correspondence courses and educational materials at INADES-formation

	1993–4	*1995–6*	*1996–7*	*2004*
New enrolments	5 835	2 987	4 080	4 694
Total correspondence students	15 737	15 698	11 853	n/a
Assignments marked	28 556	20 673	19 946	6 666
Items of educational material produced	132	239	160	n/a

Source: INADES formation 1998: tables 9 and 10; INADES formation 2004: table 8

(Perraton 1984: 247–50). While these figures are high for nonformal education, they compared reasonably well with the cost of farmer training in a residential centre (*ibid*: 250–2). Costs have since fallen: the cost per day per
participant in 1996–7 was estimated at 18 790 CFA francs (*$45*) (INADES-
formation 1998: 7). If the reduction in costs applied across the board, with
the cost for a year's correspondence course falling proportionately, it will have
come down to *$280* at that time and has probably since fallen again. The cost
is still high for an individual but may be justifiable, if somehow it can be paid,
where individuals are able to exercise influence and leverage.

INADES-formation has developed and demonstrated a methodology for
rural education using distance-teaching methods. Its success over more than
a quarter century has shown both that the method is viable and that there
is a demand for it. The weakness of the system is its unsustainable cost, bear-
able because INADES-formation has been drawing at least 80 per cent of
its revenue from funding agencies abroad. The association's current emphasis on working with groups rather than individuals may provide a mechanism for a new generation of courses to be directed to those groups, that
benefit from its experience of an effective teaching system.

The Functional Education Project for Rural Areas in Pakistan

Many of the large open universities have a commitment to rural and adult
education. In Pakistan, the act that established the People's Open University,
later renamed Allama Iqbal Open University, gave it the responsibility of
providing 'facilities to the masses for their educational uplift' (Warr 1992: 2).
From 1982 to 1985 the university ran an experimental rural education project
designed both to explore how the university might meet its nonformal
mandate and to improve the quality of day-to-day life in its project area,
around the village of Dinga midway between Islamabad and Lahore. The
project (FEPRA) worked like this:

> Turning off one alley, through a heavy wooden doorway, you emerge in
> a surprisingly spacious yard, bordered on all sides by high mud-lined
> walls. One end of the yard is occupied by the group leader's house with
> its ornately decorated veranda. The rest of the yard has a clean-swept
> surface of hardened mud. Four buffalo are lying in the shade of a large
> mango tree, chained securely to large wooden pegs hammered into the
> ground, with a pile of freshly gathered fodder nearby. There are healthy
> looking goats tethered in a corner and several hens scratching around
> for a meagre existence.
>
> A semi-circle of *charpoys* (comfortable wooden-framed beds, laced
> with string) has been arranged in front of the house. These are already
> occupied as seats by a gathering group of women ... Most are mothers
> with a babe-in-arms and young children in tow. Those who are unen-
> cumbered in this way are mostly either grandmothers, time-worn but

self-assured and comfortable, or meekly disposed unmarried girls in their mid or late teens.

One by one the latecomers join the circle of seated women and eventually the group leader, who has been patiently waiting, seated on a chair near the centre of the group, announces the start of the meeting. Beside her, on a small table, there is a cassette recorder – its plastic and chrome finish incongruous in this setting. Next to this a flipchart has been carefully set up, supported by its own two stiff cardboard covers, ready for the first page to be displayed.

The group leader is quiet and unassertive, but the group settles down to listen in what appears to be a familiar pattern. The proceedings begin with a short prayer to Allah, the most mighty and the most merciful. Then the group leader explains that today's meeting will be learning about a disease called polio, and she outlines the aims of the meeting. After this brief introduction, she switches on the cassette recorder and the programme about polio, unit two of the course on child care, begins. An announcer explains that though the name may be unfamiliar to the listeners, polio is a very dangerous disease which attacks children, and she invites the group to 'listen to an incident about this disease' ...

After [a dramatic sketch] a narrator takes the listeners through the main symptoms of polio: fever, headache and vomiting, and finally the paralysis and wasting of a limb. As each symptom is discussed, the narrator asked the group leader to turn to the next page of the flipchart so that the appropriate illustration and caption can be seen. ... Twice during the course of the programme the narrator asks the group leader to stop the tape. This gives the learners a chance to talk and think about what they have heard and relate it to their experience. ...

The programme ends with the narrator recapping the main points and bidding the listeners farewell until the next meeting. The group leader switches off the cassette, takes a pile of papers [containing reduced versions of the illustrations and captions from the flipchart] and hands one sheet to each member of the group. ... During a final discussion, one woman declares that she has not heard of this disease before, and the name seems to be new to most of the group. ... Several others agree that it is important to take precautions and they want to know where they can obtain the polio drops. Someone has heard that they were administered by a mobile immunisation team which visited a neighbouring village recently. The group leader agrees to make a note to ask about this.

(Warr 1992: ix–xi)

Pakistan is predominantly poor, rural, and with 51 per cent adult illiteracy. Only one in three women can read, fewer in the countryside. The university worked out a style of teaching, based on extensive field research, that matched village needs. Courses on child care, poultry keeping, electricity in the village, livestock management, and agricultural credit were offered to some eighty-nine groups in forty-nine villages over two annual cycles which were meshed with the agricultural seasons. Each had a similar set of elements. Teaching material was prepared at the university and presented in print, on large-scale illustrated flipcharts, and on audiocassettes. Field workers recruited and trained group leaders in the techniques of group study and supervised their work in the field. At the end of each session the group leader completed a feedback form that provided information for later sessions in the course, for management and for evaluation.

At its maximum the project was reaching about 1500 learners and it was estimated that the same structure could reach about 5000 a year. It had some success in reaching its target audience of people with little formal education: 55 per cent of learners were illiterate and 66 per cent had either not gone to school or progressed no further than lower primary level. 'But the FEPRA courses did not reach the most socially and economically deprived groups ... who make up a significant proportion of the population in the area' (Abbas *et al.* 1985: 19). Despite the project's original intention only 37 of 126 learning groups were for women, in part because of a decision to respond to demand for a popular livestock course addressed to men (Warr 1992: 23). The evaluation of the courses found that there were learning gains among participants and, 'though there was no evidence of a revolution in poultry, livestock or childcare practices in the area, there was much evidence to show that a large number of small changes of practice have taken place as a result of the courses. For example, in one village we were told that nearly 100 per cent of the mothers now take their children for vaccination as a direct result of the child-care course' (Abbas *et al.* 1985: 16). Documented changes included more frequent monitoring of women during pregnancy, increased use of oral rehydration therapy, increased immunisation of children and improved livestock breeding techniques (Dodds and Mayo 1996: 136).

The evidence is consistent in showing that the project succeeded in establishing a viable and effective system for rural education. While it was designed as an experimental project, with external finance for its initial three years of work, some elements of its work have continued since within the university faculty of mass education. It demonstrated that the university could 'act as a resource development centre, as a catalyst and as a testing ground for functional education and communication strategies for rural areas'; all legitimate and near-conventional university functions (*ibid*: 137). But we need to go on and ask a tougher question about the possibility of building a national system of rural education on the basis of the project experience.

To answer that we need to look at structure and at finance. An essential element of the project design was the employment of field workers who recruited learners, trained group leaders, and provided continuing support to the groups. The project organisers concluded that a team of two field workers could support some 5000 learners a year (Warr 1992: 40). It would be unrealistic to argue that the university should itself create a cadre of field workers on the scale needed to reach a significant proportion of the potential adult audience in rural Pakistan, a total of something over 50 million. (And yet, on those figures, a team of 2000 could reach 10 per cent of rural adults each year.) Any expansion of the project's methods would therefore demand the cooperation of the other agencies with field workers, concerned with agriculture, health, credit and rural electrification. In practice this kind of cooperation, in Pakistan as elsewhere, proved difficult to achieve. Formal agreement at senior levels did not trickle down to ensure the involvement of the local staff or relevant departments. But also, 'there were signs that FEPRA's messages, although supported by Nation Building Department head-quarters, actually challenged the working practices of ... district and field staff. This may have been no bad thing in itself, but it suggested also that the University was entering a field where there could be controversy, conflict and opposition' (Abbas *et al.* 1985: 27). Any major expansion of the system of rural education would have depended on a series of strategic alliances unfamiliar to both parties – the university and the nation-building agencies.

Would the cost have been supportable? We lack the information to give one kind of answer that would compare the economic gains from improved health and agriculture with the costs of the rural education that had made them possible. The available figures show that the cost per learner, for a cycle of eight meetings, was about £35 (equivalent to $81 assuming the reported figure was in 1985 currency) and that, if the system were expanded, the cost would fall to £10.15 ($24) (Warr 1992: 22, 41). To put the figure in context, the annual cost of primary schooling in Pakistan in 1985 was about 476 rupees ($57) per student (UNESCO 1994: tables 3.4, 4.3). The figure demonstrates the need for robust arguments based on solid evidence if a case is to be made for expanding nonformal education. But, with that caveat, and assuming the costs could be found, the FEPRA model looks demonstrably successful.

African Medical and Research Foundation

The FEPRA project in Pakistan was aimed directly at rural learners. In contrast it may be possible to apply leverage to their problems by raising the effectiveness of extension workers. This approach has been used, for example, by the African Medical and Research Foundation (AMREF) whose Distance Education Unit provides inservice education for health workers in Kenya. Its administrator tells the story of Jane, trained to examine patients and pass her findings on to a doctor who, on qualifying, was posted to a rural health post where she was the only health worker.

> She remembered that some patients with fever were given antimalarial drugs while others were given antibiotics. She also knew that aspirin and paracetamol were for fever and pain, and that sometimes multi-vitamins were given to weak patients who had little appetite. Now that she was on her own she had to make do with this knowledge. She decided that as she could not differentiate the fever-causing diseases such as malaria

and pneumonia, she would give all these drugs to any patient with fever and one of them would work. In addition she would give cough medicine and anti-diarrhoeal treatment to those with a cough or diarrhoea respectively. This was to be described by a physician and colleague in the department as a 'hit and run' prescription. As a result of this it was no wonder that there was always an acute shortage of drugs as well as a rise in drug resistance problems.

(Nduba 1996: 344)

The distance education unit has developed a programme that uses correspondence lessons, audiocassettes, a weekly radio session called 'Health is life' and organises practical demonstrations to support its other teaching methods. Evaluation has shown that the programme is achieving its aim of updating health workers' knowledge with evidence of increased skills and gains in knowledge (*ibid*: 350). It has grown from a pilot 100 students in 1980, all of them paramedical health staff, and over a twenty-year period enrolled 7991 learners of whom 44 per cent completed the course, 41 per cent were still actively involved and only 15 per cent had dropped out. While AMREF's work is largely funded by donors it has introduced 'cost-sharing measures' with its learners so that they have been asked to pay a nominal charge of Kshs1000 or $15 (*$17.50* assuming this is a 1999 figure) (Mwangi 2000: 53–60). An evaluation of continuing education in Kenya found that the cost per distance-education graduate of the programme in 1996 was KSh8500 (*$185*) (attributing all the costs to the graduates and none to those who dropped out) giving a cost per learning day of about one-sixth of that of face-to-face training seminars (Tenambergen *et al.* 1997: 39). Building on this experience, in 2003 AMREF embarked on a new, larger, project to help upgrade 26 000 nurses with certificate-level qualifications (AMREF 2003: 4). The Uganda ministry of health has used AMREF's experience and materials to run a similar programme which by 1998 had reached 5500 health workers, nearly half of the total number in the country (Bbuye 2000).

The AMREF project, and those based on it, are unusual in using distance education for the inservice education of field workers. Although there is extensive experience of supporting schoolteachers at a distance, far fewer projects have used the same methods for health workers or extension agents. (A small mystery: the three groups face similar problems of isolation, individual responsibility and a need to keep up to date. In many countries they have a similar educational background and get much the same pay.)

Adult Basic Education and Training

On the collapse of apartheid the new government of South Africa set about reforming its education system, narrowing the gaps between its privileged and deprived subsystems, and addressing the needs of the one in five adults who had never been to school. A right to adult basic education was written into the constitution.

Among its educational resources were a tradition and skills in open and distance learning. The University of South Africa (UNISA) had long been a single-mode distance-teaching university (see chapter 5). The South African Committee for Higher Education (SACHED), which operated within the law but against the regime, ran correspondence education and offered support to distance-learning students during the apartheid period. SACHED went out of business in the new South Africa but key members of its staff moved to UNISA and set about changing its practices and its philosophy. One of the products of this change was the establishment in 1995 of an Adult Basic Education and Training Institute at UNISA. Both words, education and training, were seen as important:

> Adult basic *education* refers to the educational base which individuals require to improve their life chances. Adult basic *training* refers to the foundational, income-generating or occupational skills which individuals require for improving their living conditions. Putting the two together, Adult Basic Education and Training (ABET) implies the foundational knowledge, skills, understanding and abilities that are required for improved social and economic life.
>
> (McKay 2004: 110)

The ABET Institute developed a programme relevant to 9 million potential learners who had never been to school or had dropped out of primary school. The institute set up a tiered structure to reach these learners, developing teaching materials, putting in place coordination and monitoring structures, and recruiting volunteer tutors who were then able to run literacy groups. Central to this was a training course for the volunteers or practitioners:

> The ABET Institute sees the practitioner as central to the enhancement of communities and directs its training at practitioners – in many instances nurses, community workers, literacy volunteers, trade unionists and so on – who will be able to teach skills like basic literacy, numeracy or health education but with a *developmental bias*.
>
> (*ibid*: 119)

All practitioners were required to study courses on the social context of their work, project management, and adult learning, in addition to those on teaching literacy and numeracy. Specialist courses on such topics as water and sanitation, computer studies, and business education were available for those who needed them. The ABET institute recruited and trained the practitioners but did not teach the learners directly; its aim was to empower the practitioners so that they could, in turn, empower the learners in the study groups which they were supporting. In a contrast with much distance-teaching practice, where an institution allocates students to a tutor, the ABET courses began with local public meetings in which learners and practitioners agreed the membership of groups among themselves. The institute's director commented that this was far the best, perhaps the only workable, method in a face-to-face society with multiple role relationships among potential learners and tutors (personal communication 22 September 2004). The ABET teaching system depended mainly on print and on group meetings with occasional use of videoconferencing and some use of the internet to introduce learners to the world of computers. Volunteer tutors were paid a modest monthly stipend which was nevertheless 'well received, especially in the most poverty stricken areas. As one of the volunteers points out: "At least when we wake up in the morning we will know what we are going to do on that day and this will help buy food for the family"' (McKay 2004: 133). They were mainly people who had followed the ABET tutors' course but were unemployed.

The programme aimed to make learners literate in their mother tongue and able to read as well as speak in English. There was some evidence of its success both in achieving this and in its broader aims of capacity building. The course included material on income generation and there were reports of groups moving on from learning to practice. All learners attended lessons on HIV-AIDS and the possibility was opening up of using the programme for further work here (*ibid*: 134).

The government established a South African National Literacy Initiative in 2000; it entered into a formal partnership with the institute in 2001, which committed itself to making 75 000 adults literate, a target exceeded within a few months. In the first two years of the partnership it had reached 307 000 learners at a cost of US$59 per learner (*$64* assuming this is a 2002 figure) (*ibid*: 129–32). The figure is relatively modest compared with the cost of primary schooling at $317 (*$343*) per learner (UNESCO 2005: table 11). But, given all the other priorities, South African national funds were not available to support the project at this scale. One of its main supporters since 1995 had been the British Department for International Development which, despite an expectation that funding would continue for at least another year, withdrew its support in 2002.

ABET, like FEPRA in its time, had demonstrated a methodology, brought benefits to its learners, but not solved the problem of finding sustainable finance for a nonformal programme.

Conclusion

The rural world has not been transformed through mass communications in the way that was once a hope, if never a reality. The history of mass-media projects is one of pilots that did not develop, promising beginnings that never became institutionalised, and a rural way of life that still lacks the educational resources that flow more easily to the cities. The communications sector has been moving away from public control and the public interest. With only rare exceptions, structures that link the use of mass media with face-to-face learning have not proved sustainable.

Perhaps there are new technical opportunities that will change all this. Telecentres had been established in at least twenty-one developing countries by 2001 (Latchem and Walker 2001: 4). By making available communication services including the internet, usually on a market basis, they provide an opportunity for improving access to information and potentially for more structured learning. But the evidence so far suggests two grounds for caution. First, they have seldom proved viable: twenty-six out of seventy rural telecentres in South Africa, for example, closed down in response to the problem 'that the community does not see the need for using the internet or the telecentre' (Colle and Roman 2004: 17). Second, there is, as yet, little reported experience of their use for programmes of nonformal education that build on the lessons of theory and practice in linking mediated and social learning. We come back to this in chapter 8.

One conclusion, from programmes with a record of success, is that nonformal education can be strengthened by using distance education to raise the capacity of field staff. Both INADES-formation and AMREF have succeeded in developing relationships with government extension services that enabled them to become accepted and respected trainers of field staff. It may turn out that the most effective use of the mass media is not to run programmes addressed directly to adult learners but to work in concert with the agents of various government extension services. Adult education may belong not in Cinderella's cupboard, housed in an outbuilding of the ministry of education, but in the rural health post or agricultural office.

There may be organisational conclusions too. AMREF and INADES-formation have drawn strength from their status as nongovernment organisations, and not simply because it enabled them to tap into international and charitable funding. In contrast, Allama Iqbal Open University was not able to develop a structural relationship with government that would allow its services to be applied, through other agencies, throughout the country. Articulation, between governments, agencies outside, and universities, remains a challenge but one that has to be resolved where distance education demands field support on the scale that can be offered only by a national extension agency, or broadcast support through a quasi-government broadcaster.

Conclusions about methodology are also clear: the evidence from the field continues to give support to Hornik's view that we know how to use distance-teaching methods within nonformal education. Even with the old-fashioned techniques of print, cassette, flipchart and radio, results have been achieved, in varied settings, for literate and nonliterate people, which confirm that methodology is not the problem. The combination of group study with prepared materials works in practice as predicted in theory.

But we are left with the problem of resources. While INADES-formation and AMREF have been in place for many years and can be seen as institutionalised, both have relied on external funding; FEPRA and the ABET programme could not survive the withdrawal of external funds. Governments have been reluctant themselves to fund out-of-school and nonformal education, partly because of the crippling other demands upon them and partly because they have not been convinced of the case for doing so. And yet the solid evidence of success of just these four examples suggests that, where or when resources are available, distance education can be used to attack problems of rural agriculture, health and capability. It needs to be articulated with other services, perhaps most often with extension agencies. But it would be tragic to write it off because it has generally been used on too small a scale, or for too short a time.

Schools, and schoolchildren, remain a priority. We look next at the record of open and distance learning to support schools, and to offer an alternative to schooling.

3   Schooling: the door is ajar

> What a wise parent would choose for his own children, that a nation, in so far as it is wise, must desire for all its children. Educational equality consists in securing it for them. It is to be achieved in school, as it is achieved in the home, by recognizing that there are diversities of gifts, which require for their development diversities of treatment. Its aim will be to do justice to all, by providing facilities that are at once various in type and equal in quality.
>
> R.H. Tawney 1931

Schooling is mysterious. We have all, those of us who read or write books, been there and done that. We are often critical of school's process and values (my own claimed a naval tradition and was appropriately marred by rum, sodomy and the lash) and sceptical about its outcomes.[1] The research provides reason for our doubts. And yet, even poor schools achieve some results and improve the life chances of their scholars. More schooling brings more pay, reduces infant mortality in the next generation, increases agricultural productivity. Even a short exposure to schooling changes attitudes for life (Inkeles and Smith 1974). Ministers of education have a costly, impossible, portfolio. In developing countries they face conflicting pressures to expand education and to improve it. Distance-teaching methods, of various kinds, have been used in responding to these twin pressures.

Broadcasting for reform

At various times, and in different ways, broadcasting seems to promise a fuller education to the millions outside school or the thousands inside. Between 1965 and 1981 television was used in a dozen developing countries, often with the double aim of expanding education and improving it. The American colony of Samoa was one of the first, where, in the eyes of an impatient new governor,

> there was no time for waiting, no time for 'armchair patience' – there has been too much of that for sixty years, he has been quoted as saying ...

He was turning over in his mind a daring idea: could television be used to share the best teaching, and to spread the use of English over the islands?

(Schramm 1967: 14)

He set out to build a television service, change the curriculum, and transform the island's educational service. In Colombia, with backing from the United States Agency for International Development (USAID) and staff recruited by the Peace Corps, television was used to support primary education for half the school children of the country. In El Salvador, 'AID's showcase ETV project ... not only incorporates educational media into the educational system (at the junior high school level), but is the basis for a far-reaching reform of Salvadorean education' (Carnoy 1976: 8). The French government funded an experimental television project in Niger and, with the World Bank, UNESCO and others, a project in Côte d'Ivoire intended, as in Samoa, to reform curriculum as well as structure. With rather less note and acclaim, Mexico launched a programme called Telesecundaria in 1966 to provide education to those who could not get to regular schools.

These were large and ambitious projects. American investment in television in El Salvador, whose population then was around 4 million and where the project was to serve 40 000 students, was $3.8 million in 1972 currency (*$17.7 million*) (UNESCO 1977: 110–1). The annual cost per classroom was almost 60 per cent of the full salary for a junior-high-school teacher (Carnoy 1976: 41). In Côte d'Ivoire, where the project was reaching 235 000 students by 1975, albeit with the aid of 187 expatriate staff, the planned cost represented almost a 21 per cent increase on the existing costs of primary education (Kaye 1976: 153–6; Carnoy 1976: 47). The projects were also successful: children learned, in some cases more effectively than they had before; new curricula were introduced; the logistical problems of servicing television sets in poor countries with bad roads were overcome. But the projects were always expensive and often unpopular. The expenditure might have been justified had they attracted public support and had the increased costs been balanced by reductions elsewhere. In practice, public disillusion, high costs and teacher opposition stifled them. Teachers in El Salvador went on strike. The Samoan attempt to teach directly by television, and make the worst schools match the best, collapsed into an optional extra for teachers, labelled enrichment. Despite the agencies' heavy financial and moral investment in Côte d'Ivoire, the government closed the television project down in 1981.

The rise and fall of educational television discouraged the aid community.

Anyone who was in the [World] Bank working on education projects in the 1970s will recall the apparently disastrous Ivory Coast educational television experiment. Although evaluation studies showed some positive outcomes, the project has 'sunk without trace' and educators say that never was so much wasted, including Bank funds, on such poor television broadcasts with so little effect.

(Hawkridge 1987: 2)

Scepticism about educational television, with its promise of a quick and technologically exciting way of expanding education, still left ministries in many countries with the continuing problem of numbers. As primary education expanded, so the demand for secondary education became more pressing. Where it was not possible to build, staff and finance secondary schools in pace with the increasing numbers of primary-school leavers, ministries began to look at alternative models of secondary education. The models fall neatly into three continents. In Mexico and Brazil television-based programmes seem to have been quietly successful. India, Indonesia and South Korea among others have set up open schools alongside their open universities. In Africa, Malawi, Zambia and Zimbabwe used study groups as substitutes for secondary schools; Botswana and Namibia came back to the same idea in the late 1990s.

Telesecundaria and Telecurso

The Telesecundaria programme has been running in Mexico for nearly forty years. It provides an alternative form of secondary education, parallel to that of the seventh to ninth grades of regular schools. Students attend classes, usually in premises provided by local communities, and receive some thirty television lessons a week covering the regular secondary curriculum. Coordinators are employed to supervise their work, preparing the ground before each fifteen-minute broadcast and supervising follow-up work. The coordinators, usually one in each grade and covering all subjects, supervise the work of students; 60 per cent of them are qualified as junior-secondary teachers and the others mainly professionals who cannot find work in their own disciplines. They are supplied with a monthly outline of the ground to be covered in the television programmes. The television broadcasts are backed by textbooks provided on loan to students and student learning guides (Calderoni 1998).

Telesecundaria recruited students who could not get to conventional schools and, with the expansion of regular secondary schooling, might have been expected to fade away. But this has not happened. It started with a pilot group of 6500 in 1967, rose to 29 000 by 1971 and by 1998 had some 817 000 students in 13 000 centres, 17.6 per cent of the total junior-secondary school population (Wolff *et al.* 2002: 145).

Telesecundaria is large enough to benefit from television's economies of scale. Early studies showed that its costs compared favourably with those of the regular schools (UNESCO 1977: 128). They have since risen relative to those of conventional schools so that by 1988 costs per student were higher than those of the conventional system, partly because the Telesecundaria centres are in areas with a scattered population so that class sizes are small (Nettleton 1991: 133). Over a period of more than twenty years, however, Telesecundaria's costs have been remarkably consistent, with three reports out of four giving an annual cost per student within the range *$526* to *$703* (see chapter 7 and table 7.2).

Telesecundaria continues to provide an alternative education for the more deprived children. Three-quarters of those who enter at grade seven successfully complete grade nine although the proportion going on to senior-secondary school is lower than the rate for conventional schools; there are fewer senior-secondary schools in the countryside. Telesecundaria is unusual in having become institutionalised as an alternative system of education, operating in parallel with the regular system, and using broadcasting to meet the needs of its scattered, rural, audience.

Brazil has also used television but on a quite different organisational model. The first Telecurso was launched more than twenty years ago with backing from the private Globo television network – the fourth largest in the world – and the Robert Marinho Foundation. Telecurso 2000 was set up through a partnership between these two bodies and the Federation of Industries in the State of São Paolo. The federation's members were so concerned at their workers' low levels of education that they put up US$30 million to produce a television series while Globo gave the equivalent of $60 million of commercial broadcasting time. The programme covers two levels of a streamlined secondary education together with a vocational course in engineering skills. It is aimed at people at work who, following Brazil's tradition of having open examinations, can gain qualifications in this way. Costs were estimated at about $25 per student (*$28* if these are 2000 figures) with a dropout rate perhaps as low as 17.5 per cent, for a student body of 450 000 (Oliveira *et al.* 2003: 141).

The television programmes are backed by textbooks and are used in three ways. Some learners attend *telessalas* where a group meets every day to watch the programmes for about two hours under the guidance of a tutor. Others watch the programme either individually or in small groups and contact a tutor once a week. And some, perhaps as many as 7 million, simply watch the programme and follow the lessons without any formal tutoring (Wolff *et al.* 2002; Guibert 1999).

One recent overview of the Mexico and Brazil experience concluded:

> In mid-size and large countries, television at the secondary level works: it can be used to reach underprivileged groups, either rural children or young adults who have left school. It is likely that the learning ... is equal to or greater than at conventional schools. Costs are lower than the equivalent requirements (e.g., setting up full schools in rural areas or fully operational, four-hour-long 'night schools' in urban areas). The very rigidity of the television format may be to its advantage, especially in the Mexico case, since it requires students and teachers to be punctual and to keep up with the pace of the program.
>
> (Wolff *et al.* 2002: 152)

Open schools

In contrast with Telesecundaria, most distance-education programmes at this level of education are based on print or radio. Faced with problems similar to Mexico's, of meeting the rural demand for secondary education, Asian governments that include India, Indonesia and South Korea have set about creating open schools.

India

India's educational system reflects her national contrasts, embracing class-rooms with no walls and scientific research institutes of international standing. The recent expansion of the system is as dramatic as the contrast; between 1980 and 2002 the gross enrolment ratio in primary schools rose from 83 to 107.5 per cent with the number in school increasing from 74 million to 126 million. Survival rates mean that 61 per cent of pupils are now completing primary school. Secondary education has in turn expanded with the gross enrolment ratio increasing from 30 to 53 per cent over the same period. But these achievements still leave large numbers outside school and a large back-log of children – more girls than boys – and young adults who could not complete their education or never got to secondary school. India's educational history has generated an interest in alternative forms of secondary schooling.

India began to use correspondence education at secondary level in the mid-1960s in four states (Dewal 1994: 11). A bolder initiative came in 1979 when the Central Board of Secondary Education set up an Open School, since twice renamed and now the National Institute of Open Schooling (NIOS).[2] One of the board's main functions was to act as an examining body but, as a national agency, it had the freedom to set up a school that would operate throughout India, with all the logistic complexities this entails. It now not only runs its own examinations and courses, which are available nationally, but is also responsible for supporting the development of open schooling at state level.

The institute's function was 'to provide alternative schooling to those who cannot attend schools. Its mission is to provide education for all and to achieve equity and social justice' (Mukhopadhyay 1995: 94). Most of its students are enrolled in secondary and senior-secondary courses, equivalent to tenth and twelfth grade in conventional schools, and aimed at students with some prior secondary education. Smaller numbers are enrolled in bridge courses, at around grade eight. In 1992 the school introduced vocational courses which may be combined with academic courses. While its examinations are intended to be at the same level, and of the same status, as those of other examining boards, the school has been free to develop a curriculum appropriate for its students. There are no formal entry requirements to the school, though students on senior-secondary courses need to have qualified at junior-second-ary level. Students may accumulate examination passes rather than taking all their subjects at once and can select from a wider choice of courses than are available in many schools. Until 1994 it was working only in English and Hindi, though it has since added Urdu, Marathi, Telugu and Gujrati.

The school's teaching depends on print. All courses are based on self-instructional materials which are developed by teams of writers, mainly from other educational institutions including conventional schools, the National Council for Educational Research and Training and the Indira Gandhi National Open University. There is a limited amount of audiovisual support. The school plans, develops, prints and distributes the materials to students. They are encouraged to do a limited number of assignments, included in their texts, and to attend classes, or 'Personal Contact Programmes', at study centres which are generally within a formal school. These have grown steadily; in 1997 there were about 670 study centres throughout India; between 50 and 70 per cent of students attended a study centre and generally did so for thirty days during their programme of study (Gaba 1997a: 46). By 2004 the number of study centres for academic courses had grown to 1652 (NIOS 2004). Basic figures are in table 3.1.

By 2004 ten states had themselves set up open schools, operating in appropriate state languages and working in a broadly similar way to NIOS. In 2004 the state open schools had a combined enrolment of 277 300, with the Andhra Pradesh Open School the largest institution at 106 300, which compares with academic enrolments at the national school of 318 200 (Mitra 2004: 9).

At the NIOS 54 per cent of students were on secondary courses, 36 per cent on senior-secondary and 10 per cent on vocational courses. A review of enrolments and examination results from 1990 to 1999 found that 42 per cent of students gained their certificates, while others had completed some courses but nor enough for a full certificate, although lower rates, in the range 20 to 33 per cent were quoted later (Sujatha 2002: 116–121; NIOS 2004). For part-time, disadvantaged students these figures compare favourably with those in projects in other parts of the world. One-third of the students were female, a slightly lower proportion than in conventional schools. The school has succeeded in recruiting a higher proportion of students from scheduled castes and scheduled tribes than the formal sector (Sujatha 2002: 85). Most students were from families with an income below the average (Gaba 1997a: 44).

Table 3.1 Enrolments in the open schools of India and Indonesia

	1990	1993	1996	1998–9	2004–5
India National Open School					
Study centres	161	306	671	1 000	2 735
Enrolments	40 884	62 283	93 703	122 726	259 054
Percentage female	36	34	36	32	33
Indonesia SMP Terbuka					
Locations	15	34	956	3 773	n/a
Enrolments	n/a	10 548	172 082	376 620	n/a
Percentage female	n/a	n/a	n/a	n/a	n/a

Source: National Open School 1999; NOS statistics; Sadiman 1994: 93; Sadiman and Rahardjo 1997; Panda and Garg 2003: 108; Jenkins and Sadiman 2000: 211; NIOS 2004:1.

In contrast with regular schools, the National Institute of Open Schooling draws most of its income from student fees and from the sale of books and materials; many government secondary schools are more heavily subsidised and in some Indian states are free. In 1997–8 secondary students paid 800 rupees (*$26*) if they were male and 600 rupees (*$20*) if they were female for five courses. There were reduced fees, of 550 rupees (*$18*), for 'exempted students' who were handicapped, ex-servicemen or from scheduled castes and scheduled tribes (*National Open School Prospectus 1997–8*). Some of the state open schools have followed a different approach: in Andhra Pradesh, for example, state open school courses are free.

The national and state open schools' impact is necessarily small when compared with the 81 million in formal secondary schools. And, while open schools have grown to a total enrolment of nearly 600 000, their expansion has been much more modest than forecast in 1995 when its chairman looked forward to open-school methods being used to reach 40 million students in sixteen languages within ten years (Mukhopadhyay 1995: 104).

Indonesia

Indonesia, too, had ambitious plans to expand its open school system before the economic crisis of the late 1990s.[3] It used its oil revenues to expand primary education so that the gross enrolment ratio rose from 71 per cent in 1960 to 107 per cent in 1980. Meeting the consequent demand for secondary education became a government priority both because of references to educational development in the constitution and because it was seen as necessary to future industrialisation. The expansion of junior-secondary education was, however, constrained by a shortage of qualified teachers, especially in the countryside, and a shortage of school buildings. Alongside the expansion of conventional junior-secondary schools, Indonesia therefore decided in 1984 to expand an open-school system which it had been piloting since 1979. The system needed fewer teachers and made do with more modest buildings. By 1995 the Open School had expanded from a pilot eight schools in five provinces to fifty-nine throughout the country with a total of 17 478 students. A larger number of schools, working on similar lines, had been established by local government so that the total number of students was about 50 000. Expansion then accelerated, stimulated by the formal introduction of universal basic education, which had been decreed in 1994. By 1996–7 there were 172 000 students in 956 locations and plans to increase to 410 500 students in 3270 locations by the end of the decade (Sadiman and Rahardjo 1997: 287).

The Open School's objectives 'are to extend educational opportunities to the disadvantaged, the economically deprived, and those school-age children who are not reached or served by the regular education system' (*ibid*: 10). The students are in practice mainly from poor and rural families in which the children usually have work to do within and for the family. Pupils are not locked into the fixed timetable of the regular school and can avoid daily, sometimes lengthy, journeys to a regular school.

The Open School is part of the formal school system so that students follow the same curriculum and take the same examinations. The main teaching medium is print, with materials being developed centrally and designed to promote individual learning. They are backed by twice-daily radio and television broadcasts. The Indonesian Open School differs from other models in the way it supports and teaches students. Each open-school centre is attached to a regular junior-secondary school. This base school then has the responsibility of appointing a teacher's aide who meets students and marks their assignments. Students are expected to meet for three hours daily, four or five times a week and attend a weekly three-hour session with subject specialists at the base school. Thus they are expected to have fifteen to eighteen hours of supervised study a week, which contrasts with a nominal twenty-seven contact hours in the regular schools. Open-school students can take their problems either to the teacher's aide or to the subject specialist at the weekly session.

Expenditure on the Indonesian open schools is limited to 60 per cent of the cost of regular schools. Some are financed by central and some by local government. A detailed report of the Open School from UNESCO does not tell us about the dropout or graduation rate but notes that between 1981 and 1993 5450 students graduated from the system (Sadiman *et al.* 1995: 60). For those who complete their courses, examination results are good: pass rates of 92 per cent have been achieved in the national junior-secondary examination and there was no significant difference between the academic achievements of open school and regular school graduates (Sadiman 1994: 97, 1995: 155). But the available figures do not enable us to calculate a successful completion rate or cost per student.

An Asian model

Similar approaches have been used in other Asian countries. South Korea, for example, has a system of Air and Correspondence High Schools working on a model similar to that adopted in Indonesia (Lee *et al.* 1982; Kim 1992). The schools had some 35 300 students in 1992 compared with a total of 3.6 million in regular high schools. Fees, at US$65 (*$91*), were about one-sixth of the cost of regular schools. Students worked from textbooks and self-instructional materials and were expected to follow radio lessons early in the morning and late in the evening, five days a week, while they attended the linked secondary school on alternate Sundays, adding up to 1224 study hours a year. Students could earn a living in what was left of their time.

The open-school model is not the only one adopted in Asia: Bangladesh, China and Pakistan have used their open universities to provide education at secondary as well as tertiary level and there is extensive use of correspondence education, offered without the open-school structure. But there are enough common features, in India, Indonesia and Korea, to talk of an Asian model. In all three countries central governments have created a structure that offers an alternative system of secondary education. Governments have justified the system in terms of access and economics. Indonesia sees the open school contributing to the development of the workforce while students in Korea follow their punishing course programme in the hope that a better job will follow a higher qualification. While courses are open to students of any age, most are young people who cannot get into regular secondary school. Within this model, teaching materials are produced centrally while arrangements are made for regular support to students in the field. Both Indonesia and Korea have linked their alternative secondary schools with regular schools in order to provide student support.

The Asian model is grander than some and, where we have examination statistics, the success rates do not look too bad. At the same time, the record so far suggests that it is making only a modest contribution to solving the region's educational problems. The Indonesian Open School has lived up to its name in frankness about the shortage of good managers and the difficulties of making the system work efficiently. India has not expanded its system in the way once hoped for. The most striking contrast is with Latin America. The Asian model has not managed to attract the state or private-sector funding that has gone into parallel alternative schools in Brazil and Mexico. Nor have Indonesia and the south Asian countries made use of broadcasting on a comparable scale – only in part because the linguistics are more complicated. Each open school has tried to offer alternative secondary education at a lower cost than that of conventional schools, an aim that fits awkwardly with claims of social equity. The open schools are offering a form of secondary education to students who would otherwise get none, but one which achieves higher dropout levels and lower examination passes. The most disadvantaged students get least resources.

African approaches

Subsaharan Africa had only 22 per cent of the age group in secondary education in 2002 compared with 44 per cent in south and west Asia. As in Asia, the expansion of primary education has created an unsatisfied demand for junior-secondary education. Malawi, Zambia and Zimbabwe alike set up study centres in which young people could follow correspondence lessons in order to gain secondary-level qualifications.[4] The programmes go back a long way: Malawi created a government correspondence college soon after independence and set up study centres in 1965 as a way of providing secondary education to adults in work. The adults were soon displaced by children for whom there was no room in school. Zimbabwe's study centres were started before independence, in the early 1960s. Zambia set up its system in 1974. Botswana, Lesotho and Swaziland all experimented with the use of distance teaching for similar students; more recently Botswana and Namibia have revived the idea of an alternative route to secondary qualifications.

Most students of these programmes have been primary-school leavers working at junior-certificate level and following the regular school syllabus. Malawi, Zambia and Zimbabwe all used an approach which recognised that these students needed considerable support and combined the use of printed correspondence materials with support from a tutor.

> The basic teaching–learning package is the same in the three countries. On enrollment students receive printed correspondence courses and access to a marking service. They then register in a local study center (called an open secondary class in Zambia) where they meet every day. They are supervised by individuals who are either primary school teachers or reasonably well-educated adults, and they may get the opportunity to listen to radio programs or taped instruction.
>
> (Curran and Murphy 1992: 19)

In all three countries study centres enrolled a significant proportion of students at secondary level. In 1987 14 000 students were enrolled in Malawi, 14 100 in Zambia and 41 000 in Zimbabwe (*ibid.*) (see table 3.2). The Zambia figure amounted to 7.9 per cent of the total enrolment in the final year of primary education at a time when less than 20 per cent of primary-school leavers got into secondary school (Siaciwena 1994: 106). In Malawi there were more enrolments with the Malawi College of Distance Education than in regular secondary schools. Enrolments declined but rose sharply again in the 1990s. In Zambia the number apparently fell because of the increase in private schools and the development of basic schools in which the two junior-secondary grades, eight and nine, were grafted on to primary schools. In Zimbabwe, the annual report of the ministry of education sadly noted in 1994 that, 'Many study group students, particularly those in rural areas, dropped out because of financial constraints. Enrolments in study groups declined, and some groups closed down'. Meanwhile the Zimbabwe Institute for Distance Education, 'was not operational because of financial constraints' (Secretary for Education and Culture 1994: 24).

Table 3.2 Enrolments in study centres in central Africa

	1986	1990	1991	1992	1994
Malawi[a]	14 000	28 220	35 130	35 779	57 481
Zambia[b]	14 100	11 138	n/a	n/a	n/a
Zimbabwe[c]	41 000	26 882	32 289	232 289	23 281

Notes
a. Murphy 1992: 19 for 1987; *Basic education statistics, Malawi, 1995* for remaining years; b. Murphy 1992: 19 for 1987, Siaciwena 1994: 106 for 1990; c. Zimbabwe ministry of education annual reports

That sad note echoes through the accounts of study centres. Shortages of paper, shortages of staff, shortages of vehicles, all hampered their work. The Malawi College of Distance Education estimated that it printed 500 000 fewer booklets than its students needed over a five-year period. While radio programmes were broadcast, few study centres had a working radio. In Zambia the National Correspondence College faced a continuing crisis over the production and distribution of lessons to students (Murphy 1992: 63–4). Despite the difficulties, Malawi has a complicated record of success and failure. The Malawi College of Distance Education moved from achieving poor examination results and high unit costs (in terms of cost per successful student) to one in which it was reporting junior-certificate pass rates of 88 per cent in 1996 and 84 per cent in 1997. These figures were a major contrast with those at school-certificate level where pass rates were only 11 and 9 per cent (Laymaman 1999: 3). Despite the evidence of success, at least at junior-secondary level, by 1999 the Malawi government decided that the study-centre model was outmoded and switched instead to upgrading the groups and turning them into community schools. The college was no longer in a position to supply teaching materials automatically to the centres.

Just as enrolments in study centres, and government support for them, were declining in central Africa, Botswana and Namibia decided to revive the same idea. Botswana had set up a Botswana Extension College in 1973 which was intended to offer alternative secondary courses and a nonformal programme to support agriculture, health and rural development. It was near suffocated when the government followed consultancy advice, absorbed it into the ministry of education as a department of nonformal education, and promptly dropped its nonformal work. In 1998 it escaped and by act of parliament pupated into the parastatal Botswana College of Open and Distance Learning (BOCODOL). Meanwhile Namibia, in its attempt to build a post-apartheid education system, set up a Namibia College of Open Learning (NAMCOL). Both saw out-of-school secondary education as a priority. Both colleges are parastatals and have a new commitment to a solid programme of student support. They also enjoy 'a firm and sure formula for both government subsidies and alternative fund-raising activities' (Dodds 2003: 64) so that students pay only nominal fees (see chapter 9). Table 3.3 shows figures for both colleges.

By 2005 BOCODOL was enrolling 6400 students, about 4 per cent of the numbers in regular secondary schools. They were mainly young adults of between 16 and 25, following junior-certificate courses, equivalent to the first three years of secondary school, and GCE courses, equivalent to years four and five. Botswana already has more girls than boys in secondary education and this trend is even more strongly marked in BOCODOL where two-thirds of the students were female. Following the earlier model students received printed materials and there was some audio support, with a single weekly radio broadcast and tapes distributed to study centres, of which there were some fifty; a further set of eighteen satellite centres were set up, most often in primary schools, in the remoter parts of the country. Early examination

Table 3.3 NAMCOL and BOCODOL: recent data

BOCODOL - 2005		*Male*	*Female*	*Total*
Student nos.				
Junior certificate		523	944	1 467
GCSE		1 264	2 693	3 957
Vocational		645	354	969
total		2 432	3 991	6 393
Examination results	*Candidates*	*Subject entries*	*Grade C and above %*	*Grade G and above %*
JC full certificate	198	1 584	89.4	n/a
GCSE	1 586	4 064	27.3	75.1
NAMCOL-2004		*Male*	*Female*	*Total*
Student nos.				
Junior certificate		4 724	8 584	13 308
GCSE		3 218	7 989	11 207
other		82	93	175
total		8 024	16 666	24 690
Examination results	*Candidates*	*Subject entries*	*Grade C and above %*	*Grade G and above %*
Junior certificate	13 315	29 479	11.7	88.3
GCSE	11 821	24 311	6.7	76.7

Source: Mandevu 2006a and 2006b; NAMCOL 2005.

results were encouraging with junior certificate pass rates, for those completing the course, rising from 49 per cent in 1999 to 89 per cent in 2005. Far more candidates took a limited number of subjects so that they could build up towards a full certificate. At GCE level some 27 per cent of BOCODOL's students were getting grades A to C compared with about 45 per cent of those attending conventional schools (Tau 2005; Mandevu 2006b).

The Namibia College of Open Learning has worked on similar lines (Mensah 2005). About half of its students – more at junior-certificate than at GCE level – were able to attend study centres while the rest studied predominantly at a distance. By 2002 enrolments reached 32 389 but seem now to be levelling out at about 25 000 a year, approaching 20 per cent of the numbers in regular schools; as in Botswana, over two-thirds were female. Its system of student support seems to be holding down dropout rates which were only around 20 per cent in 2004 and 2005 (NAMCOL 2005: 17–18. Both colleges have attracted more solid government support than the earlier central African study centres and have grown rapidly; NAMCOL is now enrolling a significant proportion of the total secondary enrolments. Given the difficulties under which their students were working, examination results stand up reasonably well against those in conventional schools. Both face the challenge of providing something better than correspondence education in thinly populated countries where it is consequently difficult to provide face-to-face support.

The story from central and southern Africa can stand for others: within Africa, Tanzania, Lesotho and Swaziland have also used distance education at secondary level. Mozambique has plans on the same lines. Further afield, Papua New Guinea set up an alternative secondary system, but starved it of resources. Total enrolments with its College of Distance Education were about half the figure for secondary schools. But in 1990, for its 27 780 students it received 3 per cent of the educational budget while the secondary schools got 56 per cent (Guy 1992: 36).

Five years ago it looked almost time to write the study-centre obituary. They were a valiant attempt to offer an inferior form of education, to children with inadequate primary-school results, that was still better than nothing. While they were set up by ministries of education as part of the demand-led expansion of education that followed independence, they were then treated by ministries as a poor relation of the proper schools and regarded as a second best by the public. But the record is not entirely negative and it may be that, with an increased concern for the quality of student support, Botswana and Namibia will demonstrate that the model still has enough merit to survive.

The evidence from three continents is mixed. Mexico and Brazil have developed a large-scale model, which appears to be successful and cost effective, but has not been replicated outside Latin America. While the open schools of India and Indonesia have attracted international attention, they have been running at quite modest levels in relation to the potential demand and have not attracted public or corporate funding on the Latin American lines. Despite the mixed earlier record in subsaharan Africa, there are new attempts in southern Africa to revive a long-established study-centre model At the same time, one consistent part of the common story, from central Africa to Papua New Guinea, is of an attempt to create an alternative that, despite its modest, defensible success, has failed to attract public support or ministry seriousness of purpose. The expectation that the Indian National Institute of Open Schooling should raise most of its income from student fees could be regarded in the same light. Perhaps out of sight is out of mind. The attempt to use distance education to make schooling more widely available, to the invisible children beyond the school gates, has seldom brought them to the focused attention of the education service.

Rediscovering radio

Ministries of education, for good reason, spend most of their time and energy on running schools. They are generally therefore more interested in the possibility of using educational technology to raise quality within school than to extend education beyond it. (Sometimes it is difficult to draw the distinction: television in Côte d'Ivoire was a way of creating new schools as well as transforming old ones.) Two stories need to be told, an old one about radio and a new one about computers.

Even before the collapse of television, the same American scholars who had been developing its use in the south were rediscovering radio (Arnove 1976; Schramm 1977). The United States Agency for International Development (USAID) got interested in using radio to raise the quality of primary education. It contracted with the Institute for Mathematical Studies in the Social Sciences at Stanford to design a way of using radio to teach mathematics. 'The Radio Mathematics Project, in contrast with most AID projects, did not arise from a country's request for assistance. Rather the original contractual agreement between AID and IMSS stipulated that the project find an appropriate site for its work' (Friend *et al.* 1980: 5).

Out of a possible twelve countries, and with a clearer vision of the educational possibilities than of the political future, Nicaragua was chosen in 1974. It offered a single national language, government support, a radio studio and transmitter, an appropriate national mathematics syllabus and competent local staff. Nicaragua was at that time a middle-income country with GNP per capita of US$690 ($2722). The project ran for four years until the Sandinista revolution brought it to a swift end in 1979. But that was not the end of the story: children learned effectively, the costs looked as if they might be sustainable, and the whole thing was properly researched and documented. The United States came away from the revolution with an educational model that seemed to work effectively. The story is important, and the Nicaragua experience worth revisiting, because the model has been replicated in a series of projects under the general name 'Interactive Radio Instruction'.[5]

The project started with the realities:

> In rural areas of Latin America the typical school is a small structure built of concrete blocks. It has three or four self-contained classrooms, each with a single door to the outside. There is no interior hallway. Large window openings provide light and air, but often there is no glass – the openings are covered with wire mesh. Many of the schools in Latin America have no furniture. Classrooms are empty, except for a chalkboard and maybe a broom. There is usually chalk, sometimes provided by the government but more often by the teacher, but other classroom supplies are unlikely to be available .... Children in the city schools seem to be no better provided with furniture than in the rural areas. Often in the morning you can see them walking to school, carrying their own little chairs on their heads.
>
> (Radio Learning Project n.d.: 8)

The project used radio to teach mathematics in the first four grades of primary education, in schools like this. It started with sixteen pilot schools and grew to reach about 10 000 students in five provinces. The project team, with three American and eleven Nicaraguan professional staff in the first year, went through a lengthy process of curriculum and materials development. Curriculum staff developed worksheets and recorded radio programmes which were designed to act as a surrogate teacher. The intention was to use radio for direct teaching, rather than to support and enrich regular classroom practice. The radio lessons differed from conventional educational radio in asking for an oral class response: The radio teacher stated the problem, paused for a response from the whole class, and announced the correct answer, with a typical dialogue:

> Radio teacher: Everyone tell me, how much is five times seven?
> (Pause for response from classroom)
> Radio teacher: Thirty-five. Five times seven is thirty-five
> Notice that after the pause for a response, the next words pronounced by the radio teacher are the exact response expected from the children; there are no intervening words or phrases such as 'Good' or 'Correct' or 'The right answer is…' After that, as further reinforcement, the radio repeats both the exercise and the correct answer.
> (Friend *et al.* 1980: 59)

The project was successful in various ways. Children and teachers liked it. The project gained international recognition, winning the Japan prize for educational radio in 1977. The thorough evaluation built into the system demonstrated unequivocally that the project was more effective in teaching mathematics than conventional classroom methods. It achieved comparable results for boys and girls and, by offering the same quality of teaching throughout the reception area, did something to equalise educational results in the town and the country.

The heavy investment in the development of radio programmes and workbooks meant that the costs per student were relatively high. An early but detailed study of the costs showed that if the project expanded to 50 000 students the cost per student in 1975 currency would be $5.60 ($20.25) and suggested that the unit costs might be held down 'by insuring a long life (ten plus years) for the programs, by implementing the RMP through all or most of Nicaragua and by attempting to use the same programs with only slight revision for Spanish-speaking students elsewhere in Latin America or within the United States' (Jamison *et al.* 1978: 136).

USAID was sufficiently impressed by the model developed in Nicaragua that it went on to adapt it to other countries and other subjects. Radio was used to teach English in Kenya, Lesotho and post-apartheid South Africa, science in Papua New Guinea, and mathematics again in Bolivia, Ecuador, Guatemala and Honduras. Projects were set up to teach Spanish in a number of Latin American countries and to support environmental education in Costa Rica. Some of the experience is summarised in table 3.4.

The first move was to Kenya where the ministry of education agreed to work with USAID in order to raise the quality of English teaching in the first three years of primary education. While the methodology was similar to that developed in Nicaragua, it had to be adapted to a different subject in a different continent. The programme designers introduced three innovations – a range of radio characters, the use of songs and games to engage the pupils, and a fuller role for the classroom teachers (Moulton 1994: 16).

Other adaptations of the model followed as it moved across the continents. Recently it has been used for out-of-school education in Zambia in an ambitious project, 'Learning at Taonga market', to cover the first five grades of basic education. Communities were expected to find accommodation and pupils were guided by a mentor, usually someone who had completed secondary education. The project grew from 1254 learners in 2000 to 38 913 in 2004, studying in 647 centres while the team produced a record number of 1360 individual radio programmes. The project seems to have overcome some of the logistical problems of working outside the formal school structure, though not all: one survey found that one in four centres did not have a working radio (Education Development Center 2004: 49). But it was succeeding in reaching some of the more deprived children, including AIDS orphans, and making some progress both in terms of learning and of providing a route, for some, into regular schools.

Over the course of twenty years, the series of interactive projects have developed a standard methodology and a consistent pattern of achievement. The method is based on three principles. First, lessons are designed to teach a core curriculum and do so intensively, often with a half-hour lesson every day. Second, the lessons are designed on clearly articulated educational principles, sometimes, especially in the early projects, expressed in firm behavioural terms. Third, formative evaluation is built in and quality regularly monitored (Tilson 1991: 294). Each project went through a similar process of audience research, curriculum development and scriptwriting, and piloting of materials before full-scale broadcasting. Start-up costs were therefore high.

There is consistent evidence of the effectiveness of the radio projects: children learned what they were supposed to. Studies in Bolivia, Nicaragua and Thailand for mathematics, in Papua New Guinea for science, in South Africa for English and in Honduras for Spanish showed that radio students performed better than a control group on post-test scores (Bosch 1997: 4). Evaluations have often shown larger gains in achievement than other educational innovations with gains in standard deviation units from 0.24 for English in Kenya to 0.91 for mathematics in Bolivia (Klees 1995: 400). Radio confirmed its capacity to narrow the gap in achievement between town and country and between girls and boys (Bosch 1997: 3).

The evidence on cost is also consistent; some figures are shown in table 3.4. Using a standard methodology, and taking a social discount rate of 7.5 per cent,

Table 3.4 Interactive radio instruction[a]

Country and project	Dates	Subject, level, quantity	Scale	No. of students	Cost	Comment
Nicaragua Radio mathematics project	1974–79	Mathematics in first 4 primary grades	Half-hour daily broadcasts	10 000 maximum[b]	Average cost 1975$5.60 @ 50 000 students[c] ($20.25)	Closed as result of revolution
Thailand Radio mathematics	1980–at least 1984	Mathematics in first 3 primary grades	Half-hour daily broadcasts	n/a	n/a	Adaptation of Nicaragua materials, undertaken mainly by Thai staff
Kenya Radio language arts	1980–85	English language in first 3 primary grades	Half-hour daily broadcasts	n/a	n/a	Project closed when USAID funding ended
Dominican Republic RADECO	1982–at least 1989	Reading and mathematics for first 3 primary grades	One-hour daily broadcasts	57 schools, 80 classrooms by 1989[d]	n/a	Project run for nonformal group, with auxiliary, on radiophonic school model
Papua New Guinea Radio science	1987–at least 1994	Science for primary grades 4, 5, 6	60 20-minute lessons for each grade	9 000 in 1990 40 000 in 1992 75 000 in 1994[e]	n/a	Project survived USAID cuts 1989 and funding withdrawal 1990
Lesotho English in action	1987–90	English for primary grade 1–3	n/a	200 900 in 1990 (80 500 in standard one, 63 400 in s two, 57 000 in s three)	1990$1.34 per student[f] ($1.99)	Materials adapted from Kenya and became part of regular curriculum. Reported to be still operating 1997[g]

Continued

Honduras Radio learning project	1987–	Maths primary grades 1–3 English, Spanish	465 lessons produced	100 000 grade 1, 50 000 grade 2, 30 000 grade 3 in maths 1990[h]	1990 $2.94 per student @200 000 enrolment[i] ($4.38)	Run in partnership with commercial publisher. Not institutionalised[g]
Bolivia Radio mathematics Radio health Early childhood development	1986– 1992– 1994–	Mathematics: primary grades 2–5 Health Child development for carers	Daily Weekly	250 000 enrolled in 1994[j]	1990 $2.80 per student @ enrolment of 70 000, falling to $1.28 @ 300 000[k] ($4.16 to $1.91)	Run in association with church-based NGO
Ecuador	1988–91	Mathematics	n/a	300	n/a	Pilot in 21 schools, completed by 1991[l]
Guatemala, Costa Rica, El Salvador, Dominican Republic	1988–92	Maths, Spanish	n/a	n/a	n/a	Adaptation of Honduras material Costa Rica closed down; El Salvador continued
Costa Rica Radio Environmental Education	1991–	Environmental education for primary grades 4 and 5	n/a	36 000 students in 1200 schools 1991[l]	n/a	2 pilot schemes run but not then implemented
South Africa English in Action	1992–	English language, primary grades 1–3	428 30-minute daily broadcasts and cassettes	15 200 grade 1, 9 600 grade 2 in 1995 680 000 in 2001	Cost in range 1994 Rand 3.13–8.16 per student[m] ($1.16–$3.07) cost about $3.00 ($3.09 in 2004)[n]	Project originally criticised for behaviourist approach but then remodelled and continued with NORAD and DfID funding. Faced financial difficulties after end of DfID funding

Table 3.4 Interactive radio instruction—cont'd

Country and project	Dates	Subject, level, quantity	Scale	No. of students	Cost	Comment
Lusophone Africa	1992–	Maths grades 3–4	n/a	n/a	n/a	Developed in Cape Verde for use also in Angola, Mozambique, S Tome[g]
Venezuela	1996–	Maths	275 30-minute lessons	300 000 students in 12 000 classes	n/a	Funded with World Bank loan with some recurrent funds from state budgets[o]
Zambia	2000–	Literacy, maths, science and social science, life skills including HIV-AIDS - grades 1–5	1 360 lessons	38 513 students in 647 centres	n/a	Significant external funding. Still operating in 2004[p]

Notes
a. Other projects, with less detail, are referred to in Bosch 1997 and Dock and Helwig 1999; b: Friend *et al.* 1980: 30; c. Jamison *et al.* 1978: 136; d. Radio Learning Project n.d.: 43; e. Olsson 1994: 16; f. Tilson 1991: 337 but including direct costs omitted form his figure; g. Bosch 1997: 9–10; h. Radio Learning Project n.d : 48; i. Tilson 1991: 326; j. Fryer 1995: 20; k. Tilson 1991: 307–8; l. Anzalone 1991: 48; m. Cobbe 1995 : 21; n. Potter 2006; o. Helwig *et al.* 1999: 24–5; p. Education Development Center 2004: 8.

the cost per student per annum has fallen within the range, in 2005 currency, of about *$1* to *$5*. The figures are more likely to be under than over-estimated as some are based on assumptions about expansion and about a long shelf-life for teaching materials (Klees 1995: 401). While the costs sound modest, they send a warning. With the exception of a community-based project in the Dominican Republic, these were incremental costs, generally for a single subject. To put them in context, expenditure per student at primary level in the mid-1980s was 736 shillings (*$81*) in Kenya, 146 lempira (*$174*) in Honduras and 38 maloti (*$49*) in Lesotho.[6] While radio broadcasts alone allow dramatic economies of scale, these do not apply to workbooks or to staff training.

The cost of expansion may be the main reason why many interactive radio projects have not gone beyond a pilot phase. 'Since around 1975 the United States Agency for International Development has invested more than US$50 million to test and market IRI globally. Yet of the fourteen IRI projects initiated, only two have expanded nationwide, in Honduras and Lesotho' (*ibid.*). In many cases ministries of education did not feel able to continue to support the costs of interactive radio beyond the pilot phase. In Kenya, for example, the project closed down as the USAID team left the country.

One major criticism of interactive radio is, therefore, that it has not demonstrated that it can be sustained, despite its established educational success. Another, fundamental, criticism is illustrated by the attempt to adapt instructional radio to post-apartheid South Africa.

Interactive radio started in a firmly behaviourist tradition. In Nicaragua the team identified as their first task, 'to read between the lines to determine the intent of the syllabus and to transform it into a set of clearly stated behavioural objectives' (Friend *et al.* 1980: 64). The American team 'thought of the South Africa Radio Learning Project as a fairly straightforward adaptation' of existing approaches and materials (Leigh 1995: 9). The South African reaction was different. Plans for interactive radio were seen as dangerously close to fundamental pedagogics, the theoretical foundation of apartheid education, and built on assumptions of authoritarian, teacher-centred methods. The project, and the materials, were redesigned in an attempt to reconcile constructivist principles with a radio-based style of direct teaching. Pilots were run to teach both English and mathematics, reaching a total of about 35 000 students in 600 classrooms. Since then it has expanded, with a huge increase from 41 000 students in 1996 to 227 000 in 1997 and 680 000 in 2001. In 2004 annual costs were about $3.00 (*$3.09*) per student. By demonstrating a different, livelier and more imaginative, kind of teaching the project was making classrooms more fun and contributing to the inservice training of teachers (Potter 2006; Potter and Naidoo 2006). The combination of South African localisation, and external funding from, in turn, America, Norway and Britain, moved it closer to institutionalisation than most similar projects, although not to a point at which the government was willing to meet its cost. But there was a sting in the tail. A British review of its aid priorities cut DfID funding to South Africa so that the Open Learning Systems Educational Trust, which was running the project, had to set out once again with a begging bowl.

Since the collapse of educational television, interactive radio is the only well-documented example of a coherent set of comparable projects using communication technology to raise the quality of education. If open and distance learning has a role to play in the classroom, as well as outside, then there should be lessons that we can draw from it. But it is difficult to do so. Klees has noted that it has attracted little critical analysis and that most of the evaluations have been undertaken in-house (1995: 401). And there is a contrast between its demonstrated results and its failure to expand to the scale where it will raise national standards and, benefiting from the economics of radio, bring down its unit costs. One clear lesson, broadcast alike by radio and television, is about the danger of assuming that technology can transform education easily or cheaply.

Computers in the classroom

Rhetoric about the use of computers in third-world classrooms is reminiscent of that about television a generation ago. Computers have been introduced into schools for a variety of reasons. Some early projects were designed to teach part of the curriculum with computer-based learning replacing ordinary classroom teaching. Achievements were limited and costs high. Then some projects were intended to provide a supply of secondary-school leavers with familiarity with computers or skill in using them. The CLASS project in India was launched in 1984 because of a national concern that India should be producing its own computer specialists (Sharma and Singh 1996: 256). It 'failed miserably due to problems of maintenance, electricity and lack of useful content' (Mishra 2004: 100). A project in Costa Rica was unusual in seeing computers, and in particular the computer language Logo, as central to a programme of curriculum development; its aim was to bring constructivist ideas into the curriculum generally rather than to develop computer skills (Alvarez *et al.* 1998). More recently emphasis has shifted towards the use of computers for communication, enabling teachers and children to seek materials on the internet and use computer technology to communicate with other schools.

Often the aims are mixed, or blurred. In Chile, for example, an educational reform programme was launched in 1991 to raise the quality of primary and secondary schools. It included curriculum development, teacher training and more textbooks, closer links between school and work, and measures to strengthen management: the usual mixture. As part of the reform a computer network, *Enlaces*, was set up and arrangements made to put computers into 100 primary schools and, by 2000 into all 1700 secondary schools (see also chapter 4). In contrast with earlier projects' emphasis on computer-aided learning and computer familiarity, its main goals were 'to provide teachers and students access to new and improved instructional content and methods, increased information resources for research and analysis, and improved communication for collaboration and dissemination of ideas' (Potashnik 1996: 4). A more recent project in Egypt aims not only to reach 23 000 students in 14 schools which are being provided with equipment and teacher training but also to create a databank of 6000 lessons covering the whole of the curriculum (USAID 2006).

A variety of consortia have helped schools enter this world; 'schoolnets' of this kind are organisations that encourage the use of information and communication technologies in education, promote cooperation, and may supply hardware, software and training (Naidoo 2004: 4). While there are pilot projects everywhere, the actual use of computers varies widely within and between countries. Malaysia has 90 smart schools with computers in at least 15 classrooms per school, designed to improve teaching, assessment and management, and plans for all schools to become smart by 2010 (Belawati 2004: 109); at the other extreme in 2004 only 20 of Mozambique's 7000 schools had computers (Isaacs 2004: 12). Computers, complete with electricity supply and internet connection, tend to be in urban schools, along with the children of the elite. Evidence on effects is scarce. There is rich-country evidence to show that the use of computers can help learning but hardly any that compares their effects with putting extra resources of a different kinds into the classroom.

Evidence on costs is examined in more detail in chapter 7. It offers two warnings. First, computer technologies are unusual 'when compared to other educational inputs: they are not linked to a national price structure, but quite the opposite, they tend to be similar worldwide for equipment, software, spare parts and consumables' (Orivel 2000: 147–8). It follows that, in many developing countries, the cost per hour of education using computers is likely to be high in comparison with the cost of regular teaching. Second, studies that have looked at computer use in schools over a five-year period suggest that the total cost – even excluding teacher salary costs – can reach five times the cost of obtaining the original equipment (Cawthera 2001: 5).

There are powerful arguments that developing countries cannot afford to remain on the wrong side of the digital divide; it takes only a short step – though it may be a costly one – to go on and argue that every child needs to learn something about computers at school, though a rather longer one to argue that access to internet resources is also a necessary part of school education. But at the same time the high costs, and limited information about effects, mean that decision-makers will need an assurance that these technologies look a sounder investment than television proved to be.

Conclusion

Twenty-five years ago we thought that, 'the evidence, sketchy though it is, shows that distance-teaching methods can be used to raise the quality of schools even at the primary level, extend their numbers, and increase the number of competent teachers' (Young *et al.* 1980: 80). We turn in chapter 4 to the record of teacher education. The school report is mixed.

A handful of different models have been developed to offer education outside school walls. The most successful are in Latin America where large numbers and single-language policies have allowed the use of television on a grand scale. The African and Asian record does not look so good. Open schools and study centres have often, and for good reason, been seen as a second-class alternative, unloved alike by parents and children anxious for a proper school, and by ministries of education, who have starved them of funds. Open schools in Asia have been expected to draw fees from their students.

And yet, the other side of this tarnished coin shows that models have been developed that can achieve success for at least a proportion of their students, and that may be of continuing significance where economics and geography make it difficult for secondary education to expand in pace with demand. In the north, resource-based learning, which these models depend on, is seen as a sign of innovation and not of the second-best. And, as with nonformal education, we have a much better idea, after two or three decades of experience, how to make alternative secondary education work, even if we seldom apply the lessons. It is possible that Botswana and Namibia are now doing so and will have a new story to tell the world.

The report on technology within the classroom is simpler. Communication technology, whether radio or television or computers, can bring resources into the classroom, make learning more fun, raise quality. Computers in schools have been used more to teach children about computers than to bring in new resources, though this may yet change. But the technologies have not so far been allowed to displace teachers. Without doing so, they always raise educational costs and therefore have to justify themselves against the claims of more books, better inspection and support, and even pay rises for teachers. Ministries of education, for good reason, are loath to making savings elsewhere even for technologies that have proved their success.

4   Teachers: educating the largest profession

Extraordinary demands continue to be placed on teachers. As during the period of Sandinista rule [the previous government], they are expected to be not only technically competent and inspirational instructors but also moral exemplars and community leaders and social change agents.

Robert Arnove 1994

There are three roads for a career in China: red, yellow and black. Red refers to the government career, and it leads to power. Yellow refers to a business career, and it leads to wealth. Black refers to a career in teaching, and it leads nowhere.

Chinese trainee teacher

It is certainly cheaper and probably easier to encourage children to respect their teachers than to vote them more pay. One of the constraints on the quality of education is that each improvement in the education of teachers is likely to raise teachers' pay, a major component of ministry of education budgets. Over the last forty years most countries of the south have tried to juggle between recruiting more teachers, raising the standards of their education and containing the educational budget. At the same time, teacher education has gradually been shifting from something that follows primary education – unless primary school leavers are recruited straight away as teachers – all the way to being a postgraduate specialism. Distance education has been used as one way of raising the quality of the teaching force. Tanzania and Zimbabwe used it to provide initial training to thousands of new teachers. China has trained more than a million. Pakistan has used it on a large scale for inservice training about a new curriculum. Programmes have been run for particular groups, including head teachers and managers, and for specialist skills, such as school guidance. To put this experience in context we need to look first at the purposes of teacher education and then at our understanding of its strengths and weaknesses.

What should we teach the teachers?

There are common elements to teacher education everywhere. While much recent discussion has been in terms of teachers' competencies, it is likely to include four elements: general education, teaching about the content that trainees will themselves have to teach, material about children and their education, and practical work on the craft of teaching. The balance between the four will be most heavily affected by the educational background of the students; UNESCO comments that the importance of subject knowledge 'tends to be underestimated, given that many trainees lack basic knowledge' (UNESCO 2005: 162).[1]

There are conventional distinctions between preservice and inservice teacher education. It is, however, useful to keep in mind two sets of distinctions here. The first is between initial training that is delivered preservice, usually to school leavers, and initial training that is delivered inservice, usually for unqualified teachers already working in the schools. The second distinction is between preservice education for teachers and their continuing professional development after they have qualified and begun teaching. While once-for-all, preservice, education used to be the norm, inservice education, with its promise of rapidly effecting change in the classroom, has steadily grown in significance. The two modes have also been converging so that 'the current divisions between "pre-service" and "in-service" training may prove increasingly unprofitable to maintain and that we may do well to evolve a more unified and more flexible concept of "Teacher Education and Training"' (Hawes and Stephens 1990: 93).

Both preservice and inservice teacher education have grown, more or less in pace with the expansion of schooling, although with lurches and time-lags. In an early stage of educational expansion, schools may not be producing enough qualified leavers to feed the teaching profession. Later there may be surpluses: in some parts of India, for example, teacher surplus and scarcity exist side by side. But teacher education still disappoints: it is trenchantly criticised for reasons of quantity and of quality.

The first criticism is a numerical one: over two generations it has not provided the number of teachers needed to do the job. In subsaharan Africa and south Asia in particular there are marked shortages of women teachers; in 1997 women made up only 43 per cent of the African teaching force and only 30 per cent in south Asia with inevitable consequences where 'tradition, religion or social pressure mean that only women can teach girls' (Creed 2001: 9). In many countries, schools have grown faster than teachers have been trained to work in them. Even where there are reasonable numbers of trained teachers, particular, sometimes crippling, shortages may remain. As junior-secondary education has expanded, so many countries lack specialist junior-secondary teachers, often with particular shortages in science and mathematics.

Alongside the concern about numbers, the quality of teacher education has been criticised in terms of its effectiveness, curriculum and cost.

The research evidence on effectiveness is mixed but there is all too little to show that preservice teacher education provides skills and develops attitudes that carry through into a better education for pupils in school: despite the scale of teacher education, we are not sure that it works. Three overviews of the research data (Husen *et al.* 1978; Avalos and Haddad 1978; Schiefelbein and Simmons 1981) found only modest evidence of its effectiveness. Work by UNICEF suggests that, 'in different parts of the world, primary education programmes that operate with underqualified and para-professional staff are often showing equal or even better student results than those operating with professional, certified teachers' (Torres 1996: 449). Avalos found that, 'there is little evidence about which approaches work best in training teachers to undertake the variety of roles required of them' (1991: 30–1).

This last concern may be the most serious as it means that we do not know enough about matching the curriculum of teacher education to the background of its students. Where trainee teachers have little more than primary or junior-secondary education, the best thing to do is probably to strengthen their general education. At the other extreme, where they are already graduates in a particular discipline, teacher education probably needs to concentrate more on classroom processes and practice. But we are short of any systematic guidance to help us judge the weight to be given to different components of the curriculum for particular groups of students.

One practical difficulty in developing an effective curriculum is the psycho-logical distance, sometimes open hostility, that often lies between the colleges that teach teachers and the schools where they go to work. The hidden curriculum of the school may be quite different from that of the teachers' college. Where teachers' colleges have developed ideas and approaches that are unfamiliar to schools, perhaps as part of a programme of educational innovation, newly trained teachers are likely to find there is a conflict between the culture of the colleges from which they have come and the school to which they are going.

The practice of teacher education may not fit current views of what the curriculum should be. Many distance-education programmes, along with much conventional teacher education, have taken a quite narrow view of the teacher and the curriculum. In contrast teacher educators have increasingly been stressing the need to develop trainees' capacity not only in the techni-cal skills of teaching but also in reflecting on their own work and in gaining 'the inclination and skills to analyze what they are doing in terms of its effects upon children, schools and society' (Zeichner 1983: 6). There may be a particular problem here in shifting the emphasis of teacher education where trainee teachers have themselves a limited educational background. Skills in analysis and reflection are at the core of this new curriculum for teach-ers but, 'the question is whether it is realistic and efficient to try and develop those skills in teachers who do not have a minimum knowledge base. Another way to pose the question is whether it is possible to move from a content pedagogy to an emphasis in processes without a solid content base' (Villegas-Reimers and Reimers 1996: 485–6).

If distance education is to match the curricular demands of the education service it needs, then, to be planned in a way that takes account of the trainee teachers' own educational background, the agreed aims of teacher education, and the methods that are to be used for each component of the programme.

Moving from curriculum to economics, teacher education is criticised as being costly. Costs per student are often much higher than those of secondary education, even where the content is similar (Lockheed and Verspoor 1991: 95–6). (This problem is probably most severe in Africa where the difference in expenditure per student at different levels of education is generally higher, for the countries reporting data, than in Latin America or Asia [UNESCO Institute for Statistics 2005: table 12].) As the teaching service is often the largest national profession, presenting the largest single wage bill to governments, so the costs of training the service are significant for educational budgets.

In principle, distance education should have some advantages in overcoming teacher education's problems of numbers, of effectiveness, of the curriculum and of costs. It should be able to reach the armies of untrained teachers and offer them education on the spot, without replacing them with people even less qualified. If it can realise economies of scale it may have cost advantages. It can, too,

> put information about curricula and teaching approaches directly into the hands of individual teachers rather than trickling it down through administrators or other teachers in an increasingly diluted cascade of meetings. It offers a shorter time-gap between teachers' learning about new teaching practices and the opportunity to try them out in their own classrooms.
>
> (Robinson 1997: 125)

Can it do all this? We have a variety of experience from which to draw in seeking an answer. It has been used, across much of the south, to upgrade unqualified and underqualified teachers for primary and secondary schools, to raise the quality of teaching and support curriculum change, and to meet the needs of specialist groups including head teachers. We look next at the record in addressing these three needs.

Responding to shortages of teachers

For more than forty years education authorities have used distance education to overcome critical shortages of primary-school teachers. United Nations agencies led the way. In 1963 UNESCO, with the relief agency UNRWA, set up an institute of education to train Palestinian refugee teachers. Over the next five years it reduced the proportion of untrained teachers from 90 per cent to 9 per cent (Young *et al.* 1980: 29). It may have had a ripple effect too; UNESCO analysed and published the results of the scheme and staff members from the Palestinian institute moved to comparable projects in Africa. In their turn, African governments experimented with the use of distance education for the same purpose: to provide primary-level teachers for the rapidly growing number of children in school. Projects of this kind, with students usually numbered in their hundreds, were launched in the 1960s in Botswana, Kenya,

Malawi, Swaziland and Uganda. Similar methods have been used in a sequence of African projects and programmes up to the present day.[2] Most projects used a combination of correspondence teaching, radio, and some supervision of classroom practice. They had in common, too, a high pass rate, of between 83 and 97 per cent attributable in part to the fact that teachers got a salary increase on completion (*ibid*: 34). Swaziland's experience is typical.

> The course had three elements, apart from the radio programmes. Each student attended three in-college courses, at intervals of about a year, each lasting six weeks. The first in-college course came at the beginning of a student's involvement with the project, so that she could get the face-to-face help and encouragement necessary to keep up her enthusiasm when she returned to school. After this intensive introductory course, students worked at home on the second element of the course – a series of correspondence assignments on five subjects: English, education, mathematics, science and social studies. The third element was a series of visits paid by tutors to their students while they were teaching and working through their correspondence lessons. ... Students who worked through the course were awarded certificates by the Ministry of Education on recommendation from the College [that was running the course]. Formal examinations were not held, as it was felt that, with the knowledge from three residential courses, seven or eight school visits and the record of correspondence work, project staff knew their students well enough to gauge who should and should not be regarded as a qualified teacher.
>
> (*ibid*: 31–2)

Most of these projects, like Swaziland's were conceived as one-off activities, designed to eliminate untrained teachers from the system, and to replicate the work of a teacher-training college but with much of the subject content taught at a distance. Kenya adopted a different approach, both in organisation and in curriculum. The University of Nairobi set up a Correspondence Course Unit in 1967 (later the College of Education and Extension Studies) which offered courses, using radio and correspondence, for the Kenya Junior Certificate of Secondary Education, mainly for unqualified primary-school teachers. The main aim was simply to improve the background education of the teachers, although the unit also went on to run courses on teaching methods. Over six years 8433 students were recruited on to a programme for unqualified teaches, of whom 7632 (91 per cent) gained their qualifications and were promoted (Hawkridge *et al.* 1982: 184–92).

About ten years after this first wave of teacher-training projects, the governments of Nigeria, Tanzania and Zimbabwe all decided on a major expansion of primary education and set out to train teachers through distance education. Larger numbers were involved, as set out in table 4.1. After Nyerere's government brought forward plans to introduce universal primary education in 1977 instead of 1989, Tanzania set out to train 45 000 teachers. In Zimbabwe, primary-school numbers rose from 820 000 in 1979 to more

Table 4.1 Teacher training projects in Nigeria, Tanzania, Zimbabwe

	Enrolled	*Passed examination*	*% of original enrolment*
Nigeria National Teachers Institute TCII course 1984–90	186 713	n/a	Probably in range 25 to 30
National Teachers Institute NCE course 1997–2000 cohort	8 521	2 872	34
Tanzania Teacher upgrading course 1976–84	45 534	37 998	83
Zimbabwe Integrated Teacher Education Course 1981–8	7 353	5 887	80

Source: Bako and Rumble 1993: 211, 225; Perraton, *et al.* 2001: 20; Chale 1993: 31; Chivore 1993: 46

than two million in 1989 and some 7300 trainee teachers took part in the ZINTEC project as one response to the demand for training (Chivore 1993: 42). Nigeria recruited 45 150 to its National Teachers' Institute in 1984.

Both Tanzania and Zimbabwe decided to work by setting up cooperative structures involving a number of national agencies.[3] Tanzania already had experience and capacity in administering distance education; it had introduced correspondence education to its Cooperative Education Centre, set up a National Correspondence Institute in 1970 and developed structures to run one-off radio educational campaigns. It also had a semi-administrative, semi-political structure in the country's 2400 wards, which had already been used for adult education as well as political mobilisation. In each ward there was an adult education coordinator – who had a bicycle and was to become the local tutor – at least one radio set, and a library of about fifty books (Chale 1993: 23).

The distance-education programme, which ran for eight years, was designed to offer an equivalent qualification to the two-year post-primary courses provided by conventional teacher training colleges. From the beginning, trainees worked in school as teachers but with a reduced teaching load, though one that increased as they progressed through the course. Trainees' teaching practice was assessed and they sat a formal examination at the end of the three years. The teaching system had six elements:

> together they formed an apprenticeship model of training which was partly school-based and partly study-centre based. The trainees could also study privately in their own homes. The elements were correspondence

courses; radio broadcasts followed by group discussion; face-to-face tuition in study centres; practice teaching followed by discussion and coaching; monitoring and evaluation; and a six-week residential seminar in teacher training colleges. The teacher training distance project was made a three-year course for each of the three cohorts of trainees.

(*ibid*: 26)

The projects in Tanzania and Zimbabwe are sufficiently well-documented for us to evaluate them at four levels: were they effective in supplying qualified teachers to the schools? did their students then teach effectively in the classroom? did they solve the problems of teacher supply that led to their inception? and have they had a long-term effect on the continuing structure of teacher education?

In both cases, the projects do reasonably well at the numbers game. Of the 45 534 enrolled in Tanzania, 37 998 (83 per cent) eventually passed the course and gained qualified teacher status (Chale 1993: 31). In Zimbabwe 80 per cent passed (5887 out of 7353) and there were no significant differences between their results and those of conventional colleges, either in terms of total pass rates or of the number of distinctions awarded (Chivore 1993: 53).

It is more difficult to assess teacher performance. Both projects treated teachers as apprentices. As a result they spent longer in the schools than trainee teachers at conventional colleges so that, at the end of their training, they had much more classroom experience. While the quality of the programmes was criticised, alike by parents and professional educators, what evidence we have is cautiously positive. One sceptical, retired, World Bank official returned from Tanzania praising the distance-education scheme with the comment that 'the teachers are no worse than the others' (Personal communication). In Tanzania two comparative studies were carried out in 1983 and 1989. The latter summed up the findings of both:

> Our first general conclusion must then be: whatever differences between participants of the distance programme and the residential programme that may have existed before and immediately after their training, after a few years of regular teaching the two teacher groups did not differ as regards subject matter knowledge and teaching competency in the core subjects of the curriculum; the notable exception was science in which the performance of the residentially trained teacher was superior...
>
> Our second general conclusion ... is more tentative than the first and ... needs to be further investigated in other research studies: globally speaking, the two training programmes have succeeded in developing the teachers' confidence in their own competence but the Distance Programme has been relatively less successful in reinforcing self-confidence among female teachers.

(Mählck and Temu 1989: 125–6)

We have rather less information on ZINTEC where evaluations were designed mainly to look at the working arrangements and logistics, although the limited findings on effectiveness were positive (Chivore 1993: 56). So far as it goes, therefore, the evidence confirms that these two projects did produce teachers who were competent in the classroom.

In both Tanzania and Zimbabwe the projects seem to have had an important and continuing effect on the supply of teachers. The Tanzanian teaching force grew from 29 735 in 1975 to 81 153 in 1980 and after 1985 remained at over 90 000: the 38 000 teachers trained at a distance thus made a significant proportion of the increase in numbers. In Zimbabwe, numbers rose from 21 202 in 1975 to 28 118 in 1980 and 56 067 in 1985, after which the figures levelled off. Zimbabwe used a range of different approaches for expanding its teaching force, of which ZINTEC was one. Of the 5887 teachers trained through ZINTEC, 5401 were still working in primary schools in 1994 with 270 in secondary schools (Secretary for Education 1996).

Our fourth evaluation criterion is about educational innovation where both Tanzania and Zimbabwe embraced distance education as an emergency measure but have made much more limited use of it in their regular, continuing, programmes of initial teacher training. Zimbabwe cut back the ZINTEC programme (Chivore 1993: 63). Tanzania reverted to conventional methods of teacher education, and with some success: UNESCO now reports that 100 per cent of primary teachers are trained (UNESCO Institute for Statistics 2005: table 3). Neither project led to a permanent change in the structure of teacher training.

Nigeria took a different approach and its experience provides a contrast. The federal government proposed to introduce universal primary education in 1974 which meant expanding the number of primary-school teachers from 130 000 to 310 000 and upgrading some 70 000 who had no teaching qualification. The existing training colleges were full, and were doing an inadequate job with poor pass rates at West African Examinations Council qualifications. With its oil revenues flowing, Nigeria decided to create a new, distance-teaching institution that would train teachers throughout the country.

After a slow beginning – with material writing started in 1976, formal promulgation of the institute in 1978, and teaching launched in 1984 – the National Teachers' Institute has gone on to do the job, and to become an established part of the Nigerian educational structure. It has faced problems inescapable from its location in a large federal country in which responsibility for education is shared between federal and provincial authorities. The organisation and supervision of face-to-face study, and of teaching practice, are inherently difficult. Materials are prepared centrally and distributed to students through a network of field centres, with one per state, and study centres where students are encouraged to attend Saturday sessions.

The institute's first job was to provide training for the lowest level of teachers' qualifications (Teacher's Certificate II) which conventionally required two years' attendance at a teachers' college after completing junior-secondary school.

Much of the curriculum was equivalent to that of the senior-secondary schools. By 1992 it had trained some 300 000 grade II teachers, a significant number in relation to the Nigerian teaching force which rose from 177 221 in 1975 to 331 915 in 1990. With this achievement behind it, the institute began to phase out its grade II course and introduce a course for the Nigerian Certificate of Education, a higher level qualification, demanding the equivalent of three years study after the completion of senior-secondary education. From 1994 to 2001 the institute upgraded some 20 000 teachers. It enrolled 8521 trainees, 55.5 per cent of them women, in its 1997–2000 cohort of whom 2872 gained their certificate (Aderinoye 2006).

We have some information about the effectiveness of the National Teachers' Institute in terms of success and completion rates. The limited figures on examination results for the former teacher's certificate II suggest that in 1987 and 1988 the pass rate was between 25 and 30 per cent, higher figures than those achieved by conventional teachers' colleges for the same years. By 2000 the figure for the Nigerian Certificate of Education was higher with a satisfactory completion rate of 34 per cent. The figures need to be seen in context: the institute, like the teachers' colleges generally, was offering the equivalent of a secondary-level course to students who were either experienced but unqualified teachers, with limited education some years behind them, or young people who had failed to get into conventional senior-secondary schools.

Nigeria's experience is interesting in that it chose to establish a free-standing institution for teacher training that was neither a temporary consortium to solve an emergency, as in Tanzania, nor a university, with its danger of academic drift. (The first principal of the institute was adamant that it should remain a specialised agency, avoiding the seduction of university status.) The innovation of distance education has been institutionalised.

Much of the African experience, including that in Nigeria, Tanzania and Zimbabwe, has been about training for unqualified teachers, who have themselves completed only primary or secondary education. It can be seen as a catching up, or an emergency response, relevant only while the education service is unable to provide enough potential teachers with a fuller conventional education behind them. Teacher-training programmes of this kind, using distance education, continue. The rapid expansion of primary school numbers in Malawi, after Banda, led to an unmanageable demand for teacher training. Malawi therefore adopted a training structure in which training college students matched 11 weeks in college with four terms of self study in school and five terms of supervised teaching practice. Costs were modest, and there was a prospect of dramatically expanding the number of trained teachers, if it were possible to overcome problems of logistics and of the supervision of teaching practice (Stuart and Kunje 2000: 49–59; Lewin and Stuart 2003: 152–60). After the fall of Amin, Uganda, similarly, needed to expand its teaching force: only 71 per cent of the age group were going to primary school in 1991, of whom a third dropped out before completing the seven-year primary cycle. Nearly half the teachers were untrained and many of them could not afford to attend a residential college (Wrightson 1997: 2–3). The Uganda government has therefore run distance-education courses to offer a curriculum parallel to that of the regular colleges. A Mubende Integrated Teacher Education Project ran from 1992 to 1995 with 900 trainees and was followed by a similar Northern Integrated Teacher Education Project from 1993 to 1997. Its aim was to upgrade 3040 serving, untrained, teachers who generally had completed five years of secondary education, in ten districts of northern Uganda. Course materials were in print, covering over three years the ground covered in a residential two-year course. They gave relatively heavy weight to pedagogy – 40 per cent as compared with 60 per cent on subject content.

The project was unusual in the structure it developed, with apparent success, for student support. The term 'integrated' in its title meant that it was integrated with the work of the ten regular teacher-training colleges within the northern region where trainees attended tutorials and twice-yearly residential sessions. Tutor-counsellors were appointed with three functions: to administer the scheme on the ground; to teach the ten to thirty students in the area at their fortnightly session; and to visit them,

> sharing problems, such as – the in-laws have taken my wife away, what should I do? – I have raised most of the money needed to purchase a paraffin study lamp but I need a final, small amount. What do you advise? – my brother has just died of AIDS, I will be unable to attend the next tutorial or submit my [tutor-marked] assignment. What should I do? My sister's dowry is being paid this weekend. I would like you, my tutor to come and attend the celebrations. ...
>
> A student in a remote and sometimes inaccessible location (especially during the wet season) who received a visitor, whether impromptu or planned, feels deeply cared for. ... There is a strong correlation between care and learner motivation.
>
> (*ibid*: 6)

In keeping with this emphasis on personal contact and local support, the project guided and monitored teaching practice. Personal tutors observed trainees' practice monthly with a school practice workbook being maintained for each student, to the satisfaction of the regional Institute of Teacher Education which moderated the programme, as it did the work of regular teacher training colleges.

Success in the project gained trainees status as qualified teachers. After three years the completion rate was 88 per cent (2750 of 3128 teachers enrolled) and it was anticipated that some 75 per cent of those who had started on the course would pass the final examination. This would give a unit cost of about $2000 (*$2420*) compared with about $2500 (*$3030*) for a two-year residential course (*ibid*: 5). This compares favourably with the earlier and smaller Mubende Integrated Teacher Education Project with its 900 students whose costs were greater than those of the residential equivalent.

Although there is probably more literature about distance education for teachers from Africa than from Asia, large numbers of Asian teachers have also got their qualifications through distance education. In Sri Lanka, for example, a programme in the 1980s allowed experienced but unqualified primary-school teachers to gain a teaching qualification while continuing to work at school. Some 5000 teachers graduated from the programme between 1984 and 1988 with 85 per cent of them doing so within three years (Nielsen and Tatto 1993: 97–8). More often Asian ministries of education have called on their open universities to play a role in teacher training alongside their degree and diploma courses for the general public.

China, understandably, offers the largest example. In 1979 it established its network of radio and television universities (see chapter 5). Within that framework a China Television Teachers College started work in 1986 to offer inservice courses to both qualified and unqualified teachers. In doing so it makes extensive use of television, the main teaching medium; by 1995 it was offering 750 hours of programmes a year on a dedicated television channel. Some printed material is made available to students and there are opportunities for face-to-face sessions at study centres; plans are reported for the development of ict-based distance education.

One of the purposes of this activity was to meet the needs of the 1 056 000 unqualified primary and secondary teachers who, in 1998, were mainly working in rural areas. Between 1987 and 1999 717 300 primary-school and 552 000 secondary-school teachers gained qualifications in this way (Zhang and Niu 2006; Perraton *et al.* 2001: 13–14).

Professional development, curriculum change and raising quality

Alongside these programmes of initial teacher training, distance education has been used for the continuing professional development of teachers, for upgrading, and to support curriculum change, all directed to teachers who already have a basic qualification.

Upgrading

The establishment of large open universities in the 1970s and 1980s provided a mechanism for a number of Asian governments to raise the quality and standards of their teaching force. Indonesia gave this job to the newly established Universitas Terbuka. In 1989 the Indonesian government raised the level of the basic qualification for junior-school teachers to that of a Diploma II, requiring two years of post-secondary school training. At that time it was estimated that some 273 000 teachers had qualifications below this level (Nielsen and Tatto 1993: 100). The qualification is now required for primary-school teachers, of whom there are over one million. The Universitas Terbuka therefore introduced a distance-education programme, heavily based on printed materials, which took two forms, offering tutorials in the towns and support by radio and television for students in the countryside. The curriculum had three elements: general education, with about 10 per cent of the weight, some 70 to 80 per cent on subject knowledge of the subjects being taught by students, and the balance on education and on teaching processes. No teaching practice was included on the grounds that the teachers already had the necessary skills (*ibid.*). In 1996 Indonesia reported that 76 149 students had graduated from the course, 244 482 were still enrolled on it leaving 552 000 still awaiting training. Another 238 000 were over 46 and so exempted (Asian Development Bank 1997: 363).

An evaluation of the Indonesian programme, which compared it with a conventional course for the same qualification, looked at the effects of both programmes on teaching in languages and in mathematics and found:

> that the one-year programme has made a considerable difference in the language programme participants' subject mastery and teaching skills, but relatively little difference in practical skills. In contrast, the one-year programme in mathematics has had virtually no impact on subject-matter mastery and teaching skills, but a small impact on practical skills. In both cases, the impact on practical skills seems to be constrained by the fact that learners entered their respective programme with relatively high marks in practical skills.
>
> (Nielsen and Tatto 1993: 121)

The limited effect on mathematics was matched in a parallel study in Sri Lanka and fits with a finding in Tanzania. Generally, the researchers found that the distance-education courses compared favourably in terms of cost with those of conventional colleges, although they did not quote completion rates, and concluded that 'using the standard of cost-effectiveness, our findings seem to justify the use of distance education for the inservice training of teachers' (*ibid*: 127).

Although it starts from a much lower base, with much worse enrolment ratios in primary school, Pakistan's experience matches that of Indonesia. The federal ministry of education saw that the Allama Iqbal Open University offered a way of providing inservice education on a new curriculum to its primary-school teachers. The university introduced a Primary Teachers' Orientation Course in 1976 to train 150 000 teachers as quickly as possible in the new curriculum. Their own background education was limited; teachers generally did a nine-month course after ten years of schooling. Of a sample of students on the university course, 8 per cent had been to school for less than ten years and 17 per cent were untrained (Robinson 1993: 238). As in Indonesia, the course concentrated on subject knowledge rather than teaching method and did not include any teaching practice. The courses were written in Urdu – a second language for most students but a third for others – and used print backed by between eighteen and twenty-four 15-minute radio programmes.

The Primary Teachers' Orientation course ran for ten years and was acclaimed a success in reaching a significant proportion of its target audience who could not have been reached in any other way. It recruited nearly 84 000 students, or just over half of its target audience. Of these, 56 per cent completed the course and 38 per cent qualified and got their certificate. Though lower than the target, the figures are large in comparison with the annual output of teachers' colleges. The course was revised and relaunched with increased student–tutor contact and more supervision. A further 50 000 teachers were recruited and, with a high pass rate and completion rate, another 33 000 qualified over seven years (Allama Iqbal Open University 1999: 38). While it was not formally evaluated,

> teachers who completed the course had, through the course assessment, demonstrated their understanding of the course content; but the nature of this understanding could not always be tapped fully by the limited scope of the multiple-choice questions frequently used. Few assignments appeared to focus much on the application of theory to practical action or to call for evaluation by teachers of their own practice.
> (Robinson 1993: 252)

The open universities dominate the account of distance education for teachers in Asia. In India, for example, alongside programmes from Indira Gandhi National Open University (IGNOU), a third of students at Yashwantrao Chavan Maharashtra Open University were on teacher-education programmes (Manjulika and Reddy 1996: 101–4).

Different mechanisms have been used in other parts of the world. Within Latin America, alongside the conventional work of teachers' colleges and universities Brazil has experimented with a television-based approach to the inservice education of teachers. The programme, A-Plus, is run by TV-Futura, a non-profit television channel run by a consortium which shares the values of public-service broadcasting and whose members are drawn from the private sector, nongovernment organisations and chambers of commerce. The consortium is managed by the Fundação Roberto Marinho, which is itself affiliated to the major communications group Globo. The programme has three elements: broadcasts, a magazine to support them, and a network of community officers whose job is to visit the schools.

> Its purpose is to help educators deal more critically and effectively with practical matters of concern to them and the community. The 15-minute daily TV programmes have a magazine format, combining general educational news with an in-depth documentary. Each programme shows two examples of real-life applications of the programme topic, for example, a method of literacy teaching or using videos in the classroom or conducting PTA meetings …. Follow-on activities and monthly meetings are organised around these programmes for teachers' groups

that opt in to the 'plus' part of the programme. A-Plus provides 60 Community Officers who facilitate the Community Mobilisation Network which supports this activity. The programme has no set curriculum but aims to be responsive to teachers' needs, drawing on several sources of guidance.

(Perraton *et al.* 2001: 7)

Some 8600 institutions were taking part in the mobilisation network in 2001; over 40 000 teachers were involved in the use of the programme as a result of their work; the general audience for the programmes, many of whom were teachers, was estimated at 2 million. A-Plus was seen as unusual in its context because,

> unlike the majority of teacher training programmes, A-Plus allows teachers to observe, discuss, probe and interact with what other teachers are doing or trying to do. In general, teacher training is confined to situations in which teachers are exposed to theories about teaching, abstract discussion about general issues, or are being directly taught. Seldom do they have the opportunity to watch and interact with their peers – a fundamental tool for the creation of a learning community.
>
> (Oliveira 2006)

The scale on which A-Plus was operating, and its roots in a successful broadcasting service, meant that the programme had the high fixed costs associated with television but costs per viewer of only a few cents a year. The annual community network costs were estimated in 2001 at US$18 (*$19.78*) per teacher or 60 cents (*$0.66*) per potential beneficiary (Perraton *et al.* 2001: 8). This is a modest figure when set against public expenditure on primary education, which was estimated at $290 (*$319*) per pupil (UNESCO 2004: table 17).

Brazil's use of television for teachers is not unusual, especially in large countries where production costs can be spread across large audiences, and illustrates a fairly unstructured approach to teacher upgrading. But it is unusual in its organisational structure, with its mix of private and public-sector agencies.

On a smaller scale, the Shoma Education Foundation was set up in South Africa with private-sector backing as a non-profit organisation to support the continuing professional development of teachers. It developed computer-based teaching programmes which reinforced video lessons that were distributed by satellite. Teachers watched the videos, discussed the content, and worked individually at their computers. In 2002 Shoma was reaching fourteen centres, operated by provincial education departments, and reaching some 5000 teachers a year. Teachers involved in the project 'were unanimous in their praises', although attendance at sessions sometimes dropped to 20 per cent, and there was some evidence of teachers' changing their practice in response to the course (Capper 2002a: 44–8). The positive evidence needs to be set against its relatively high costs at $198 (*$218*) per teacher which leave its sustainability uncertain.

Curriculum change

Ministries of education wanting to change the curriculum have to find a way of ensuring that changes made at headquarters affect schools wherever they are. They may use a cascade approach in the hope that, at the politest, innovation will trickle, from government guru to the remotest schoolteacher. In principle distance education offers an alternative approach. In South Africa, the OLSET programme provided on-the-job training for teachers who were working with its radio-based classes for children (see pp 53–4).

In Chile, too, the *Enlaces* project included training for the teachers involved with it (see pp 54–5). The web-based course was based on an existing face-to-face one, with the same content and was designed mainly for primary and secondary-school teachers interested in learning how to use information and communication technologies in their teaching. Members of the Instituto de Informática prepared the course material and served as tutors on the course which had annual enrolments, between 1997 and 2000 of about 100 students, about three-quarters of them teachers. The programme required 1068 hours of study on the part of the students over a period of fifteen months; satisfactory completion led to the award of a diploma from the Universidad de La Frontera. Though valued by employers the diploma does not earn a title or lead towards a further degree qualification (Perraton *et al.* 2001: 11).

The programme had several strengths: a good reputation, popularity among its students and their head teachers, and evidence of quality. Unfortunately, but not unusually, there is little information on its effect on classroom practice. And it was expensive, costing $860 in fees (*$971*, assuming these were 2000 figures) – the sole source of finance – or about 10 per cent of a teacher's salary. Recruitment may have been limited by price as well as by the restricted value of the diploma offered. Dropout rates at around 50 per cent may have been forced up by students who could not keep up their payments.

We come back to the balance between payment and benefit in chapter 10. Despite its difficulties the project in Chile is a useful demonstration of a deliberate and rational choice of technologies, learning about computers through a computer network, and of a more direct alternative to cascade training.

Specialist courses

In contrast with these general programmes for continuing professional development, some courses have more narrowly focused aims. A certificate course in guidance, for example, is available from IGNOU while various courses have been developed for managers and head teachers. Trinidad and Tobago developed plans with the World Bank for a course in administration that was to become a necessary condition for promotion. In cooperation with the francophone agency RESAFAD, Burkina Faso trained three cohorts of head teachers through distance education between 1997 and 2000 reaching a total of 1275 heads at a cost thought to be significantly lower than a residential alternative. The project reached about a quarter of the total number of head teachers but reliance on external funding meant that, when this came to an end, the scheme was closed down (Perraton *et al.* 2001: 10). It is surprising that there is not more experience with specialised courses of this kind, designed to strengthen school management, increasingly seen as a crucial variable in raising the quality of schooling.

Individual professional advancement

Throughout the world universities have developed courses in response to demands from individual teachers, seeking a more advanced qualification, rather than as part of a national upgrading programme. Courses have been offered at various levels. The Sukhothai Thammathirat Open University in Thailand, for example, offers a teaching certificate programme, a four-year degree programme which runs over a period of four to twelve years, and a two-year programme, running over two to six years, giving qualified teachers advanced standing. The university has gone on to offer master's programmes in administration and in curriculum. Some 40 700 students enrolled in the school of education over eight years; in 1987 education was the third largest school, after management and law, with some 15 per cent of all enrolments (Brahmawong 1993: 71). In India, by 1996 sixteen dual-mode universities and three open universities were offering BEd programmes for teachers; several MEd programmes were available and IGNOU offered a postgraduate programme in higher education (Sahoo 2000: 136).

Similarly, there had been a proliferation of courses in teacher education in the new South Africa, most of them designed to raise the general educational standards of teachers. In 1995 nearly 130 000 teachers, 70 per cent of them women, were studying education courses at a distance. The figure had increased by 23 per cent over the previous year (Gultig and Butcher 1996: 84). Courses were being provided by colleges of education, three universities, a technikon and a number of private colleges which had 19 per cent of the enrolments. The expansion illustrates a demand for education but an appraisal, carried out by the South African Institute for Distance Education bluntly illustrates its weakness:

> The system is large, of questionable quality, and expanding rapidly. It is dominated by a few large providers, but also has many small and probably uneconomic providers. It wears its apartheid history strongly: in the didactic nature of most of its teaching, in the remnants of Fundamental Pedagogics philosophy in courses, and in the dominance of white male managers. The system is, at the same time, characterized by fragmentation

(little collaboration between institutions; 'compartmentalization' of courses within institutions) and a bland uniformity (many courses containing similar content presented in very similar ways).

Unusually high pass and throughput rates are achieved at most institutions despite a lack of attention to student support, either in texts or by way of contact tutorials. While large providers are able to administer their courses relatively efficiently, little attention seems to be paid to ongoing quality assurance.

(*ibid*: 83–4)

Dual-mode universities as well as open universities have offered degree courses for teachers. In Africa, the University of Lagos and the University of Nairobi stepped cautiously towards wider-ranging external degree programmes by introducing bachelor's degrees for teachers, aiming mainly at teachers in secondary schools.[4] When the University of Nairobi launched its BEd programme in the late 1980s there were some 19 300 teachers in secondary schools of whom 8600 were not educated beyond A level. The degree course provided a general education, initially in the humanities and social sciences but oriented towards education, which would provide graduate status, justifying increased pay, to students who worked through it and passed. It had 3000 applications, accepted 600 of them, and intended to continue recruiting at 600 a year. The course was mainly print based, with some audiocassettes, and compulsory residential sessions (Odumbe 1988).

The course was designed to run over six years and follow the same curriculum as the residential BEd also offered by the university, though at a slower pace. Teaching practice was included and assessed in the last two years of the course. Students were expected to attend residential sessions on campus, amounting to 21 days per year, and weekend sessions, although the number of these was cut down and students faced many problems in getting to them (Dodds and Mayo 1996: 117). In the first year 515 students were recruited. A review of their progress suggested that some 54 per cent would complete the course and graduate (Makau 1993: 339). While we have no data on the effect of the programme on students' classroom performance, their degrees were recognised by the Teachers Service Commission as being equivalent to the internal BEd, so that their salaries were increased; self-report was, as usual, positive.

The external BEd programme had significantly lower annual costs per student than the residential equivalent, although the economies were not as dramatic as had been forecast. Estimates showed that with an enrolment of 515, the cost per graduate was K£8091 (*$11 464*) compared with K£9582 (*$12 960*) for the full-time equivalent. This figure, however, omits the important opportunity cost of students' time. These were real costs where students gave up offering private tuition in order to have time to study and if they were included the cost advantage of studying at a distance would be eroded (Makau 1993: 335–9). Nevertheless, if we omit opportunity costs, then even with the modest enrolment of 515 students, the external degree was at a cost advantage, while the cost would drop as numbers increased.

The Nairobi course, and many others like it, offered a qualification to school teachers, which brought them individual benefits and could be expected to raise the quality of teaching in schools. It was not conceived as a way of making major changes to the educational service.

Effects, outcomes, costs and organisation

We began with a critique of teacher education in terms of numbers, effectiveness and curriculum and a concern about its costs. In trying to assess the distance-education experience we are limited by the shortage of good evaluation. Many projects have little or no formative evaluation. Only a very few studies have tried to examine outcomes with any sophistication. Few have followed students on into the schools to see whether graduates of programmes were better teachers in the classroom. Hardly any have looked at the three levels of teachers' knowledge and practice, examining knowledge and understanding, knowledge applied to practice, and practice and performance including the demonstration of competencies and skills, for which Robinson has argued (1997: 130–3). For the most part, therefore, we have to rely on much more partial evidence.

Numbers first, where distance education has a positive record. The experience of China, Pakistan and Tanzania, for example, show that distance-education methods can be used on a scale that makes a difference to national numbers. An earlier review summed it up:

> Many of the programmes started with a numerical imperative. ... The teacher upgrading project in Tanzania for example, was conceived in order to train between 35 000 and 40 000 teachers needed for universal primary education at a time when the conventional colleges had only 5000 students in total. The first and simplest measure of success is one of reach: distance-education programmes have a reasonable record of success in reaching audiences. ... The audiences were not always as large as had been intended. ... [They] are sometimes large in relation to those in conventional institutions but may be small in relation to the total size of the teaching force.
>
> (Perraton 1993: 391–2)

It is more difficult to answer questions beyond the simple ones about reach. One of the difficulties in reaching comparative conclusions is the shortage of evidence on the effectiveness of conventional approaches to teacher education. In examining distance education against the high aims with which this chapter began, we can often find only quite modest indicators, mainly comprising completion rates, examination results, and in some cases learning gains, and, more rarely, demonstrated effects on teachers' classroom practice.

The same review noted that completion rates varied widely within a range from 42 per cent at the National Teachers' Institute in Nigeria to 83 per cent in a programme in Nepal, rather lower than earlier projects which were in the range 77 to 97 per cent. In nine cases where there were data on examination pass rates, figures falling between 50 and 90 per cent confirmed that distance-teaching methods were getting students through their examinations. Evidence on teaching practice is mixed. In Tanzania, students trained at a distance tended to perform better than those trained conventionally on a number of measures of classroom performance but rather worse academically and in their command of the subject matter. While it was not possible to make this kind of comparison in Zimbabwe, studies of teachers' classroom effectiveness showed positive results while the examination performance of pupils taught by ZINTEC teachers were in line with the national trend. Findings from Indonesia and Sri Lanka were more complex; distance teaching seemed to be at a disadvantage in science though doing reasonably well for the study of mother-tongue languages. In Sri Lanka distance education performed better than the alternative in teaching language and in developing professional attitudes towards education while in Indonesia neither distance nor conventional education were effective in changing trainee teachers' attitudes. All this led to the conclusion that: 'The research findings are notably undramatic; the differences between trainees studying in different ways are relatively small and, so far as they go, do not suggest that distance education must be ruled out, or ruled in, for any particular educational purpose' (*ibid*: 391–6). The results are summarised in table 4.2.

On curriculum the evidence is of potential rather than achievement. The capacity of distance education to reach students and improve their general education or subject knowledge, suggests that it may yet offer a way of effecting major changes in the curriculum. But we have seldom seen this happen on a large scale. One reason may be organisational, that most projects and programmes have been run with quite limited aims, to help the unlucky and less educated remote teachers catch up with the better educated and luckier urban ones. They have not changed the curriculum, or the culture of education, because they were not meant to.

Enough distance-education programmes for teachers have been run for us to reach some conclusions about costs. An earlier study showed that, 'where data are available, costs for distance education appear to have been lower than the alternative; where we have detailed figures it is reasonable to conclude that distance-education programmes can be designed for teachers which will cost between one-third and two-thirds of conventional programmes (Perraton 1993: 385). The findings were qualified in four ways: that some projects were too small to show economies; that projects with high levels of student support were likely to have high variable costs; that they omitted opportunity costs; and, to revert to one of our starting points, that the economics of some projects looked attractive because the costs of conventional teacher education were so high.

Table 4.2 Outcomes of some teacher education projects

Project, date, purpose	Numbers	Outcomes	Costs
INITIAL TRAINING PROJECTS			
Botswana, Swaziland, Uganda Inservice upgrading of unqualified primary school teachers 1967–78[a]	Each in range 600 to 1 000	Successful completion rate 88–93%. Anecdotal evidence of impact on classroom performance.	n/a
Kenya Programme for unqualified primary school teachers, to improve general educational background and achieve secondary examination passes 1967–73[b]	8 433 over 7 years; annual enrolment 850 to 2 000	91% passed examination and gained promotion. No firm evidence on classroom performance.	Cost per enrolment relatively high in comparison with alternatives
Tanzania Training of primary school teachers for introduction of Universal Primary Education 1976–84[c]	45 534 in 3 annual cohorts	83% qualified. Positive evidence on classroom performance. Weaknesses in science teaching and self-confidence among female teachers.	Cost per successful trainee about half cost of residential course
Zimbabwe Integrated Teacher Education (ZINTEC) for secondary school leavers, trained on the job for expansion of primary schooling 1981–8	7 353 over 4 years	80% pass rate. Positive evidence of classroom performance but difficult to draw comparative conclusions.	n/a
Nigeria National Teachers' Institute training primary school teachers TCII course after 2 years secondary education 1984–90	186 713 over period	Success rate thought to be in range 25 to 30% of those entering; compares favourably with alternative; no evidence on classroom practice	Cost probably lower than conventional college

NCE course 1997–2000[d]	Annual cohorts in range 7 300 to 8 500	21 000 students graduated 1994[c] Dropout rates 27–39%; pass rates 55–66%	
China Courses for unqualified primary and secondary teachers from China Television Teachers' College (part of China Central Radio and Television University) 1987–99[e]	n/a	717 300 primary teachers gained certificates 552 000 secondary teachers gained diplomas	CCRTVU cost per graduate reported as between 1/3 and 2/5 cost at conventional institutions
Malawi Inservice Integrated Teacher Education Programme 1997–2000[f]	Aimed at 18 000 untrained teachers with annual cohorts of 7 500	Apparently no formal evaluation	Cost of two-year full-time training would be 3 to 4½ times as expensive
Uganda Northern Integrated Teacher Education Project for primary school teachers 1993–95[g]	3 128 enrolled	88% completed course; 57% of original enrolment passed examination; some evidence of improved skills in teaching competencies	Cost per student about $2000 compared with $2500 in conventional college
PROFESSIONAL DEVELOPMENT PROGRAMMES			
Pakistan Primary Teachers, Orientation Course (Allama Iqbal Open University) introducing new curriculum to primary school teachers 1976–86	83 658 total	56% completed course; 38% of original enrolment passed examination Positive self-report on usefulness. No direct evidence of classroom effects	AIOU graduate costs 45–70% of conventional university costs
New PTOC 1991–8[h]	50 138 enrolled	79% completed, 66% original enrolment passed	

Continued

Table 4.2 Outcomes of some teacher education projects—cont'd

Project, date, purpose	Numbers	Outcomes	Costs
PROFESSIONAL DEVELOPMENT PROGRAMMES—cont'd			
Indonesia Universitas Terbuka upgrading course for lower secondary teachers 1985–	c 5000	Positive effects on subject mastery and in theory and practice in skills; relatively poor results in mathematics; apparent decline in attitudes towards teaching	Cost about 60% of equivalent
Sri Lanka National Institute of Education training primary school teachers with secondary level qualifications 1983–88	c 5000	Positive effects on subject matter and in theory and practice in skills; less successful than conventional college in mathematics	Cost 1/6 to 1/3 of alternative
Brazil A Plus television-based programme of continuing education for teachers[i]	TV audience of 13 million. 40 000 teachers have participated in training activities	Anecdotal evidence that programme seen as useful and valuable by teachers	Unit costs around $20 per teacher, <10 cents per viewer per programme
Burkina Faso Professional development of head teachers 1997–2000[j]	1 275 head teachers	High completion rate. Positive self-report and some evidence of more efficient school; management	Costs lower than face-to-face alternative

Source: This table is adapted from tables 13.1 and 14.1 in Perraton 1993, expect where shown.

Notes

a. Young *et al.* 1980: 34; b. Hawkridge *et al.* 1982; c. Aderinoye 1995: 208; d. Perraton *et al.* 2001: 20; e. *ibid*: 14; f. Lewin and Stuart 2003: 152–61; g. Wrightson 1998: 43-4; h. Allama Iqbal Open University 1999: 38; i. Perraton *et al.* 2001: 8; j. *ibid*: 10.

We look at the cost issues in more detail in chapter 7. They give two bits of guidance for planners. First, one of the reasons for the economic advantage of distance education for teachers is that programmes have, characteristically, had high completion and success rates. This has kept the cost per successful student close to the unit cost per student. Second, even without the rigorous evaluation for which we have argued, it is reasonable to believe that support for students in their own classrooms is critically important both to get results and to keep up motivation and with it a good completion rate. The cost evidence can encourage planners not to stint on field support for students.

Teacher-education programmes have used a range of different organisational models. Some, though often with limited success, have created an ad-hoc structure, as in Tanzania and Uganda. In many cases distance education has been made the responsibility of an existing college or, increasingly, of an open university. Then, there is also documented experience of multi-country programmes, as with the programme in Burkina Faso, of nongovernment activity, as with OLSET in South Africa, and of consortia and partnerships. These six models are set out in table 4.3. Each has advantages and drawbacks: local culture, needs and circumstances will determine choices between them.

Within each organisational model planners have tried, with varying success, to integrate supervised classroom practice with a distance-learning approach. This has not been a universal feature: a certificate in guidance offered by IGNOU, for example, had no teaching practice because it was addressed to qualified and experienced teachers. In place of visits to teachers' classrooms a course in Belize used micro-teaching sessions within a period of in-college study. An IGNOU diploma course included a block of teaching practice after academic blocks of study, though this left the problem of inspecting and supervising what is happening in the classroom and ran the risk of separating theory from practice. Many programmes, as in Tanzania and Zimbabwe, have relied on visits by college staff and locally based inspectors to supervise and sometimes examine classroom practice, with all the logistical complexities this incurs. In Britain, school-based mentors were given the job in a postgraduate certificate of education programme and Malawi considered a similar approach, partly in response to the difficulties of arranging school visits by lecturers. More usually, developing-country educators have not felt they could recruit enough qualified school-based mentors to make this a practical option.[5]

Conclusion

Distance education has gone some way to establishing itself as a significant and legitimate way of training teachers. The evidence on its success is probably no worse than the comparable evidence on conventional teacher education. It can have economic advantages. And yet it remains on the sidelines, more often used as an emergency response than integrated into the normal structure of teacher education.

Table 4.3 Some models for organising teacher education

Model	Example	Comments
Ad-hoc arrangements made by ministry of education	MITEP Uganda	While this makes it possible to deploy resources quickly it may not be a sustainable model
Single or dual mode teachers' college	NTI Nigeria Belize Teacher Training College	The Nigerian case is the only example of a specialised distance-teaching teachers'college
Single or dual-mode university	IGNOU UWI	Many universities with distance-teaching capacity have been asked by MOEs to run programmes for teachers
Multi-country programme	RESAFAD head teacher training University of the South Pacific	Can share international resources and be of particular value for small states
NGO single-purpose project	OLSET	Speed and vibrancy of NGO activity has to be balanced against problems of sustainability and of coherence with government activity
Consortia and partnerships	A-Plus Brazil	If problems of integration can be overcome, a partnership of this kind may, as in Brazil, bring together an NGO a broadcasting station, schools and a private-sector publisher

Source: Perraton *et al.* 2002: 29

There are two challenges facing distance education here. First, it still needs to establish its legitimacy and sustainability. In doing so, it will need not only to establish the cost-effectiveness of its approaches to getting students through examinations, but also to demonstrate its relevance to classroom realities. While classroom practice is only one component in teacher education, it is a critical element in many programmes, and its comparative neglect may have reduced the acceptability of distance education. For an effective and integrated programme of teacher education we need to identify which aspects of the job can best be done at a distance and which in some other way and, imaginatively, to work out a varied approach to use the various tools and media available within distance education (cf. Robinson 1997: 132). Legitimacy will then demand a programme that is sustainable and that effectively links theory and practice.

Close links between college and classroom are needed if practice and theory are to inform each other, and if teachers are to avoid dismissing anything taught at their college as irrelevantly theoretical. At the same time the organisation of teaching practice presents severe problems to conventional colleges of education which are magnified where students are learning at a distance, often a long way from their tutors. One of the weakest features of many programmes has been the organisation and supervision of teaching practice: it fell away in Zimbabwe, contributed to a very high level of cost in Tanzania, caused major difficulties in Malawi, and was simply left out of account in many other programmes. The remaining step to be taken in establishing legitimacy is to find effective ways of linking school practice with the other elements of teacher education. Only if this step is taken will projects have the assurance of continuity that makes them sustainable.

The second challenge may be even more demanding. If teacher education is to take account of the critique with which this chapter started, and move away from a top-down approach, encouraging trainee teachers to analyse and reflect upon their own experience, then mechanisms need to be found for regular two-way interaction between students and tutors. But this seems at first sight to be at odds with the idea of a distance-education programme, based on centrally produced materials, and seeking to achieve economies of scale. Various ways have been sought of resolving this dilemma. In some cases the new technologies allow for interaction, sometimes with remote students, that would not be possible otherwise, where the necessary equipment is in place and the costs are sustainable. Audio feedback links have been used with satellite broadcasts. Written assignments and local or regional face-to-face sessions allow for tutor–student interaction. The strongest case for using distance education in the education of teachers may, in fact, be that it will centralise and industrialise those parts of teacher education to which this is appropriate, and so allow time and resources to be devoted, in greater measure, to interaction and reflection.

5 Higher education: beyond the courtyard wall

As far as I have been able to find out ... plans for university expansion are completely inadequate. ... What can be done? The first step would be to create further new universities more cheaply than in the past. ... The second would be to make fuller use of existing universities ... The third step, not as far as I know suggested before, would be to establish an 'open university'.

Michael Young 1962

With startling imagination the Wilson government took on the educational establishment, who were opposed to the idea, and set up the world's first open university in 1969. They even suggested, with a mixture of vision and eurocentricity, that it would 'have much to contribute to students in many other parts of the world as well as those studying in the United Kingdom. In the developing countries in particular there is an urgent need not only for elementary education but for a highly trained core of men and women, equipped to provide leadership in national life' (HMSO 1966). University open and distance learning has, in the event, expanded dramatically in the south not because of enrolment on to British courses but because the successful launch of the British Open University gave it an unprecedented legitimacy.

The idea of an open university got rapid international attention. The government of India organised a seminar on the open university system in December 1970 'to which experts from the UKOU were invited to consider the feasibility of starting an open university in India' (Manjulika and Reddy 1996: 22). By 1975 open universities of one kind or another had been set up in Canada, Germany, Iran, Israel, Pakistan, Spain, and Thailand: the idea was adopted alike by secular democracies and fading autocracies, by states that were rich, middle-income and poor. Thirty years later there are over 40 open universities while a far larger number of conventional universities have established open-learning programmes, with students numbered in tens or hundreds of thousands.

The Asian open universities

Asia led the way. Their open universities are the largest demonstration of open and distance learning of the last quarter century.

China and India

The two Asian giants exemplify the history; both set up open universities as a response to inherited educational needs. China's higher education collapsed during the cultural revolution (1966–76), after which the universities were able to enrol only 5 per cent of secondary-school graduates. Economic growth and social development demanded educational expansion and a national television network provided an opportunity to establish radio and television universities (NIME 1993: 39). They began to enrol students in 1979 and by 1990 had enrolled 1.83 million students, produced 1.25 million graduates and had 420 000 students on roll. Today China has three parallel distance-education systems: the television universities, correspondence education offered by dual-mode universities, and a newer programme entitled 'modern distance education' using online courses.

The Chinese television universities are significantly different from most open universities in the south. Most students are enrolled full-time and have in the past received a salary and benefits similar to those of other full-time workers. They attend classes in which they work from printed texts but also follow broadcast lessons which are distributed terrestrially and by satellite and made available by videocassette. Learning is a classroom activity. The strength of the system lies in its use of centrally prepared materials and its capacity to expand university-level education with more modest, and less costly, buildings than conventional universities.

Indian independence led to an expansion of secondary education and a consequent unmet demand for tertiary education. In developing its Third Five Year Plan (1961–6) the government explored the idea of responding to that demand with correspondence courses to be run by existing universities (Manjulika and Reddy 1996: 19). The University of Delhi set up the first school of correspondence courses in 1962, to be followed by another twenty by 1980. Today more than a hundred universities have followed their lead (Panda 2005: 209).

The system attracted criticism as well as students. Correspondence education had low status and was used by some universities mainly as a way of raising revenue, with fees for off-campus students cross-subsidising the more favoured students on campus. The Indian government decided to start again and in the late 1970s edged towards establishing a national open university. In 1982 it was overtaken by the government of Andhra Pradesh which set up its own state open university, later to be renamed Dr B. R. Ambedkar Open University after the Harijan leader in the national independence movement and main author of the Indian constitution. It is a measure of the credibility and political status of open and distance learning that proposals for a national open university got the name of Indira Gandhi after her assassination in November 1984. With the prestige of her memory, the university was established in September 1985.

It enrolled its first 4500 students a year later, 50 000 by 1990 and over 360 000 by 2004. The memorials to Dr Ambedkar and Mrs Gandhi have been followed by nine other state open universities. More are to come: by 2007 each of India's 29 states is expected to have an open university so that the distance-education system meets at least 50 per cent of the increase in higher education enrolment (*ibid.*). The Indira Gandhi National Open University (IGNOU) has a unique status; it acts as a university grants commission to the other open universities, distributing funds to them, offering staff training and 'promoting, coordinating and determining the standards of distance education in the country' (Kulandai Swamy and Pillai 1994: 71).

Expansion across a continent

China and India are not alone. Most of the large Asian countries have set up open universities and there is enough similarity between them to talk of an Asian model, or pair of models one illustrated by Indian experience, dominated by the use of correspondence lessons, and one by Chinese, originally dominated by broadcasting. Pakistan was first, where Bhutto launched a People's Open University in 1974. It survived the coup against him though the name, with its echo of his People's Party, had to go and it is now safely named Allama Iqbal after the national poet. In Iran the Shah chose the doublespeak title 'Free University of Iran' for an institution that would not survive his fall and was 'seen as a means of keeping students out of the campuses where it is likely that they will be politicised' (Rumble and Keegan 1982: 298). The new Iran later came back to the idea of distance education, establishing Payame Noor University in 1987. South Korea, Israel, Sri Lanka and Thailand all launched open universities or their prototypes in the 1970s, Indonesia, Taiwan, Turkey and the Palestinian authorities in the 1980s, Bangladesh and the Philippines in the 1990s. Large numbers of students were enrolled. In Thailand 56 per cent of higher education students were studying at its two open universities in 1985. In Turkey the figure rose from 9700 students, or 4 per cent of the total, in 1980 to 308 000 or 26 per cent in 1994.[1]

The similarities between them are a consequence of design as well as geographical accident or shared history. Formal and informal contacts have tied them together. Academic staff in Pakistan were well informed about distance education in India, even when political contacts were at their most difficult. The founding Vice-Chancellor of Indira Gandhi

National Open University helped plan the Bangladesh Open University. An Asian Association of Open Universities was set up in 1987 and brings the key players together every two years. Basic facts about their development are in table 5.1.[2]

The growth of the open universities was part of a more general expansion of higher education. Most were set up in the fifteen years between 1972 and 1987. They grew fast in the 1980s, a decade when the east Asian economies were growing in GNP per capita at 6.1 per cent per annum, and south Asia at 3.1 per cent. Until the stock market collapses of 1997, they were seen as buoyant exemplars for the rest of the world in contrast with the sluggish OECD economies, and at a time when subsaharan Africa and Latin America were in decline (Ashton and Green 1996: 73). Educational policy was seen as central to economic development and countries as different as China, India, Iran and Turkey allowed higher education to grow more rapidly than GNP per capita, alongside some of the Asian newly industrialised countries. This process has continued: between 1995 and 2003 the higher education systems of China and India were growing at more than 10 per cent per annum. Indeed, while open-university enrolments expanded more rapidly than the conventional sector in their first few years, the reverse became the case in some countries. Between 1985 and 1995 China's conventional universities expanded more rapidly than the radio and television system while in both Iran and Thailand distance education contracted in the 1990s.

While the expansion of open universities was, at least in part, a reaction to the perceived needs of the economy, governments justified their establishment on three grounds: to help economic development, to respond to public demand, and to widen access for new groups of students. China's policy in 2005, for example, was summarised as 'putting great efforts into developing ICT-based distance education and e-learning as a way of meeting the growing demands for higher education and the need for qualified personnel in a rapidly expanding economy (Ding *et al.* 2005: 63).

Many of them had explicit economic and developmental ends. In Turkey, as the open university got under way, the largest single group of students were doing degrees in economics and business, presumably seen as contributing to economic development. The Payame Noor Open University in Iran seeks first to promote science and culture and then 'to provide skilled manpower in areas critical to national integration and development' (ICDL 1997). Its first courses were in chemistry, education, mathematics and Persian to be followed by biology and geology (NIME 1993: 117). The first objective of Sukhothai Thammathirat Open University in Thailand is 'to provide and promote university and professional education so as to enable the people to raise their educational standards in response to the needs of society' (Iam Chaya-Ngam 1987: 322).

The other two justifications – demand and access – are reflected in several of the open universities' founding charters. India's Yashwantrao Chavan

Table 5.1 Basic facts about some Asian open universities and distance-education departments

(figures in thousands)

Country, institution and date of foundation	Total student numbers 1990	Year	Most recent data		
			Total student nos.	Annual enrolment	Annual graduation
Bangladesh Open University 1992[a]		1995	42.3	n/a	n/a
China Radio and TV University 1979[b]	407.7	1996–7	526.6	197.1	187.9
Correspondence education 1953[b]	562.5	1996–7	896.3	286.4	12.3
Modern distance education 1998[c]		2003	2 290.0	n/a	n/a
India IGNOU 1985[d]	52	2003	1 013.6	316.5	81.9
Dr B. R. Ambedkar OU 1982[e]	38	2000–1	450.0	106.7	3.0
YCMOU 1989[f]	9.6	2000–1	486.7	113.5	60.7
Correspondence Departments 1960[g]	450.1	2001	904.1	438.8	78.6
Indonesia Universitas Terbuka 1984[h]	n/a	2005	n/a	250.0	n/a
Iran Payame Noor University 1987[f]	32.5	1998	147.8	n/a	n/a
Israel Open University 1974[j]	15.8	1992–3	19.0	8.1	0.4
Korea National open University 1972[k]	160	1997	208.9	70.0	n/a
Pakistan Allama Iqbal OU 1974[l]	235.2	2003	456.6	n/a	86.2
Sri Lanka Open University 1980 (SLIDE 1976)[k]	14.4	1998	20.0	n/a	n/a
Thailand Ramkamhaeng University 1971[k]	n/a	1992	302.9	210.0	n/a
Sukhothai Thammathirat OU 1978[k]	n/a	1998	200.0	80–90	n/a
Turkey Anadolu Open University 1982[k]	673.6	1992–3	304.5	n/a	n/a

a. Rumble 1999: 168; b. Ding 1999: 182–5 with earlier figures from Central Radio and TV University 1993; c. Ding *et al.* 2005: 66; d. Panda 1999: 204, IGNOU *Profile 2003*; e. DEC 2001a. f. ICDL 1997, DEC 2001a; g. Panda 1999: 202, DEC 2001b but later figures are for central universities only; h. ICDL 1997, UT website; i. ICDL 1997, 1999, NIME 1993; j. Herskovic 1995; k. ICDL 1997, 1999; l. *Vice-Chancellor's reports*

Maharashtra Open University (YCMOU), founded in 1989, has three objectives:

1. To make higher, vocational and technical education available to large sectors of the population.
2. To give special attention to the needs of the disadvantaged groups, in particular people in rural areas and women.
3. To relate all courses to the developmental needs of individuals, institutions and the State.

(ICDL 1997)

Asian open universities vary in the weight they have given to each of the three broad aims. For some, the demand was led by secondary-school graduates who could not get into conventional higher education. Secondary-school leavers are the main source of enrolments for the correspondence institutes in India where most students are below the age of 21 (NIME 1993: 75). Similarly, the first aim of the Korean Open University is to provide 'opportunities for higher education through distance methods to those high school graduates, who for various reasons cannot receive or have had to interrupt college education'. Indonesia, too, set high-school graduates as its primary target audience, although it then had difficulty in recruiting them (NIME 1993: 104).

A concern for access has led some open universities and distance-teaching systems to adopt mechanisms and policies to promote educational equity, or at least to attempt some balancing. Some Chinese universities charge tuition fees at half the normal rate for distance education learners in western China (Ding *et al.* 2005: 67). In Pakistan, Allama Iqbal Open University (AIOU) 'has the declared aim of providing educational uplift of the masses' (ICDL 1997). The main aim of the Dr B. R. Ambedkar Open University is 'to promote equality of educational opportunity for as large a segment of the population as possible ... and particularly including housewives and other women' (ICDL 1997). Plans for the Bangladesh Open University included, alongside 'students in rural areas and in particular women' such unconventional university audiences as 'untrained teachers at primary and secondary level [and] extension agents in agriculture, family planning, health and rural development' (Ali *et al.* 1997: 19).

We can go on to ask who the students are, what they are studying, how they are doing so, and how effectively.

Courses and students

The open universities vary in their range of courses and so in the students they recruit. All have significant programmes at first-degree level: without this they would miss the title, kudos and funding that go with the name university. Generally the courses fall into four main clusters: secondary and nonformal work, certificates and diplomas, degrees, and teacher education. First, in both Bangladesh and Pakistan, the open universities have a significant proportion of enrolments at secondary level and for nonformal courses. Then, second, many universities offer a range of certificate and diploma courses, which may be around the level of conventional degree work. Some of these are providing an initial professional qualification while others are programmes of continuing professional development. Teaching of this kind may be on a bigger scale than conventional degree work. The Shanghai TV University, for example, moved into professional and continuing education offering a variety of certificate and diploma programmes. This reflected a general shift by the radio and television universities, from degree to vocational diploma and certificate courses (Weixiang and Hawkridge 1995: 31). Third are the degree courses where most of the emphasis is on undergraduate degrees but some open universities have significant enrolments for higher degrees: these were 29 per cent of the total at IGNOU in 2000. Fourth, many universities have become involved in programmes of teacher education, often on a large scale, such as the Primary Teachers' Orientation Courses in Pakistan, described in chapter 4. The Bangladesh Open University incorporated existing programmes for teachers when it was set up, while Universitas Terbuka developed plans to teach a million school teachers (NIME 1993: 105).

The balance between these four kinds of course, and that between different subjects within them, reflect the purpose for which the open universities were established. Degree programmes have been important to universities set up mainly to widen access; so have secondary and nonformal programmes for a different group of students; vocational programmes have dominated where this fitted national policy; and a new vocationalism may have encouraged the growth of certificate and diploma courses. In India, for example, the largest enrolments have tended to be on first-degree courses in the arts and in commerce though computer studies are growing in terms of student numbers and popularity. Turkey began an associate degree programme for nurses in 1991 with the aim of training 100 000 nurses over ten years (Demiray 1995: 271). The recruitment of students at any one institution is affected by its profile of courses, and by social factors beyond its control. A study in Sri Lanka noted that 64 per cent of students on a technology programme were in jobs involving technical work, while 80 per cent of those studying tourism were in the private sector. Appropriately those on a 'Certificate Programme in Wild Life Conservation and Management' appeared to be a mixed bag' (Jayatilleke *et al.* 1997: 80).

For many institutions we can describe the students in two words, young men. Despite their differing priorities, and the different matches between courses and students, the Asian open universities have generally recruited students below the age of 30 and recruited more men then women. In China and Korea, where open universities offer an alternative route to degrees for school leavers, they form a large proportion of students. Universitas Terbuka in Indonesia has not found it easy to retain school leavers but 26 per cent of its students are between 19 and 24. As table 5.2 shows, between 60 and 90 per cent of students are below 30 in most open universities.

With some exceptions, the gender balance within open universities tends to reflect the national balance within higher education. In India women have made up about a third of enrolments in both conventional and distance education, but with the proportion gradually increasing. Whereas IGNOU had only 22.5 per cent women students in 1994, by 2004 the proportion had risen to 37.4 per cent by 2004 (Manjulika and Reddy 1996: 98; Panda 2005: 212). (Indian dual-mode universities have been more successful than open universities in recruiting women.) Indonesia reports a similar change with female enrolments rising from 25 to 48 per cent of the total over about fifteen years. In both Bangladesh and Pakistan the proportion of women has been rising: at AIOU it rose from 30 to 53 per cent between 1990 and 1995. The relatively high figures may reflect the particular value of open and distance learning in overcoming constraints on mobility (Raza 2004: 22). Sri Lanka had more women than men on a BSc science programme – perhaps remedying problems in the conventional system where the reverse was the case. The proportion of women students is influenced by the kind of courses offered by a university as well as by national culture. The move towards vocationally oriented courses in agriculture, or in computer studies, has tended to attract more men while courses in education, food and nutrition and nursing at IGNOU had female enrolments of between 59 and 89 per cent (*ibid*: 23).

One of the justifications for open universities is that they allow people to work and study at the same time. This has been a marked feature of the Korean Open University where the expanding economy meant there was a clientele of young high-school graduates, in employment, who also wanted to get a degree. In China many students attend full-time while on paid leave from their regular employment, an option that is not available in the other countries of east and south Asia. In India Dr B. R. Ambedkar Open University found that 65 per cent of its male students were employed while 68 per cent of its females were unemployed (indeed classified by the oxymoron 'unemployed housewife') (Manjulika and Reddy 1996: 93). This varied experience suggests, again, that the employment status of open university students reflects national social conditions more then any preference for a particular method of learning.

Earlier Indian evidence also suggested that distance education was doing no better and no worse than conventional education in reaching the most deprived groups. While 'the major purpose of distance education is to provide education to those who, for one reason or another could not take advantage of the facilities provided by the formal system' enrolment in fact 'reflects the urban and upper-class bias of the university system as a whole' (*ibid*: 62). In 1992–3 IGNOU had only 21 per cent rural students and only 8 per cent from scheduled castes and scheduled tribes. This, however,

Table 5.2 Students at some Asian open universities

Institution	Date	No. (1000s)	Age %	Female %	1st degree %	Higher degree %	Teaching qualifications %	Certificate, diploma %	Secondary nonformal, other %
Bangladesh: Open University[a]	1995	42	n/a	25 to 30	50		n/a	16	34
China: Radio and TV U[b]	1990	420	Many school leavers	28					
China Modern distance education[c]	2003	942	n/a		58	1			42
India: IGNOU[d]	1994	300	37% <26; 31% 25–30	23	43	29		29	
	2001			28	46	29	n/a	25	0
India: Dr. B. R. Ambedkar OU[e]	1993–4	60	31% <20; 81% <30	33	95			5	
India: YCMOU[e]	1993–4	38.3	45% <26; 15% 26–30	22	59	7		34	
India: Correspondence[c] Depts	1992	547.6	n/a	34					
Indonesia: UT[f]	1991	30–36	26% <25; 37% 25–30	25					
	2005	48							

	Year		Age						
Iran: Payame Noor U[g]	1996	117	70% 21–30				39		
South Korea: National OU[g]	1996	210	61% <30			57			
Pakistan: Allam Iqbal OU[h]	2003–4	456.6	n/a	52	47	7	11	0	34
Sri Lanka: Open University[i]	1991	16.2	n/a	25			16	59	1
Thailand: STOU[j]	1995	216.8	11% <21; 64% 21–30; 25% 31–40						

Notes:
a. Ali *et al.* 1997 with teaching qualifications included in degree total; b. NIME 1993; c. Ding *et al.* 2005 with 42% students on vocational courses; d. Manjulika and Reddy 1996, *Annual report 2001/2*; e. Manjulika and Reddy 1996; f. Daniel 1996, UT Website; g. Daniel 1996; h. *Vice Chancellor's report*; i. Wijeyesekara 1994; j. ICDL 1999.

probably reflects rational choice by students in these categories: there were untaken places within conventional universities reserved for scheduled castes and scheduled tribes (Fielden *et al.* n.d.: 70). Dr B. R. Ambedkar Open University increased its proportion of students from scheduled castes and scheduled tribes from 9 to 13 per cent over seven years, while two state open universities report similar difficulties in recruiting rural students: YCMOU, for example, intended to target rural students, and teaches in the local language, Marathi, but found that 71 per cent of its students were urban (Manjukika and Reddy 1996: 93, 106). More recent figures, however, show

> that for at least three open universities rural enrolments were higher than for conventional institutions while IGNOU, by 2004, had increased its rural students to 25 per cent; socially deprived students were 15 per cent of the total and backward class students 16 per cent.
>
> (Panda 2005: 212).

As far as the evidence goes, distance education in Asia seems to have been widening its appeal to some disadvantaged groups.

Methods

Although there are differences of emphasis that reflect their differing aims, Asian open universities generally use the same teaching methods, linking print, broadcasts or recordings, and opportunities for face-to-face study. Today, many are exploring the use of e-learning. There are two main variants: the Chinese radio and television universities and Ramkamhaeng University in Thailand rely heavily on classroom sessions, taught by radio and television, while most of the others assume that their students will work at home. One teaching system can stand for many, comprising:

> a multi-media integrated approach suitable for the conditions available in a developing country such as Sri Lanka. Printed material forms the major component of the study package. This includes printed texts, assigned books and recommended reading. The student is expected to devote about 55 per cent to 70 per cent of study time to the printed material. The second important component is face to face contact, either at day schools or demonstrations, and practical work, depending on the needs of the particular course. Face to face contact sessions are highest in English language programmes while demonstrations and practical work form an important component in science and technology programmes as well as in teacher training programmes. Approximately 15 per cent of study time is expected to be devoted to these. Face to face sessions are used for group interaction, discussions, and counselling.

The use of audio-visual material as an integral part of the study pack-age is less frequent and varies from relatively high in English language and law programmes to about 5 per cent in others. ...

Assignments and periodic assessment through examinations form a compulsory component of the study package in all programmes. These are used as a teaching learning device as well as for continuous assessment of student progress.

(NIME 1993: 395–6)

Familiar stuff: the open university gene seems to reproduce with few muta-tions. But the other model is different. Students of the Chinese television university in Shen Zhen in 1993 were attending classes in an echoing brick and concrete building with the institutional feel of an English technical college of the 1950s. Television lessons, with talking head and blackboard, showed the same physics curriculum you would find anywhere, followed by a familiar noisy move from one classroom to another at the end of fifty minutes. The teacher was on the screen, in the only apparent difference from a conventional class. In Thailand about a third of the 300 000 students of Ramkamhaeng University regularly studied in the same way attending lecture halls – said to accommodate 3000 to 5000 students each – which were linked by closed-circuit television. Another 40 per cent attended irregularly. Self-help was part of the system so that 'those students who have a good under-standing of the course act as tutors and volunteer to tutor other students' (NIME 1993: 414). The Korean Open University assumed most students would work at home but had the same heavy reliance on broadcasting, with ten hours of radio lectures a day. Each semester students had to attend a five-day summer or winter school, where three days were devoted to teaching and two to assessment (*ibid*: 147–55).

Correspondence study, in your own time, may be less demanding. And it is what most people get. Some years ago IGNOU used 100 tons of paper a year and in 2003 despatched 978 000 packets to students; the Universitas Terbuka in Indonesia has a formal agreement with the post office where students can register, pay their fees, and order course texts; AIOU puts print at the top of its list of teaching methodologies. Despite rhetoric about other technologies, and despite evidence of the potency of mixing media, the methodological achievement of the open universities has been to move from a person-based educational system to a print-based one. Most open universities have been making quite modest use of radio or television.

Many express hope for the use of the internet though it is a long way from displacing print. At IGNOU, for example, 'the online programmes have been successful in reaching the digitally rich who have access to the Internet or can manage to visit learning and teaching centres regularly, though issues like digital access and exclusion, content design, design of a university-wide platform and learning management system, and both teacher and learner capacity building need to be addressed simultaneously (Panda 2005: 214). China has also begun to experiment and by 2004 had developed 321 online curricula. Its use of the internet was, however, essentially ancillary to other teaching methods rather than a substitute for them; 'more than 90 per cent of e-learners have the opportunity to acquire a face-to-face tutor, and more than 80 per cent have at some time taken part in learning groups' (Ding *et al.* 2005: 69).

Face-to-face study is the third horse of the distance-education troika. And here, too, open universities have been disappointed in what they have been able to achieve. Allama Iqbal Open University noticed as one of its major weaknesses the logistical difficulties which meant that 'provision of face-to-face contact between the teachers and the students tends to be minimised' (NIME 1993: 290). In Indonesia only 10 per cent of students attended tutorial sessions (Setijadi 1987: 126). In India the open universities have developed structures for contact with students. IGNOU allotted 10 per cent of total study hours to counselling, established regional offices and, by 2003 had 1068 study centres. But it has been difficult to get the system to work. Inevitably most study centres are in towns: even if they were evenly distributed throughout the country each would have to cover an area of over 3000 square kilometres. As a result students have had difficulty reaching study centres; attendance at tutorial sessions is 'thin and varied' while some centres lack 'qualified counsellors and other technical facilities' which reduces the value of what they can offer to students (Manjulika and Reddy 1996: 124). Many sessions were not working well, degenerating either into lectures, rather than counselling and something 'more like intense/ crash courses' (Panda *et al.* 1999: 254).

The logistics of linking print, broadcasts and tutorials have proved daunting everywhere and it is neither surprising nor discreditable that they continue to plague under-resourced universities working in some of the poorest countries of the world. There is a dilemma here, too. The highly structured system based on broadcasts as the main teaching medium, developed in China but with echoes in Korea, seems to have solved many of the problems of integrating the media. But it demands capital investment in buildings for students to attend – even if the timing of broadcasts allows dual use – marked dedication from students, and possibly their willingness to attend classes full-time. Structure may be in conflict with flexibility, flexibility with effectiveness.

Effects

The open universities have become multi-purpose organisations. They have attracted students – sometimes by the half-million – and awarded degrees. In many cases governments have given them a specific role, in meeting workforce demands, as well as a general one of widening opportunities for higher education. They have been working long enough for us to ask how well they have done so. Part of the answer is that they have become an established part of the educational system with the legitimacy implied by their founding acts. If their purpose was to enable citizens to register for a degree, in larger numbers than was possible through the concurrent expansion of the formal university system, then the numbers in table 5.3 show their achievement. But we need to know more than this and at least to ask how effective open universities have been in producing graduates or certificate holders.

There are some technical difficulties in finding an answer. Students may take varying periods of time to complete their degrees so that members of a cohort who all begin studying in the same year may graduate between three and ten years later. Then, too, in comparing different universities we are seldom matching like with like. Many open-university students are older than students in conventional universities. Where they are the same age, they are usually at an educational disadvantage; those who have done best at school tend to go on to conventional universities. It has been argued, too, that it is unrealistic to calculate a successful completion rate by reference to the total number of students who initially enrolled where a large number give up study in the first month or two.[3] To compound these difficulties, many universities have been reluctant to publish figures even though, 'if open universities are to advocate a different funding structure or to bid for more funds, they will also need to make their case by producing fuller data than have usually been available on completion rates and costs per graduate' (Mugridge 1994: 121).

The limited evidence available is mixed. To begin with the positive, China has long demonstrated that its model of distance education, with many students working full time, can produce results that stand up well in comparison with those of conventional universities. In the late 1980s more than 80 per cent of students in the radio and television universities graduated within the minimum time. The volume of graduates was enough to be economically significant: some 17 per cent of all university graduates, or 1.5 million in total, were from radio and television universities between 1982 and 1991 (Ding 1994: 161–5).

There is positive evidence, too, of the efficiency of university programmes of teacher education and some other vocational subjects. Many of these were inservice programmes that guaranteed improved status and pay at the end of the course. With that incentive, Anadolu Open University reported a completion rate for its teachers' courses of over 90 per cent as compared with 24 per cent for its courses in economics and business (Daniel 1996: 192). The Bangladesh Open University reported a 52 per cent pass rate for its BEd course (Rumble 1999: 174); the Korean Open University had a success rate of between 53 and 68 per cent for a two-year course in primary education (Kim 1992: 61–5). Raza (2004: 36–7) found 43 and 70 per cent successful completion rates for two different cohorts on the Open University of Sri Lanka's bachelor's in nursing.

Table 5.3 Outcome data from some open universities

Country and Institution	Type of course	Date	Enrolment	Graduation	Pass or completion rate%	Conventional university rate%
Bangladesh						
Open University[b]	Cert in English	1996	7 333	3 841	48	n/a
	BEd	1996	11 195	5 401	52	n/a
	Certificates and diplomas	to 2003	23 580	5 023	3–54	n/a
	BEd	1992–2003	49 969	26 230	52	n/a
	Grad dip management	1995–2003	12 623	123	1	n/a
China						
RTVUs[c]	Equivalent jr college degree	1996–7	197 100 p.a	187 900	70–80	n/a
India						
BRAOU	First degree[d]	1991–2	n/a	n/a	23	55–60
	BA[e]	1993–4	30 000	3 500	12	
IGNOU	First degree[d]	1991–2	n/a	n/a	23	55–60
	Management programmes[f]	1987–93	44 731	17 708	40	
	Diploma progs[f]	1987–93	5 015	853	17	
	Cert in food and nutrition[f]	1987–93	19 213	3 740	20	
	Certs and diplomas[g]	1996–2001	9 288	1 679	18	n/a
	First degrees[g]	1996–2001	6 250	1 056	3–39	n/a
	Postgraduate[g]	1996–2001	4 767	987	6–34	n/a
YCMOU[d]	First degree	1991–2			34	55–60
Indonesia						
Universitas Terbuka[h]	Two-year degree	1984–8	65 000	n/a	1	n/a
	First degree	1984–90	n/a	n/a	5	n/a
	First degree	1991–7	9 288	1 679	18	n/a

	Years			Rate %	
South Korea KACU[i]					
Two-year degree	1977–85	10 837	3 684	34	n/a
	1980–8	17 104	5 150	30	n/a
Five-year degree	1981–91	28 266	4 111	15	n/a
	1983–91	35 698	3 511	10	n/a
Pakistan AIOU[j]					
BA	1981–6	53 697	15 895	30[k]	n/a
MBA	1986	600	277	46	n/a
Sri Lanka[g] OUSL					
Certs and diplomas	1994–2000	6 666	1 257	3–65	n/a
First degrees	1994–2000	220	90	7–70	n/a
Postgraduate	1994–2000	1 469	924	33–65	n/a
Thailand STOU[l]					
2-year degree programme	1980–2	82 139	9 594	12	85
	1982–3	69 561	17 236	25	85
Two-year prog	1980–7	50–80 000 p.a	n/a	38	
Three-year prog				20	
Four-year prog				15	
Various[m]	1984–91	n/a	n/a	17	

Notes:

a. Rate is for graduation or certification except where shown; b. Rumble 1999: 174, Raza 2004: 39; c. Ding 1999: 180–2; d. Ansari 1994: 83; e. Fielden *et al.* n.d.: 96 (including both the 2500 who had graduated and a further 1000 who were expected to). f. Fielden *et al.* n.d. 63; g. Raza 2004: 32–8; h. Wilson 1991: 261, Belawati 1998: 82, Belawati 2001: 183; i. Kim 1992: 61–5; j. Sargant *et al.* 1989. Figures for BA are the total shown in their table 2. k. Figures apparently relate to single courses of which students had to take eight to graduate. l. Wichit and Tong-In 1985: 11–13; Smith n.d.: 160; m. Belawati 1998: 82.

But these are the exceptions and much of the scattered evidence is much less positive about the efficiency of the open universities. In many, dropout rates are high, graduation rates relatively low, and where we have data, the quality of graduates' degrees is below that of conventional institutions (Ansari 1994: 82–3). Available figures are in table 5.3.

Early figures from Korea, Indonesia and Thailand show graduation rates that are usually below 20 per cent. Over a period of nine years in which the Korean Open University offered a two-year degree programme, the success rate within five years of enrolment varied between 30 and 36 per cent. A five-year degree programme had a lower success rate: in 1991, after ten years, only 15 per cent of the first cohort of students had graduated (Kim 1992: 61:5). The graduation rate at Sukhothai Thammathirat Open University rose from 12 to 25 per cent between 1982 and 1983, as it relaxed restrictions on how long students could take over their degrees, but then apparently fell back to 17 per cent (Belawati 1998: 82). In Indonesia, dropout from the university's first cohort of 65 000 students who enrolled in 1984 meant that only 9117 (14 per cent) were still active by 1988 when a successful 443 graduated (Wilson 1991: 261). Of degree students registered between 1984 and 1990 only 5 per cent had graduated by 1995 although rates later improved to 18 per cent by 1997 for two cohorts recruited in 1991 and 1992 (Belawati 1998: 82, 2001: 183).

Several studies reported successful completion rates in south Asia of between 10 and 40 per cent compared with rates of 55 to 60 per cent in conventional universities in India; they appear to be slightly lower than figures for distance-education students in eight dual-mode universities where graduation rates were in the range 28 to 40 per cent (Ansari 1994: 82–3; Fielden *et al.* n.d.: 63, 96). We have important new data for south Asia from comparative studies of the national open universities in all four countries done by Raza (2004). At IGNOU she found completion rates were generally higher for master's and postgraduate diplomas than for first degree courses with three programmes out of five having rates between 28 and 34 per cent; the fairly specialist Bachelor's of Library and Information Science, which could be completed in one year, had a completion rate of 39 per cent while the other bachelor's degrees varied between 3 (computer applications) and 14 per cent (arts). Certificate programmes in food and nutrition, guidance, and tourism had completion rates of 25, 22 and 12 per cent. Detailed figures are in table 5.4. These figures are generally consistent with those reported by Lakshmi Reddy (2002a) who was using a different methodology and by Reddy (2002). The Open University of Sri Lanka is more successful in its BA programme, with a 51 per cent completion rate by 2000 for its 1996 BA cohort and higher figures, of 64 and 65 per cent, reported for its master's in technology and postgraduate diploma in education. Certificate programmes generally reported rates in the 30 to 40 per cent range though with worse results for professional engineering and better for preschool education. There are more limited data for Bangladesh where

Table 5.4 South Asian open university completion rates

	Year of enrolment	Enrolled	Graduated by 2001		Period of Completion
			No.	%	
Indira Gandhi National Open University Certificates					
Food and nutrition	1996	2 432	610	25	6 months to 2 years
Guidance	1996	628	138	22	6 months to 2 years
Tourism studies	1996	833	100	12	6 months to 2 years
Diplomas					
Computers in office management	1996	1 507	432	29	1 to 4 years
Nutrition and health education	1996	977	93	10	1 to 4 years
Rural development	1996	1 777	306	17	1 to 4 years
Tourism studies	1996	1 969	225	11	1 to 4 years
Bachelor's degrees					
Arts	1996	9 816	1 409	14	3 to 8 years
Computer applications	1996	2 661	76	3	3 to 6 years
Commerce	1996	4 018	316	8	3 to 8 years
Library and information science	1996	1 249	490	39	3 to 4 years
Science	1996	2 358	105	5	3 to 8 years
Tourism studies	1996	1 280	62	5	3 to 8 years
Postgraduate					
PG Diploma computer science	1996	2 453	424	17	1 to 4 years
PG Dipioma distance education	1996	516	173	34	1 to 4 years
PG Diploma higher education	1996	494	28	6	1 to 4 years
PG Diploma journalism and mass comm-n	1996	1 257	349	28	1 to 4 years
MA Distance education	1996	47	13	28	1 to 4 years
Open University of Sri Lanka[a] *Certificates and diplomas*			*Graduated by 2000*		
Certificate in preschool education	1994	581	480	65	1 year minimum
Certificate in professional english	1994	2 817	346	12	1 year minimum
Certificate in entrepreneurship & small business	1994	840	250	30	1 year minimum
Certificate in wildlife Conservation	1995	56	18	32	1 year minimum
Certificate in tourism	1994	72	21	29	1 year minimum
Diploma in technology	1994	1 524	39	3	2 year minimum
Diploma in management	1994	776	103	13	2 year minimum

Continued

Table 5.4 South Asian open university completion rates—cont'd

	Year of enrolment	Enrolled	Graduated by 2000		Period of Completion
			No.	%	
Bachelor's Degrees					
Arts	1996	63	32	51	3 year minimum
Technology	1994	83	6	7	3 year minimum
Nursing	1994	74	52	70	2 year minimum
Postgraduate					
Master's technology	1994	11	7	64	1 year minimum
PG Diploma technology	1994	46	15	33	1 year minimum
PG Diploma management	1994	34	13	38	2 year minimum
PG Diploma education	1994	1 376	889	65	2 year minimum
Bangladesh Open University *Certificates and diplomas*			*Graduated by 2003*		
Certificate of education	1998–	7 348	1 592	22	1 year minimum
Certificate in english language proficiency	1994–	11 834	2 507	21	1 year minimum
Certificate in Arab language proficiency	1996–	2 045	446	22	1 year minimum
Certificate in pisciculture and fish processing	1999–	356	192	54	1 year minimum
Certificate livestock and poultry	1999–	446	209	47	1 year minimum
Certificate in management	1995–	1 401	40	3	1 year minimum
Diploma in youth development	1999–	150	37	25	1 year minimum
Bachelor's degrees					
Education	1992–	49 969	26 230	52	n/a
English language	1997–	2 172	67	3	n/a
Agricultural education	1997–	7 506	740	10	n/a
Arts social science	2000–	13 708	n/a	n/a	n/a
Postgraduate					
Graduate diploma in management	1995–	12 623	123	1	$1^1/_2$ to 2 years

Source: Raza 2004: tables 4.4, 4.6, 4.7
Note:
a. Quoting for each qualification data for the longest period shown by Raza.

the most successful programmes were the more vocationally oriented with completion rates for a BEd at 53 per cent and for certificates in pisciculture and in livestock and poultry at 54 and 47 per cent. Figures from Pakistan 'although not as comprehensive, indicate a similar magnitude of failure to complete'; two-and-a-half years after enrolling on a BCom course, which could be completed in two years, '58 per cent had achieved no credits, while 9 per cent had completed' (Raza 2004: 41).

Four conclusions follow. First, shorter courses have higher completion rates than longer. This is borne out both by the data from Korea and Thailand for degree programmes of different lengths, and by the higher figures recorded in India for certificate and diploma programmes as contrasted with degree programmes. Postgraduate programmes also tend to have a higher completion rate than undergraduate programmes, either because the students are more sophisticated learners or, perhaps, simply because of the comparative demands of short and long courses. Second, successful completion rates for degree courses are often little over 10 per cent. We are short of data but the figures suggest that the open universities are, because of this low rate, disappointing many students and contributing far fewer graduates to their economies than their large enrolment figures would lead one to expect. Third, in absolute terms, they are nevertheless making those contributions. Raza, for example, found that, over a period of five years, AIOU was producing 8 per cent of all bachelor's degrees and 14 per cent of MPhil's produced by Pakistani public-sector tertiary institutions (Raza 2004: 30). Fourth, dropout rates are more important than failure rates in explaining this. They demand further examination.

Few institutions publish dropout rates but it is possible to draw inferences from the number of students admitted and the numbers graduating. By the late 1990s many of the open universities had reached consistently high annual enrolments, even if not a steady state. But table 5.5 shows the regular disparity between student admissions and graduations. The evidence on dropout is consistent with our estimate of successful completion rates. It led Lakshmi Reddy, writing from within one of the universities, to the sad conclusion that 'on the whole 91 per cent of the students enrolled are going as wastage i.e. either as drop outs or those who could not complete the programmes within the prescribed maximum durations' (Lakshmi Reddy 2002b).

The pass rates achieved have a significant bearing on the economics of using distance education for higher education, examined in chapter 6. It seems that the size, and central political direction, of China have brought the expected economies of scale to the television universities with costs per student and costs per graduate that compare favourably with the alternatives. In other cases the evidence is mixed, with dropout rates possibly eroding the economic advantage that comes from lower costs per student.

Table 5.5 Admission and graduation rates at two universities

	1999–2000	2000–1	2001–2	2002–3	2003–4
IGNOU[a]					
Admissions	196 650	291 360	298 987	316 547	334 315
All qualifications awarded	53 328	62 369	78 068	81 931	74 603
AIOU[b]					
Admissions	310 890	357 595	335 025	399 560	512 635
All qualifications awarded	62 540	89 069	80 114	89 069	95 787

Notes
a. IGNOU Convocation Reports; b. VC Report Executive Summary 2003–4 and 2004–5.

Other approaches

The rapid growth of open universities in Asia has tended to eclipse other uses of distance education. In India, though students may pay higher fees and get poorer materials from distance-education departments than from open universities, there were 147 472 enrolments in the six central universities offering distance education, leaving aside the far larger number of institutions funded by individual states (DEC 2001b: 24). While some may be 'oases of excellence in a desert of education' (Shukla 1992) many are not: students are required to pay a higher proportion of the total cost than at the open universities, and dropout rates are high (Manjulika and Reddy 1996: 64–5). Despite this, and a heavy reliance on correspondence as almost the only means of teaching, the limited evidence suggests the results of correspondence departments compare reasonably well with those of open universities. There is a similar story from China where, alongside the 206 100 students who entered the television universities in 1996, there were 212 300 enrolments in correspondence-education departments attached to universities (Ding 1999: 181–5); while by 2005 much interest was focused on more advanced technologies, dual-mode approaches were still a significant part of the system (Ding *et al.* 2005: 64–5). Costs were reported to be lower than for conventional universities and Tongji university reported an 80 per cent graduation rate (NIME 1993: 32–9).

Some Asian countries have adopted a different approach. For many years Universiti Sains Malaysia was the sole dual-mode university in Malaysia until a government change of policy moved the rest in the same direction as well as to the establishment of an open university in 2000. The university has steadily provided distance-education courses with a measure of success but on a scale that is dwarfed both by Malaysian external enrolment at conventional universities and by the activities of the Asian open universities. Hong Kong, with a population of 6 million, never needed an open university comparable to those of its giant neighbours and adopted a different approach. It built on the foundations of the Open Learning Institute of Hong Kong which began work by importing existing courses from outside the territory, rather than producing its own. Rapid expansion was followed by local adaptation of the materials. It gained university status in 1997 and is unusual, in the region, in being financially self-sustaining: with the exception of some capital grants, student fees pay for everything (Murphy and Fung 1999: 193–4).

The Asian open universities dwarf the rest. There are no distance-teaching institutions on the same scale in Africa, or Latin America. Here the story is of more modest open universities and of dual-mode universities, some limited to specialist and narrowly focused courses.

Africa

Open universities do not dominate distance education in Africa, as they do in Asia. Although distance education was widely adopted in the first decades after independence, at secondary level and for teacher training, African governments did not follow that experience by establishing open universities in the 1970s or 1980s. We can infer good reasons for this: there was less unmet demand for university places than in much of Asia. While Indonesia had only 100 000 places in state universities for the 600 000 annually sitting university entrance (Wilson 1991: 266) in Zimbabwe some 5100 students in 1989 got the qualifications needed for university entrance at a time when the university had a total of 9300 students (Zimbabwe Central Statistical Office 1993). (The expansion of secondary education is changing this picture in some countries; in 2000 Nigeria had room in its universities for only 12 per cent of those qualified to enter [Commission for Africa 2005: 137].) There was little money, too: the reduction in educational expenditure per head made the 1980s a bad decade for educational innovation. There may be a cultural factor at work as well: the francophone world seems to have been fairly resistant to the idea of establishing open universities so that 'despite the internet's recent and significant breakthrough, the development of open and distance learning has not achieved a scale comparable to that which is seen in anglophone African countries or in other continents' (Rumajogee 2003: 104).

Until recently, and with the important exception of the University of South Africa, tertiary-level distance education within Africa has been dominated by the work of dual-mode universities, which have either run specialised programmes, most often in education, or sought to offer a range of courses parallel to their regular ones. Ghana, Kenya and Nigeria have all set up university distance-education programmes for teachers (see chapter 4). Distance-education units have been set up in Namibia, Swaziland, and Uganda among others. But the numbers involved are relatively small and most universities are offering only a narrow range of courses. An external programme at Makerere University was launched with 246 students (Aguti 1999a: 7) and one at the University of Swaziland with 150, though these built up over nine years to 1595 in 2004–5. The University of Lagos and the University of Zambia have longer experience than most of running distance education; their story yields some general conclusions.

The University of Lagos set up its Correspondence and Open Studies Institute in 1975 with its initial courses in business studies and education. Over the years it enrolled between 1000 and 2700 students annually and, though plagued by dropout, produced 2000 graduates in ten years and achieved pass rates, for those who completed the course and sat the examinations, of between 75 and 79 per cent (Dodds and Mayo 1996: 110).

But the Lagos story illustrates the difficulties that have bedevilled many dual-mode programmes. The institute faced severe problems in getting materials written where academic staff saw this as an activity that brought them much work and little reward. (They were partially solved by the appointment of a senior staff member who, as a grey-haired Anglican priest who also had high status within Yoruba society, could bring several kinds of authority to bear). The difficulties have persisted: in 1989 only one-third of course units were available to students. Then it proved impossible for the university to provide the necessary supervision to study centres outside Lagos, or to pay a marking fee high enough to ensure that assignments were marked. Funding became more difficult; while the programme began with a government subsidy, this was withdrawn in 1989 with a requirement that the programme should become self-supporting. With three-quarters of all students in Lagos, the programme became, in effect, a part-time on-campus course, run through Saturday study-centre meetings (Fagbamiye 1995: 74ff.).

Cost data for Lagos shows that the cost per graduate is probably slightly lower than it is for full-time students. (Cumming and Olaloku 1993: 375).

The University of Zambia had distance teaching written into its founding charter (as a result of the presence of an Australian from a dual-mode university on its planning commission) and has run a modest programme since its foundation in 1967. It is used as a route both into full-time study and out of it. A quota of students who complete two years of a degree can move into full-time, on-campus study, while students who do not complete their degree on campus can sometimes do so at a distance. Numbers have been modest, though significant in relation to the size of the university: the programme began with 152 students in 1967 and has since then built up to between 600 and 800 students. The distance-education students, however, made up 37 per cent of the total number of students in the two university schools in which they could enrol. An evaluation in 1991 reported pass rates of over 87 per cent and that dropout rates had been reduced to 10–15 per cent (Tate 1991: 22). These figures have been achieved despite Zambia's chronically weak economy and within tight constraints on the distance-education department. The directorate of distance education suffered from low status, a lack of staff training on distance education, and the fact that academic staff saw face-to-face teaching as their main responsibility. Some of these problems are structural: the university inherited an Australian organisational model in which the renamed Directorate of Distance Education was simply an administrative and distribution unit with no pedagogical functions. Quality suffers (Siaciwena 1996: 15).

The reduction in the range of courses offered at a distance has brought the University of Zambia closer to universities which, in contrast, decided to go for a niche market. Zambia has, however, institutionalised distance education as part of the regular university structure and, for students in education, humanities and social sciences, provided a genuine alternative route to higher education in a country where the gross enrolment ratio in higher education was still below 3 per cent in 2000.

The dual-mode universities may be losing their dominance. Madagascar and Tanzania set up open universities in 1992 to be followed by Zimbabwe and, more recently, Nigeria. The Centre National de Télé-Enseignement de Madgascar offers mainly professional and vocational courses and had some

7000 enrolments in 2000 of which 2813 were in law and 2616 in management (Valérien *et al.* 2003: 37).

The Tanzanian open university was, with reason and difficulty, created by act of parliament in 1992. The reasons and difficulties come from the same source: Tanzania is among the poorest countries in Africa – and the world – and sent only 30 per cent of those qualified for entry on to university. When the Open University began to recruit students in 1994, the conventional, public, universities had a total of only 3670 students (Mmari 1999: 111). Tanzania already had experience of using distance education for secondary education, for teacher training and in support of its cooperative movement so that there was relevant experience and expertise within the country. But the logistics of establishing the university, of getting course material developed, and of establishing viable regional centres, have inevitably been difficult.

By 1998 the university was recruiting some 5700 students to degree courses in the arts, social sciences, commerce and law. Two of its degrees, a BA (education) and a BCom (education) were mainly for teachers. Degrees were planned to take a student six years but exceptions to this meant that the first degree ceremony was held in 1999, five years after the first students began their courses. The university introduced a foundation course to provide an access route for entrants with a limited educational background. In response to demand it moved on to introduce degree courses in law and a small range of postgraduate courses in areas such as tourism and community economic development. Enrolment had grown to 16 000 by 2004 (Komba 2004).

The Open University of Tanzania is different from many of its peers both in its scale, which is modest in comparison with the Asian giants though not with other universities in East Africa, and in its student enrolment. Partly because of the large proportion of serving teachers among its early students, two-thirds were over 35 (Mmari 1999: 114–5). The university has had difficulty recruiting women so that the total was at around 10 per cent and had risen only to 26 per cent by 2004. Unlike the Asian open universities, it has concentrated mainly on degree work. Unlike most of them, too, it has from the outset been keen to acquire and use materials from other institutions. These have included the University of Nairobi, and IGNOU; other possibilities, including the University of Abuja in Nigeria and the University of South Africa were being explored (*Open University of Tanzania Newsletter*, 25, 1998).

Nigeria has made three attempts at setting up an open university. As far back as 1981, during civilian rule, Nigeria decided to have an open university, appointed a vice-chancellor, and put the necessary legislation to parliament. In a demonstration of independence – apparently related to a different issue before parliament at the same time – MPs rejected the legislation (Rumble and Harry 1982: 24). This left the vice-chancellor designate a sad figure, looking for his university. The proposal was revived but again turned down, this time by the military (Ajayi *et al.* 1996: 141). With civilians back in power the idea has been revived and both planning and staff training are continuing, with advice and support being provided by the Commonwealth of Learning.

South Africa is different in the scale of its distance education and of the literature about it.

As many as 43 per cent of higher education students study at a distance, or 29 per cent of full-time equivalents. The University of South Africa (UNISA) dominates the story just as its brutalist concrete building dominates the south of Pretoria. Its roots can be traced back to 1873; since 1946 it has been a correspondence-based university and in 2001 had 133 555 students. During the apartheid years the region had an ambivalent attitude to UNISA, at once a pillar of Afrikaanerdom and a useful provider of courses not available elsewhere. In the 1980s it was joined by Technikon South Africa and VISTA university but, in 2004, university mergers meant that UNISA was again the only dedicated distance-teaching university. During the 1990s, however, distance education expanded rapidly within nine conventional universities so that by 2001 they had 73 084 students, or 11 per cent of their total numbers in terms of full-time equivalents (CHE 2004: 8–10). The government of South Africa was sufficiently concerned about the quality of their work, and the economics of small-scale courses, that in 1999 it placed an embargo on distance-education programmes in dual-mode institutions (*ibid*: 21).

The scale of South Africa's distance education, and its role in widening educational opportunity, led the ANC to commission an international review of its strengths, weaknesses and potential (SAIDE 1995). Government planning documents for the new South Africa provided a framework for distance education and a further review by the statutory Council on Higher Education followed a decade later (CHE 2004). One consequence is that we are better informed about open and distance learning in South Africa than in many other countries, whether in the south or the north.

Over 80 per cent of the students are studying at undergraduate level. UNISA students, most of them working for conventional degrees or diplomas, are mainly young with a high proportion under 30; 36 000 of them were under 23. Students at the dual-mode universities, many of them doing BEds while working, tended to be older. Partly because of the scale of the teacher-education courses distance education was attracting a higher proportion of female students than conventional education (*ibid*: 84). The Council on Higher Education was concerned, however, at the balance between subjects with commerce, management and the humanities dominating the enrolments in contrast with national priorities; distance education was not doing the job of widening access and developing skills in science and technology – only 6 per cent of the students at distance universities in 2001 – or health with only 1 per cent (*ibid*: 11).

UNISA was long criticised for the lack of support it gave to students, offering correspondence courses and little else, but launched on a process of change of both values and methods as South Africa itself changed. But by 2004 much remained to be done. Programmes offered by the dedicated distance-teaching institutions provided 'very poor quality support to rural students, with support only offered in a very limited number of urban centres' (CHE 2004: 87). None of the programmes examined in the study required students to attend face-to-face sessions, in two programmes out of four, assignments were optional and there was no formative assessment. Students signed up at the beginning of the year, were automatically entered for the examination at the end, and that was about it (*ibid*: 100).

One of UNISA's weaknesses, to which its record on student support contributes, is its poor success rate. The report commissioned by ANC found throughput rates in the mid-1990s of 5 per cent in science degrees and 10 per cent in commerce. These cannot be attributed simply to the poor previous education of black South Africans: its pass rates for white students in commerce and science did not rise above 12 per cent. Education was better at 37 per cent (SAIDE 1995: 7–8). The 2004 council report looked again at throughput rates, examining data from ten case studies of which four were from dedicated distance-teaching universities and six from dual-mode. The dual-mode institutions, dominated by vocationally oriented courses in health and education and with relatively low enrolments, had through-put figures of between 46 and 85 per cent while rates of only 5 to 25 per cent were reported from UNISA and the institutions now merged with it (CHE 2004: 100).

Ex Africa semper aliquid novum. The new public concern for distance education in South Africa, and the large numbers enrolled, may yet lead to improvements in its record.

This African account has been predominantly bleak. Before attributing that fact to the inherent weakness of distance education, we should set it against the recent experience of conventional higher education in Africa. An analysis in 1996 noted that:

> The cruel 'winds of stringency', consequent upon the severe economic recession of the past two decades or so, and the prevailing unjust economic order, continue to blow unabated across the African continent with devastating consequences for the universities and other institutions of higher education in most African countries. ...

> The damage sustained by under-resourcing the universities during the years of economic decline, in almost all Sub-Saharan African countries, has been massive generally and in some areas debilitating. In fact, the first impression one gets of an African university campus in the 1990s is one of an all-pervading state of physical, managerial, and intellectual dilapidation. For the concerned Africans anywhere and the most senior academics in the older African universities, there is indeed an unmistaken sense of loss, amounting almost to grief, as they compare the present

state of their universities with the vigor, optimism and pride which these same institutions displayed twenty or thirty years ago.

(Ajayi *et al.* 1996: 145)

Tragically, the Commission for Africa painted the same picture a decade later when 'many of Africa's higher education institutions are still in a state of crisis. They lack physical infrastructure, such as internet access, libraries, textbooks, equipment, laboratories and classroom space. ... They lack human resources, such as teachers, lecturers, and administrative and managerial systems' (Commission for Africa 2005: 137).

Distance education is not immune to these problems. The African experience has been one of modest institution building in which distance education has been able to attract only limited institutional or public support. Funds for work off-campus have been scarce. Where distance-education programmes have been started, they have generally attracted smaller proportions of the total enrolment in higher education than has been the case in Asia. The exception is South Africa where the institutional structures look stronger but where universities are still on the elusive quest for quality.

Latin America

Latin American economies suffered nearly as badly in the 1980s as those of subsaharan Africa and open universities launched with enthusiasm and generous funding in the 1970s made only modest progress in the 1990s. In Venezuela, for example, a new government and increased oil revenues led to the establishment of an open university in 1977, for which government support later fell away. In Costa Rica there is a similar account of early optimism leading to modest outcomes. As a result, the number of students using distance education at tertiary level in Latin America is relatively small (Duque 1999: 225).

When the Universidad Estatal a Distancia (UNED) was established in 1977, the Costa Rican economy had been growing at 5.8 per cent per annum and GNP per capita was US$1393 (*$4471*). By 1995 the growth rate over the previous decade was down to 2.9 per cent while GNP, at $2610 (*$3332*) had fallen in real terms, and had only recovered to $4070 (*$4400*) by 2002. At the time of its foundation in 1977 the three existing universities were admitting some 10 200 students out of 25 000 qualified applicants and the buoyancy of the economy made it seem reasonable to find a way of expanding university places. The university opened in 1978 with 1284 students. Numbers rose steadily to 10 223 in 1986 and have remained at around 10 000 since then. Courses are mainly in print, with a limited amount of support by radio and television. The university has established study centres throughout the country. An early cost study suggested that if UNED could increase its number of students and hold back its dropout rates it might show economies as compared with conventional universities.

In practice, however, the university has managed to do neither of these things. Although many of its students are teachers and public servants, who might expect promotion and more pay on graduation, it has achieved relatively low graduation rates. With the openness to be expected of a country so civilised that it abolished its army, Costa Rica has also earned the gratitude of researchers by publishing its figures. Between 1988 and 1992 it managed to reduce the dropout per course from 39 to 28 per cent. But, over the whole period from 1978 to 1993, 84 per cent of the 83 000 students it enrolled dropped out (Ramirez 1994: 69–70). The difference between the rates for individual courses, and for the student body as a whole, may suggest that completing a full degree at a distance is simply too demanding for many students. Ramirez concluded by suggesting a change of direction towards offering shorter programmes of high demand, courses that would have more recognition from other institutions, and nonformal programmes (*ibid*: 73).

One study suggests that Costa Rica's difficulties typify distance education in Latin America. Casas, writing from the Venezuela Open University, noticed that distance education was beginning to get academic acceptance, that some material of good quality was being produced, and that its cost advantages had been demonstrated so that it might reduce demands for public funds. But he went on to identify a set of negative factors: high dropout rates, low academic quality in many educational materials, a restricted choice of courses which reduced their chance of meeting student needs, conservatism in the choice of teaching technologies, and inadequate attention to vocational education. He saw some features as characterising Latin America: 'the existence of a cultural value inherited from Spain, known as "nominalism", which means that things, laws and institutions, are represented more by the name than by reality' and that, 'even today, for many sectors of these societies, provision of a degree seems to be more important than the acquisition of knowledge.' (Casas 1995: 393–4). Perhaps it is the brilliance of Latin American football that has allowed these qualities to spread to the rest of the world.

Regional universities

Finally we move from land to sea. The two Commonwealth regional universities can claim to be the world's biggest. The University of the West Indies serves a region from Belize to Trinidad, a distance of 3000 km, and always taking two days. The territory of the University of the South Pacific stretches 6500 km from east to west. Their populations are comparatively small, with some 5 million in the Caribbean and 1.4 million in the Pacific, so that there is an economic and educational case for organising higher education regionally. Each has three campuses and a presence in each territory it serves. Although it was an Australian historian who coined the term 'the tyranny of distance', it might well have been a university administrator. The cost, and difficulty, of serving their scattered communities has led both universities to explore using telecommunications for both administration and teaching.

The University of the South Pacific moved first, launching inservice courses for teachers in 1971, only a year after its formal establishment. Despite the problems of organising correspondence across the inevitable distance, students from Fiji, Kiribati and the Solomon Islands were enrolled on a print-based course. Over the years, courses were gradually expanded and extended. The programme began with certificate and diploma level work but moved on to degree level. The latter became of increasing importance as the university scaled down sub-degree teaching, so that degree courses, which made up only 25 per cent of the distance-education work in 1979, had become 53 per cent ten years later (NIME 1993: 341). Courses rely heavily on print, but this is backed by tutorial sessions in the university's local centres and by summer schools. The expansion of the university's degree courses has had two effects. Degree course enrolments rose from 11 888 students in 1989 to 16 317 in 1997 (Matthewson and Va'a 1999: 286). External students were between 54 and 65 per cent of the total in the 1990s. By 2004 there were over 15 000 students on 150 courses. Students can move from off-campus to on-campus study to complete their degree so that a majority of students for a first degree today do some of their degree at a distance and some on campus.

The university's move into distance education was driven by geography, but has been helped by technology. In 1972 NASA made the experimental communication satellite ATS-1 available for educational use, positioned it over the Pacific, and agreed that the university should use it to link its centres. The satellite remained in use for over a decade – longer than the engineers had predicted – and the university then made new arrangements for satellite communication through INTELSAT. Despite poor quality reception the satellite links were invaluable for overcoming a sense of isolation and for administration, as well as for teaching (NIME 1993: 336–7).

The University of the South Pacific has demonstrated the value of distance education for its scattered community. It has found ways of surmounting the difficulties inherent in running a system across its region that serves the needs of scattered students, which is compatible with the assumptions of its teachers on-campus. Its satellite links help control the system but do not run it.

The University of the West Indies is nearly sixty years old and, like its Pacific sister, is driven by its regional needs. Alongside its three campuses it has appointed resident tutors who have become, in the jargon of small-states management, multi-functional administrators: they may do everything from advising the minister within their own territory to opening the mail and registering students. Over the years, the university built up several parallel systems for meeting educational demands in its noncampus territories. The first system was that of the resident tutors, who had considerable freedom to respond as they thought fit to the needs of their territory. Then, students were given the opportunity to challenge the university's first-year examination and, by sitting a challenge examination, to establish that they could enter the university at second-year level. Pressure from the noncampus territories led to the establishment of an office dedicated to providing services to them which varied from supporting the development of franchised, first-year, degree courses to arranging tutorial visits by regular academic staff. And from 1983 the university began to experiment with the use of telecommunications to offer teaching to off-campus students through the University of West Indies Distance Teaching Experiment or UWIDITE.

Again, an initiative came from America to provide satellite links between campuses and off-campus centres. Gradually classrooms were equipped with loudspeaking telephone equipment so that it was possible for a lecturer in Barbados, Jamaica or Trinidad to teach a class on line to sites all round the region. A programme of courses was developed, concentrating mainly on diploma and certificate courses and inservice courses for teachers. The network was managed and controlled from the largest of the three campuses. As in the South Pacific, the telephone network proved of at least as great value for administration as for teaching, saving time and airfares. The vice-chancellor led the way with a weekly meeting with his pro-vice-chancellors.

But there were inbuilt weaknesses in the system. Again like the Pacific, the last mile of telephone link was over landlines so that the sound quality varied from just tolerable to barely comprehensible. Motivation can overcome some of the problems: you listen hard to a teleconference about pay or conditions of service but it is not easy to learn accountancy by listening to a distorted, telephoned, lecture. Alongside the technical difficulties there were managerial ones. UWIDITE began as an experimental project, designed to seize an opportunity and explore the potential of a new type of communication, rather than something that was embedded in faculty processes. Its staff were not in a position to command academic resources or to establish tight links between the regular work of the university and UWIDITE. As a result the network was used spasmodically: the education faculty began to use it, mainly for inservice teacher education; some sessions were offered to the challenge students, mainly in the social sciences and humanities; in some cases, especially in education, teaching material was duplicated and distributed to students. But this was all short of being an integrated programme of distance education: tellingly academic staff talked of 'lecturing on UWIDITE', regardless of the appropriateness of the medium for delivering lectures.

In the early 1990s the university decided to restructure its distance-education programme. With a loan from the Caribbean Development Bank it upgraded and extended the audioconference network and launched a programme of course development with the intention of offering a range of degree programmes off-campus, in parallel with those on campus. The context of this was a determination to increase the production of graduates, where the region was falling behind the newly industrialised countries of Asia, and to improve access for students in the noncampus countries of the eastern Caribbean, whose numbers had been falling as a proportion of the whole student body. Following a review of its governance structure the university brought together all its off-campus work whether done through the work of resident tutors, or by supporting other tertiary institutions, or through distance education.

The new structure meant that there was a distance-education department and a pro-vice-chancellor with overall responsibility for noncampus countries and distance education, creating an appropriate framework within which the university could become a fully dual-mode institution. But this is easier said than done: while the structures for off-campus work were in place, its development depended crucially on the support of academic staff and their willingness and capacity to develop the necessary teaching materials. Progress has been modest and by 2005 it was generally possible to do just the first year of a narrow range of degrees or a small number of certificate programmes. Although the University of the West Indies is serving countries that are, generally, wealthier than those in the South Pacific, and ones that have a stronger infrastructure of schools, it lags behind the University of the South Pacific in integrating distance education with its other activities.

Conclusion

Several common strands run through this varied experience. The creation of open universities has demonstrated a government commitment to open and distance learning which has given it a new legitimacy. For their part, they have become stable institutions, that look as if they are a permanent part of the educational structure and are often enrolling up to 15 per cent of university students, and occasionally many more. They have developed methods of working that appear to be sustainable and mean that they can offer education to large numbers of students who would not otherwise get to a campus. At the same time, they seem to have had only limited success in reaching the more deprived audiences – not always their mandate – and in getting students to complete their courses and graduate. They have usually recruited about the same proportion of women as conventional universities.

Alongside the open universities, a growing number of institutions are now working in more than one mode, teaching students off campus as well as on. Many have found the transition from single mode to dual mode difficult, demanding changes in practice for academic and administrative staff. The problems of transition mean that some have limited their response to work in particular niches – most often in teacher education – while others have sought to offer a wide range of courses, only to retreat to a niche offering as logistics constrain them. The danger is then that the scale on which they operate is too small to be viable in economic terms or to establish the legitimacy of the off-campus mode. The University of the South Pacific may be the most dramatic example and exception. Despite all the difficulties of operating over its forbidding distance it has got to the point in which both modes now have a sort of parity, at least in student numbers, and it is normal for any one student to have done part of a degree in each mode.

In both kinds of institutions it seems that many are called to enrol but few are chosen to graduate. Such evidence as we have – and there is not enough of it – is consistent across open and dual-mode universities that successful completion rates on many courses are disturbingly low. Recent data from south Asia and South Africa show continuingly low graduation rates for first degrees while suggesting that shorter courses, and postgraduate courses, are likely to be more successful. Vocational courses, including those for teachers, in which students may gain promotion or more pay on completion, form the major exception with successful completion rates several times those achieved for other courses. But the general conclusion has to be that the methods of open and distance learning, held out as a promise of grand educational expansion, have failed to meet the hopes of the majority of higher-education students. Acclaim for the large numbers of enrolments needs to be tempered by a concern about their results; we look at the economic consequence of this in chapter 7 and come back to it in chapter 11.

6 Crossborder enrolment: virtually wandering scholars

> I do not want my house to be walled in on all sides and my windows to be stuffed. I want the cultures of all the lands to be blown about my house as freely as possible. But I refuse to be blown off my feet by any.
>
> Mahatma Gandhi

Distance education need not respect frontiers; growing numbers of students and institutions are using technology to leap across them. The Briggs group which planned the Commonwealth of Learning (see chapter 9) predicted this with their 'long-term aim that any learner, anywhere in the Commonwealth, should be able to study any distance-teaching programme available from any bona fide college or university in the Commonwealth' (Briggs *et al.* 1987: 60). Technology assists it. The General Agreement on Trade and Services, GATS, encourages it. While much of the discussion, and more of the activity, has been about higher education, there has also been some crossborder activity at school level.

There has sometimes been more rhetoric and optimism than reality. When he announced the British e-university in 2000 the secretary of state for education gave it £62 million (*$107 million* at 2003 prices) and explained that 'such investment can only be justified if one can be confident of reaching a large market at home and overseas' (Blunkett 2000). Sadly it did not work like that and, five years later, with £50 million (*$73 million*) spent and only 900 students recruited, the project was closed down (Education and Skills Committee 2005). Despite, or even because of such failures it is worth asking whether international enrolment matters for open and distance learning in the south.

To answer that question we need to identify the actors who are driving the process and distinguish between the different organisational models they are using. At university level three groups have been active. First, both open and dual-mode universities have seen e-learning as a useful new tool for reaching their existing cadres of off-campus learners. Second, some activity has been stimulated by individuals keen to exploit a new way of teaching and with a personal interest in the technology. Third, universities have seen the new technologies as a way of competitively expanding their recruitment. In Australia, for example, as federal funding fell from 90 per cent of income in the early 1980s to below 54 per cent in 1997, universities saw e-learning as one way of expanding student numbers, including international students, while holding back costs (Perraton 2004a: 37–8).

Much of this activity has been driven by the industrialised countries who, seeking income and influence, want to recruit international students and see virtual technologies as an auxiliary to conventional student mobility. In some cases they have done this through partnerships with, or franchises to, developing-country institutions. But universities in the south are also actively seeking to work across borders. Even in the apartheid years the University of South Africa recruited students across southern Africa. With the newer technologies Indira Gandhi National Open University (IGNOU) wanted in 1998 'to transform itself into a global virtual university serving "anyone, anytime, anywhere"' and by 2005 had formal agreement to offer its programmes in Africa through a pan-African communications network (Dirr 2001: 100; Dikshit 2006: 73).

Four models

Schools and colleges are using the internet as a vehicle for open and distance learning for two different purposes: to distribute teaching material, thus replacing technologies from print and post to television, and to allow or ease communication between tutor and student. The two activities have different educational and economic effects and have different emphases within four models of crossborder teaching: simple crossborder enrolment, international dissemination, collaboration, and the creation of dedicated cooperative agencies.

Simple crossborder enrolment

Scholars have always wandered. While enrolment by computer may lack the excitement of walking with dusty feet from Paris to Padua, it may work out cheaper and does not demand a passport. And it is responding to both demand and supply. Malaysia and Singapore, for example, are anxious to increase their higher education enrolment ratios more rapidly than the growth of their own universities will allow. One of their responses is to encourage crossborder enrolment through distance education (Olsen 2002: 4). But the process has probably been stimulated as much from the supply side, with expansionist policies at both conventional and open universities.

Partly in response to student demand, conventional universities have begun to use the internet for internal communication and for contact with their students. Lecture notes have gone on to websites not as a result of grand university policy but of student expectation. At the same time, universities have seen the technologies as a way of recruiting and reaching out to new groups of students, both within and beyond national frontiers; once time, energy and money have gone into the development of computer-based materials for use on campus it is natural to ask how far they could be used off campus. Australian and British universities have been particularly vigorous in recruiting online students internationally with an estimated 31 000 and 77 000 students respectively (Garrett and Verbik 2004: 7). In Britain at least, postgraduate rather than undergraduate studies dominate with universities finding niche markets. The Wye campus of Imperial College, for example, with long-established and widely recognised courses in agricultural sciences, was a pioneer here. Sunderland university offers master's courses at a distance in computer studies, Staffordshire sustainable development and Cardiff palliative care – among many others – all reflecting areas of particular expertise on campus. This postgraduate emphasis does not always match with demand: the south-east Asian demand, for example, is mainly for undergraduate courses (Olsen 2002: 12).

Open universities, and dual-mode universities with major open-learning programmes like Deakin and Monash universities in Australia, have also moved into crossborder enrolment. They have seized on the new technologies as offering an alternative to print, radio and television on which they had previously relied, with the intention of expanding their student numbers and of working across frontiers. In 1999, for example, the University of Southern Queensland saw itself as 'a regional university with an international mission' with 15 000 off-campus students of whom nearly 3000 were studying abroad (CVCP 2000: 133). At the same time the open universities have been cautious in switching technologies. From the Open University in Britain to the Indira Gandhi National Open University in India, print is still the dominant mode of teaching. Where they have switched from print to the internet this has sometimes simply been for ease of distribution.

There are the beginnings of crossborder enrolment by open universities in the south, alongside the vigorous activity from the north. The national open universities of both India and Pakistan are teaching students of the south Asian diaspora, particularly in south-west Asia. IGNOU is working with partner institutions to support its students in Abu Dhabi, Dubai, Qatar, Kuwait, Oman and Bahrain as well as in the Maldives, Mauritius and the Seychelles. In cooperation with the Commonwealth of Learning, and with funding from the Rajiv Gandhi Foundation IGNOU has also recruited internationally for a master's programme in distance education. These may be growth points for the future, especially for universities working in an international language: first-degree courses for nationals working abroad, or members of a national diaspora valuing their cultural inheritance, and master's programmes in specialisms where the university has particular strengths.

With a handful of exceptions from south Asia, all these examples could be seen as manifestations of old-fashioned trade in advanced goods from rich countries to poor. The trade is more benign than the export of Birmingham brass or rifles. It can make education available to people in the south who would otherwise have narrower opportunities of getting it. But there is a double price: the south has to pay the north, and the ready availability of courses from the north may make it more difficult for institutions in the south to develop their own courses and their own expertise in developing them.

Dissemination

Several agencies have seen the new technologies principally as a means of making their teaching materials more widely available, using the internet for print or multimedia courses in much the same way as broadcasters have used radio frequencies. While this may be regarded as distribution rather than teaching, it is potentially significant both for individuals, with free access to international teaching materials, and to institutions considering how this new supply may affect their day-to-day work.

The export of teaching materials, or franchising, offers universities a way of increasing revenue without the risks of overseas recruitment. The Spanish Universidad Nacional de Educación a Distancia has made materials available to Latin America. In Malaysia, Macau, Hong Kong and Singapore, institutions have been set up that rely heavily on imported materials to serve local students. More recently institutions have begun to make teaching materials freely available, rather than selling them. The Massachusetts Institute of Technology (MIT) has been the pioneer in making all its teaching materials freely available on the internet. It appears to have been of particular interest to newly developing open universities in the Arab world but also to be generating interest in subsaharan Africa. MIT's example has been followed internationally so that material from some twenty Chinese universities is going on the web and there are proposals for promoting open educational resources in Latin America and Spain. The British Open University is reported to be planning to do the same thing. A programme to fund the development of teaching materials for teacher education in southern Africa, TESSA, has been developed by the university in association with overseas partners and with funding from the Department for International Development.

These examples have been followed in the south, with IGNOU leading the way. At a meeting of the Pan-African Parliament in 2004 the President of India suggested the development of a satellite and fibre-optic network to improve communication between Africa and India. IGNOU has now developed proposals to use the network to deliver programmes, initially in English but with the hope of later moving into other languages. The network is intended to link two institutions in India with three universities in Africa and 53 learning centres, one in each member country of the parliament. IGNOU, which already has experience of working on the development of distance education in Ethiopia, is to provide the educational content for the network (Dikshit 2006: 72–4).

Collaboration

Alongside the simple enrolment of students across borders, and the dissemination of teaching materials, institutions have begun to work together through a variety of partnerships and collaborations.

Many of these are within a framework of north–south cooperation or export rather than of indigenous or cooperative southern development or south–south cooperation. The Monterrey Institute of Technology, for example, a well-established and high-status private university in Mexico, has worked with the University of British Columbia to develop five web-based courses at master's level in educational technology. The programme enabled Monterrey to extend its teaching into an area that would not otherwise have been possible. Significantly, however, all the teaching material was developed at the University of British Columbia, in consultation with colleagues from the Monterrey Institute. The new technologies have facilitated inter-university cooperation but one that still follows the same pattern of the north–south export trade (Bates and Escamilla de los Santos 1997).

More recently two projects launched from Canada and Britain have tried to use the technologies for institutional capacity building as well as for teaching students across borders.

Canada launched a 'Canada Caribbean Distance education scholarship programme' in 1998 designed to enable students in four Caribbean countries to follow distance-education courses offered by Canadian universities. The scheme was administered by the Commonwealth of Learning and was intended both to respond to educational needs in the Caribbean and to develop institutional capacity there. Sixty-seven students from Dominica, Jamaica, St Lucia and St Vincent followed courses in teacher education from Memorial university in Newfoundland, information technology from Athabasca university in Alberta, and tourism management from Mount St Vincent university in Nova Scotia. The courses used the internet both for the delivery of materials and for student support. Each course included a short face-to-face session within Canada. The graduation rate was high with 67 of those enrolled (87 per cent) graduating. The whole project cost some Cdn$1.7 million (*$1.3 million* at 2000 expenditure) suggesting that, with these relatively small numbers, the cost per student was just below Cdn$26 000 (*$19 744*), quite close to the cost of a one-year master's course offered conventionally within Canada (Jean-Louis 2001; Department of Foreign Affairs and International Trade n.d.).

The programme was seen as contributing successfully to the development of skills within the Caribbean and expected to do so without encouraging the brain drain. In terms of capacity building within the region its effects are less clear: the University of the West Indies was hardly involved in the scheme and did not feel that the region had any sense of ownership of the project. Despite claims of success from the funding department, it seems to have been a one-off and Canada has not repeated, leave alone institutionalised the project.

The Commonwealth Scholarship Commission in the United Kingdom picked up the idea of the Canadian scheme. After over forty years of experience of supporting conventional student mobility it decided in 2001 to experiment with the use of open and distance learning through university partnerships between British and southern universities. The scheme had two aims: to provide scholarships for distance-learning students of British universities, who could pursue postgraduate degrees in subjects relevant to the millennium development goals, and to raise capacity within overseas universities. It was expected that the overseas partner would provide much of the necessary student support and would gradually reach the position where it could offer a similar course without further help from its partner. One of the first partnerships it supported was, for example, between the agricultural Wye campus of Imperial College and the University of Pretoria for students studying agricultural development and sustainability. This grew out of existing links between the two departments and, as the partnership has developed, has facilitated Pretoria's development of master's level courses; the universities are thus moving towards a position in which materials may be developed by either but offered by both. Over the period 2002 to 2006 the Commission has funded some 515 students in thirteen partnerships between British universities and partner universities in Africa and Asia.

Arrangements for student support have varied. Students in Delhi working with Jadavpur University in Kolkata and Staffordshire University found that, given the distances, it was easier to get help from Staffordshire than Kolkata. In contrast, in a course on computer science offered by Sunderland University with the Jomo Kenyatta University of Agriculture and Technology, students were willing to travel long distances for face-to-face sessions at the university campus in Nairobi. In two cases, groups of students attended a one-term residential course at the home university in Britain as part of a course which was otherwise taught at a distance. The students – studying education from Pakistan and sustainable development from India – were enthusiastic about this short, manageable, period of study abroad; the Commission was faced with assessing the benefits of this move from fully distant learning to blended learning. By 2006 annual expenditure on the programme was approaching £1 million (*$1.8 million*).

Alongside this scheme, the Commission was sufficiently encouraged with progress to fund a second strand of distance-learning scholarships, offered by British universities but without a local partner so that all the student support is provided from Britain. Some 25 students on five courses were supported in 2006, the first year of the scheme.

All these were students on master's courses, mainly in health, education, agriculture and technology, and were the equivalent of one-year full-time courses but taken over a period of several years. As a result, it is too early to know what graduation rate will be achieved. This is likely to be lower than the graduation rate for conventional master's courses but, given the cost of travel and subsistence in Britain, the cost per graduate is expected to compare favourably with the cost of conventional study. It is also difficult to assess the strength of the institutional capacity building that is a feature of the scheme, but already clear that this may be taking more varied forms than had been expected. A link between the nursing department of Dundee University and Chainama College in Zambia, for example, has resulted in raising the qualification level of the college staff, many of whom have enrolled on the Dundee courses. Distance learning has, unusually, helped to concentrate scholarship programmes within particular institutions rather than reaching out to scattered audiences.

Schemes of this kind demonstrate one way of escaping a catch-22 of crossborder enrolment: students have often been able to tap neither local funding for their fees, because they were studying with a foreign institution, nor international funding, because scholarship agencies have funded only students who travelled to study. If the British scheme succeeds in its twin aims, of teaching students and supporting institutions, it will be a useful new modality for crossborder education while leaving for researchers intriguing questions about the less easily quantifiable benefits of studying in a foreign country actually rather than virtually.

Cooperative agencies

The potential for crossborder learning, combined with the technological opportunities, has encouraged some groups to go beyond collaboration and on to the creation of new institutions. Writing in 2001 Farrell identified the process:

> Over the last two years there has been an explosion of new organisational forms in education, particularly at the post-secondary level and in the area of company staff training. These new organisational forms are the result of partnerships between businesses and institutions, joint venture initiatives between and among institutions and organisations, new consortia arrangements and a huge increase in the number of new 'for profit' education and training organisations. They are developing for a variety of reasons: to gain market share in a globalised educational world, to take advantage of value-added partnership opportunities, to reduce costs and share risk, and to profit from a burgeoning demand for lifelong learning.
>
> (Farrell 2001: 9)

Most of these new ventures are in the north and primarily concerned with demands for education and training in the industrial north. But both the public and the private sector in the north have their eye on potential enrolments in the south. One American consultancy, for example, offered guidance to the 'savvy higher education institution' wanting to explore and enter the global market for online learning which, 'over the next 20 years ... is estimated to exceed $215 billion, with rapid growth expected from cross-border delivery of higher education' It singled out China as a target arguing that, 'tertiary enrollment in China, for example, doubled from a rate of six per cent of the higher education age population in 1999 to 12 per cent in 2002. Although the number of higher education institutions has also grown, capacity still falls short of demand' (Hezel and Mitchell 2005).

Alongside these northern ventures there are examples of partnerships that are at least in principle dominated by southern interests. Probably the best-publicised example is the African Virtual University, established by the World Bank in 1997 but now an independent agency with its headquarters in Kenya. The bank argued that a virtual university, using satellite communication and computer networks to share teaching, could help the beleaguered universities of Africa improve the quality of their teaching in science, engineering and business and expand enrolments in these areas. The World Bank and other funding agencies provided start-up funding, apparently of between $5 million and $10 million but with the intention that it should in due course become self-supporting. Its starting point was that it would be a virtual institution, avoiding the costs of buildings. The virtual university would develop, or buy in, computer-based teaching material and make this available to African universities by franchising existing courses or developing new ones on demand. The plan envisaged that:

> In the early stages of the project, the courses will be bought from established producers of course and educational materials: curriculum products; reference materials and databases; multimedia conference proceedings; multimedia learning packages; software application tutorials; and computer simulations. In later stages AVU will engage in the production of top quality instructional material in Africa by Africans.
>
> (Baranshamaje n.d.: 4)

As well as being a broker the university would also have a quality-control function, work with its African partners in developing student support, and help them with their management (*ibid.*).

The African Virtual University was established in three phases: a pilot, testing feasibility, an operational phase in which some complete degree courses would be made available, and a third 'transition to Africa phase' in which materials would be originated within Africa. In the pilot phase (1997–9) equipment was set up, with 27 satellite receiver terminals initially being installed in 15 countries (World Bank 1998: 55). Television-based teaching was carried by satellite from universities in Canada, Ireland and the

United States to universities in five of the countries involved. In some cases there was an audio feedback link providing one-way video and two-way audio. Courses were at undergraduate level in mathematics, physics, chemistry and computer science. At Makerere University in Uganda, for example, 324 students took part in twelve courses in the trial phase in 1997–8 (Aguti 1999b: 5). Alongside this import of television courses, AVU began to offer digital access to on-line journals and to train staff on the use of the technologies the virtual university would use.

In the operational phase the university has continued to expand its network of study centres based at partner universities and in 2006 had 57 centres in 27 countries. It had, by this time, switched its emphasis from television-based to online courses but had made less progress than had been intended in developing courses within Africa; it was then offering degree programmes in computer science from the Royal Melbourne Institute of Technology in Australia and Université Laval in Canada and in business studies from Curtin University in Australia. Its certificate courses were from institutions such as the New Jersey Institute of Technology and the Indiana University of Technology. Enrolments were at a more modest level than had been forecast with a cohort of 302 students, for example, enrolling on the Laval course in 2005 (African Virtual University 2006).

The African Virtual University has been enormously successful in raising funds, announcing $7.22 million from the African Development Bank in 2005 to go alongside its funding from AusAID, the World Bank, CIDA, DfID and the Hewlett Foundation (*ibid.*). If it works, it will be a dramatic demonstration of the economies to be achieved through crossborder enrolment applying computer-based technologies. But several doubts remain: about the appropriateness of the technologies within the African infrastructure, about the pace of development, and about the costs. Many will want reassurance that internet-based teaching will work effectively not only in metropolitan campuses but beyond. The university's development has been slower than it hoped: a presentation in 2004 looked forward to 20 000 enrolments on its undergraduate programmes by 2006 – a far larger number than that which seems to have been achieved – with over 95 000 students to be enrolled by 2009. This has a significant bearing on its costs where it was looking forward to a reduction of costs to $368 per student by that year, brought down by economies of scale. This figure excluded the costs of operating learning centres – the variable costs for student support (African Virtual University 2004).

An evaluation of the university's progress was carried out for a group of its funders in 2004 but has not been made public. Its absence does nothing to resolve doubts about the university which seems, so far, to have been a relatively expensive way of making available rich-country courses through high technology to small numbers of students. Faith as well as hope is needed to reassure us that it will prove a successful model for crossborder learning.

Does it matter?

We may be moving towards international and virtual, or at least semi-virtual, universities. But, at present, virtual mobility is much less significant than real mobility. UNESCO figures show that, considering only for countries receiving at least 1000 students, over 2 million university students were studying outside their own country in 2003. If we assume that their fees, living costs and travel amounted to only $20 000, then the world's total expenditure on student mobility is likely to be approaching $40 billion. It seems unlikely that international enrolment at a distance is even as much as 3 per cent of this figure.[1] In part the scale reflects the economics: internationally priced courses are too expensive for most students in the developing world, except where scholarships are available. Beyond that:

> Very few universities have developed truly global support structures; the training programmes within globalised industries are probably closer to realising this aspect of global education. Whilst the Internet (in the form of electronic mail) provides a relatively trouble-free mechanism for administration, sending in assignments and receiving one-to-one tutoring, none of these features scale up to handling large numbers of students. Indeed, what we find most commonly, is that any course or programme operating globally, is only doing so with very small numbers of students (typically under 100, and usually closer to twenty). Frequently the course is administered and tutored by the course author – what can be categorised as a one-man band.
>
> (Mason 1998: 13)

But it all matters for at least three reasons. First, if some of the beginnings of crossborder enrolment are robust and successful, they open up educational opportunities that would not otherwise be available. Technology can help education make us free, if only we can find the right structures for it, and do it at a reasonable price. Second, and in contrast, there are real dangers of hegemony and homogenisation. An online forum organised by the International Institute for Educational Planning found that:

> While many participants viewed freely accessible OER [open educational resources] like MIT OCW [open courseware] as powerful tools for expanding capacity in less developed regions, some participants expressed unease about the impact of importing educational content on indigenous scholarship. It was suggested that the lack of technological and academic infrastructure to support the creation of local online content in many regions may make OER knowledge-sharing one-sided. Participants called for a move away from a provider/user model that generally casts developing countries in a passive role as a consumer of OER to one that facilitates collaborative development.
>
> (OBHE 2005)

Third, and alongside issues of cultural protection there are issues of learner – or consumer – protection, given new urgency and prominence by decisions to make education a tradeable service within the framework of GATS.

Here, while international law to control trade is well-developed, we are far short even of agreed codes of practice for overseas enrolment. Some territories have succeeded in controlling the activities of off-shore universities. In Hong Kong, for instance, an ordinance restricts the activities of institutions elsewhere in the world (or in mainland China) who want to enrol students in Hong Kong on distance-education courses (Blight *et al.* 1999: 26). The British and Australian agencies concerned with the quality of higher education claim the right to supervise universities' crossborder teaching: the right is sometimes contested and difficult to enforce. UNESCO, with a historical concern for the international recognition of degrees, has developed a set of guidelines in association with OECD, designed to encourage good practice and safeguard the interests of students and other stakeholders including higher education institutions (UNESCO/OECD 2005). But there is a long way to go and the individual learner, faced with enticing advertisements from bogus and genuine universities, has no ready way of telling one from the other, or of comparing the qualities of different offerings from the genuine.

Crossborder enrolment remains small, in comparison with the numbers involved in the national programmes reviewed in the previous three chapters, and did not merit a chapter in the last edition of this book. But it looks like a major growth point and one where, unusually, its greatest significance may be at the highest levels of education, in widening access to postgraduate study. As with other kinds of open and distance learning it raises questions about costs, technology and politics to which we next turn.

Part II
Explanation

7 Costs: what the figures say

The Errols are formidably Britannic. They are, for example, *both* economists.
Why *both*, I ask myself? One of them must feel permanently redundant.
                                                          Lawrence Durrell 1958

We get ideological arguments for open learning, economic ones for distance
education. If it can produce similar results to those of conventional education
at a lower cost, then distance education has a powerful appeal.

There are grounds for thinking that distance education may have economic
advantages. There are two cornerstones to the argument. The educational
cornerstone is the theory of media equivalence, that there are no significant
differences in the effectiveness of different educational media. A long line of
experiment and research has demonstrated this. It began with comparisons
between radio and classroom learning in the 1930s, continued through
studies of television as it was being introduced into education, and even
continues today.[1] The consequence is that, if you can learn from print, or
from a broadcast or cassette or computer, as well as you can from a teacher,
there should be no educational objection to substituting another medium
for the teacher. (There may be social objections to this easy substitution.)
If there is no teacher you do not need a school, college, or hall of residence
in order to study: educational theory can help us reduce capital investment.
The economic cornerstone was laid by Adam Smith and tapped into place
by Henry Ford. Distance education allows a new division of labour, in which
a group of teachers and producers manufacture teaching material, an organisational machine distributes it, and another group provides a minimum of
individualised tutorial support to the students. Economies of scale become
possible, provided there are enough students to justify the manufacturing
cost of the first group and student contact is kept down in order to contain
the costs of the second.

While open and distance learning has relied on the strength of this case,
it provokes a set of questions: does the evidence in fact support it? If it does,
are there economic arguments for using one approach within open and
distance learning rather than another? Do the economics of open and distance

learning influence the pattern of funding? All but the last of these can, in principle, be answered by cost-effectiveness analysis in which we compare the costs of different approaches to achieving the same result. To fill out the picture, we might want to go on to cost-benefit analysis in which, as well as comparing the costs, we compared outcomes in financial terms. In principle cost-benefit analysis would enable us to compare the economic case for – say – investing in more secondary education or in strengthened agricultural extension by calculating the financial benefit that could be attributed to each investment. In practice, there are severe difficulties in using cost-benefit analysis within education and, with minor exceptions, we make no attempt to go down this contended road.

To answer the first question we need to compare the cost of open and distance learning with that of conventional education, overcoming practical, technical and sociological difficulties as we do so.

The main practical difficulty is a shortage of data. Managers are seldom interested in economic analysis; they want to make the best use of their own budget rather than compare it with somebody else's. Governments and institutions are often interested in only part of the story. International agencies blow hot and cold. The World Bank and UNESCO carried out a series of case studies between 1975 and 1985 (Jamison *et al.* 1978; Jamison and McAnany 1978; Perraton 1982; UNESCO 1977, 1980, 1982); the Commonwealth Secretariat and the Commonwealth of Learning looked at teacher education in the early 1990s (Perraton 1993); the European Commission and the Department for International Development have sponsored some more recent work (Hülsmann 2000; Raza 2004). As a result we have a modest number of cost studies, that use a standard approach, and a larger number of partial accounts, that are often methodologically less rigorous. They help fill out the picture but are of limited value because they concentrate on recurrent costs and leave aside capital costs. Many of the studies are quite old but, where technologies have not changed, are still relevant to the analysis. As noted in chapter 5, where institutions have made data available about their students and their costs, they have often omitted any data about graduation rates. Without these we can compare costs per student but not costs per graduate.

The technical difficulties follow. Conventional and distance education are likely to make different use of capital so that, unless we have a sense of the amount of capital needed for either approach, we can draw only limited conclusions. (Where data are available, information is needed about the discount rate that is to be used in calculating an annual cost.) Where we have expenditure across a number of years, or a number of countries, we also need to convert costs to a standard currency in order to make comparisons. In principle this should create no major problems. In practice, arbitrary but necessary decisions can have a large effect on the results. If, for example, we are looking at costs in Côte d'Ivoire for a financial year 1993–4, international comparisons of the cost will be affected by use of the 1993 conversion rate of 50 CFA francs to one French franc or the 1994 rate of 100.

Sociological factors make it difficult to compare like with like. If, to take the simplest example, we want to compare the costs of educating twenty people to degree level at an open university or a conventional one, we would want to ensure that the two cohorts were similar in age and educational background and, if possible, in economic circumstances and motivation. But the real world is not like that: students at a distance tend to be studying part-time, not full-time; often they are older; quite often they are poorer or live in more remote places; where they are the same age, those with the best educational record tend to go to conventional universities and those who have done less well in their school examinations to the open university.

The costs of distance education tend to behave differently from those of conventional education. One major difference is that distance education may make it possible to expand education without investment in buildings: open universities need a headquarters, and may need local centres, but do not demand a programme of campus building commensurate with the number of students they are to teach. A second major difference lies in their expenditure on staffing. Generally, staff costs, which dominate educational recurrent budgets, rise with student numbers and are held back only by uncomfortable expedients such as cramming more into a classroom or introducing shift teaching. (There are still limits to hot-seat classrooms.) Distance teaching can hold down expenditure per student but needs a higher investment in course development. A higher proportion of the costs of distance education therefore tends to be fixed, and a lower proportion to vary with the number of students. As the number of students on a course increases, so the cost per student declines, something that does not happen to any significant extent with classroom-based education.

To examine the economics of distance education, and make sound comparison with alternatives, we need to look at its fixed and variable costs. Fixed costs are those that remain the same regardless of the number of students, for items like the cost of the headquarters and material development, while variable costs are those that vary with the number of students, notably tutorial costs and some of the costs of printing and distribution. With a large enough body of students, high fixed costs – for making television programmes for example – can be justified because they are spread over such a large number of people.

We have just enough data to use this approach and reach some conclusions about the comparative cost effectiveness of open and distance learning in the different sectors of education discussed in chapters 2 to 6.

Basic education

The difficulties in reaching conclusions are at their most extreme in looking at basic education where we have the most severe shortage of data and cost-effectiveness analysis is most difficult to apply. It lends itself to comparing the costs of teaching a student, or producing a graduate, on and off campus, or looking at the consequences of using radio or television as a component within a course. In applying it to basic education, especially for adults, we have no obvious point of comparison. The rural education project in Pakistan (chapter 2), for example, was not like anything else that was happening in Pakistan at the time so that comparisons with alternatives are arbitrary and difficult. Primary schools give one possible point of reference: there may be a partial overlap between the content of adult basic education and of primary education. But there is a lot that is different: you could not in practice expand adult basic education by sending all adults to school. Where the content of basic-education programmes is also offered in residential or face-to-face centres it may be possible to use their costs as a comparator. In other cases, distance-education approaches may be compared with those of conventional extension agencies.

Early studies reached one important conclusion about radio: because of its large audiences, and modest production and transmission costs, the cost per listener tends to be very low. A study in Malawi found that, in 1980 currency, it cost K956 (*$2707*) to produce one hour of broadcasting. For about $260 000 (*$613 665*) per year Malawi was reaching 300 000 farmers a year by radio for 4½ hours a week (Perraton *et al.* 1983: 175). The cost per unit hour per listener was less than half a cent.

Several other sources of data make it possible to reach some general conclusions. One source is the radio school movement of Latin America which offered basic education to adults, using radio and print, supported by a network of *animateurs*. Cost studies were made of two radio schools – ACPO in Colombia and Radio Santa Maria in the Dominican Republic – which were using similar methods to offer a primary equivalence course to adults. ACPO had 170 000 students and Radio Santa Maria 20 000. With such a large body of students, ACPO's costs fell below those of conventional primary schools in Colombia while Radio Santa Maria's costs were comparable to those of regular schools, and lower than those of evening classes organised for adults. Costs for radio schools were, in 1978 currency, between $20 and $35 (*$60–105*) per student per year (Perraton 1984: 170).[2] These are unusual findings and, with reduced enrolments in later years, radio school unit costs probably rose in real terms.

Detailed figures are available for a small number of nonformal projects and programmes. Costings for a radio education campaign in Zambia in 1982 suggest the level of cost that may be expected for a short, intensive programme of radio education. Some 5000 adults attended ten weekly group meetings to follow radio programmes and use printed materials about the cooperative movement in a campaign designed to encourage active membership of cooperatives. The cost per participant was, in 1977 currency, $8 (*$26*). The cost of teaching the same material in a farmers' training centre was over three times as great at $27 (*$86*). Primary-school costs were then $55 (*$175*) so that, measured in terms of costs per student learning hour, the cost of the campaign was significantly greater than the cost of primary education (Perraton 1984: 231–5). Again, the costs of radio broadcasts formed a small proportion of the total expenditure.

Figures are also available for the Functional Education Project in Rural Areas in Pakistan with a cost per learner of £35 in 1985 currency ($55) for eight meetings. This compares unfavourably with the cost of primary schooling at some $37 per student but may well compare favourably to other approaches to adult education.

Some figures are available for the costs of using distance-education methods for training extension and outreach workers discussed in chapter 2. A cost study of the work of INADES-formation in Cameroon found that the cost for each student, who was using correspondence lessons and attending three seminar sessions was (in 1977 currency) $365 ($1172), although it may have fallen significantly since then, perhaps to around $280. This cost is high in comparison with much basic education and, indeed, with many other distance-education projects. But INADES-formation was training agricultural extension staff as well as farmers. If its approach is seen as a way of raising the effectiveness of these staff, the costs look more reasonable. Figures for health education bear this out. AMREF had costs per successful student in 1996 of KSh8500 ($185), a figure that needs to be seen in the context of the multiplier effect of training rural health workers. It is very close to the cost reported by the ministry of health for using the same approach in Uganda in 1998 of $152 ($181) where comparable residential seminars cost about $400 ($477) (Bbuye 2000: 112). The Adult Basic Education and Training project at the University of South Africa had costs of some $59 ($64) per learner; this figure included all the materials provided to learners and stipends paid to their tutors (McKay 2004: 132).

The figures are summarised in table 7.1. Three conclusions follow. First, the cost of distance education for adult basic education generally compares favourably with other methods but, with important exceptions, unfavourably with the cost of primary education. One exception, in their heyday, were the radio schools of Latin America offering something like primary education, at competitive costs. The costs of radio are so modest that its comparative educational neglect is puzzling and disturbing. But, second, the costs of much distance education are such that it is difficult to see how basic-education projects could be replicated on a national scale. Where distance education has been used for basic education, its success has depended on providing student support along with the use of mass media. Different strategies have been used to mobilise that support: religious structures were used for this in Latin America, political in the case of the radio campaigns in Tanzania. Running a functional education project throughout Pakistan would have needed a comparable support structure. All of these put up the variable costs of projects, reducing the possibility of getting economies of scale. Third, the experience of AMREF, INADES-formation, and ABET, in the east, west and south of Africa, have demonstrated powerful arguments for using distance-education techniques as a way of training field workers.

Table 7.1 Costs of some adult basic education projects

(currency: 2005 US$)

Country and Project	Scale and duration	Cost per learner	Cost comparison
Colombia and Dominican Republic Radio schools in Latin America (e.g. Acción Cultural Popular, Colombia, Radio Santa Maria, Dominican Republic	ACPO: 190 000 students; RSM 20 000 students. One year course offering equivalency to primary education	In range $60 to $105 per student per annum	Cost at ACPO less than for primary schools. At RSM comparable with primary, lower than evening classes
Zambia Radio education campaign on cooperative movement	4 730 participants	$26 per student	Cost per learner lower than cost of training at farmer's centre, higher than primary school costs
Cameroon INADES-formation, courses in agriculture for farmers	573 students in Cameroon (some costs shared with other countries). One year course with correspondence lessons and 3 seminars	About $1172 per student. Costs may now have fallen significantly	Course cost about one sixth of one year's residential course but very high in relation to primary costs
Pakistan Functional Education Project for Rural Areas	1 500 students. 8 meetings at weekly intervals	About $57 per student	Cost probably low in comparison with alternatives, high as compared with primary schools
Uganda Distance education programmes, Ministry of Health, Uganda	5 500 health workers	$181 per student	Cost for residential seminar covering same ground $477
South Africa Adult Basic Education and Training, University of South Africa	307 000 adults	$64 per learner	Cost below 20% of cost of primary schooling

Source: chapters 2 and 7

The South African experience is another rare exception in which this approach brought the cost per learner down below the comparable cost of primary education. This, rather than direct education to adults, may be the most promising way forward.

Schooling

There is a stark distinction between the costs of two approaches to using open and distance learning for schooling. Where it is used to offer an alternative to schools, we may expect the cost per student to be lower. Most of the evidence comes from ministries of education whose interest in open and distance learning is to provide an alternative to school: generally they are not interested in alternatives that cost more; it makes sense to build more schools instead. Projects that use broadcasting, or some other technology such as computers, to raise the quality of schools, are likely to raise costs; they have seldom been introduced with the intention of eliminating staff costs and therefore generally amount to an add-on cost. The data in table 7.2 show how costs compare with alternatives.

Out-of-school projects tend to have lower costs than conventional schools, even where they are offering something like full-time school equivalence, because both salary and accommodation costs are lower. By employing unqualified or underqualified monitors, rather than tutors, it is possible to hold down staffing costs and, with adequate numbers, meet the costs needed to generate teaching material. In Korea the picture is clear cut: students worked with such diligence that the cost advantage remained even when measured in terms of cost per examination success. In Malawi and Zambia, the cost per student at correspondence centres was always lower than the cost in regular secondary schools. But, as noted in chapter 3, the lower examination pass rate meant that, in 1978, the cost per pass was higher at the correspondence centres. A remarkable improvement, coupled with an increase in student numbers, meant that ten years later the correspondence centres were at an advantage in terms of cost per pass as well as cost per student. In Zambia, it was estimated that the cost per pass between the two sectors would be about the same if the correspondence centres had a successful completion rate of between 5 and 14 per cent (Perraton 1983b: 11–12). Recent data from Botswana and Namibia, where distance education has been more generously funded, suggest that costs per student are lower than in conventional schools; costs per successful learner may be lower if retention and pass rates are high enough. In Namibia, estimates in 1998 suggested that the cost per learner per subject was N$578 (*$124*) while the cost for achieving a pass in the school system was N$1805 (*$243*) at junior certificate level and N$1989 (*$259*) at the higher general certificate level.

The picture from Latin America demonstrates how broadcasting becomes affordable when enrolments are high enough. In Brazil, two early projects

Table 7.2 Costs of some school equivalency projects

(currency: 2005 US$)

Country, project, date	GNP per capita at date of study		Student no	Cost per learner	Comparative cost
	Current $	2005 $			
Brazil					
Bahia State, Madureza, 1976[a]	1 410[b]	4 526	8 000	$499 per student following three courses	Higher cost per student than alternative
Minerva 1977[c]	1 410	4 526	118 118	$58 per student following group of courses for 1 year	Cost 65% of private-sector alternative. No evidence on cost per successful student
Telecurso 2002[d]	2 830	3 060	>200 000	about $400 in telessalas	Comparable to cost of conventional schools
India					
National Open School 1990[e]	360	536	40 884	$53 per student per year	Cost 63% of cost of government school
National Open School 1998[f]			132 222	$33 per student, $97 per successful student	Cost per student estimated at about half cost of government schools with similar examinations results
South Korea					
Air Correspondence High School, 1976[g]	980[b]	3 145	20 000	$204 per student p.a.	Cost per student 24% of alternative; cost per successful student 29%
Malawi					
Correspondence Study Centres 1978[h]	150[b]	482	2 884	$476 per student; $3549 per examination pass	Cost per student 62% cost at day school; cost per pass 81% higher
1988[i]	160	263	17 000	$128 per student; $451 per pass	Cost per pass now only 34% of day school rate

Mexico					
Telesecundaria 1975[j]	1 160[b]	4 193	33 840	$703 per student	Cost per student 76% of alternative
1981	3 170	6 782	170 000	$1106 per student	Cost per student 9.5%higher than alternative
1988	1 860	3 058	>400 000	$526 per student	Cost per student 16% higher than alternative
1997[k]	3 680	4 460	817 200	(recurrent)$584	
Zambia					
Correspondence Study Centres, 1981[l]	600	1 284	11 800	Cost per student in range $122–347	Cost per student between 7 and 21% cost of day school
Namibia					
NAMCOL 1998[m]	1 940	2 315	10 300	Cost per distance-education learner $124 per subject	Government schools unit costs per exam pass $243 to $259
Botswana					
BOCODOL 2004[n]	4 360	4 489	6 000	Recurrent cost for 4 subjects $243 to 259(P1108–1180)	Primary school cost about 2000$188 per student ($212)

Notes:

a. Oliveira and Orivel 1982a: 78 taking the cost for three subjects at Cr$2200 and converting at the 1977 exchange rate of Cr$14.144=$1.00; b. 1977 figure; c. Oliveira and Orivel 1982b: 49 using the one-year course figures of 1977Cr$258; d. Wolff *et al.* 2002: 151–2; e. Gaba 1997b: 125; f. Sujatha 2002: 136–41; g. Lee *et al.* 1982: 152–7; h. Costs of MK133 and MK931 reported in Wolff and Futagami 1982: 95–8; i. Costs of MK133 and MK931 reported in Murphy 1992: 91; j. Rumble 1997: 136–7, taking an average of his two costs for television; k. Wolff *et al.* 2002: 145–6; l. Perraton 1983b: 10–11; m. NAMCOL cost of N$578 in Du Vivier 1998: 46; NAMCOL's calculation of comparator at N$1805–1989; n. BOCODOL 2004: 7–8.

were developed to offer an alternative form of junior-secondary schooling, both using radio with relatively high fixed costs for making programmes. The project in Bahia, which was operating in a single province, had costs per student higher than those of alternatives whereas the national Minerva project, with larger student numbers, was able to justify the broadcasting cost, as was the more recent Telecurso project where *telessalas*, at which monitors supported the students, had costs comparable to those of regular schools (Wolff *et al.* 2002: 151–2). Telesecundaria has higher unit costs than regular schools mainly because its class sizes are lower, but it operated on a large enough scale to justify the investment in television programmes (*ibid*: 145–6).

There is a growing amount of data on the costs of using technology to raise the quality of teaching within schools. Costs for a range of interactive radio projects are available and are set out in table 7.3. The costs have

Table 7.3 Comparative costs of technology in school

(currency: 2005 US$)

Country and start date of project	Technology	Student numbers	Cost per student for technology	Cost as proportion of government primary school expenditure[a]
Bolivia 1986	Interactive Radio Instruction (IRI)	250 000	4.16	1.3%
Honduras 1991	IRI	200 000	4.38	2.0%
Lesotho 1987	IRI	200 900	1.99	1.5%
South Africa 1992	IRI	24 800	Between 1.05 and 2.73	0.3%, taking upper estimate of cost
2001	IRI	680 000	3.00	
Various[b]	IRI	100 000	9.84	n/a
	IRI	1 000 000	3.95	n/a
Venezuela 1996	IRI	360 000	2.13	
Chile 1995[c]	Computer assisted instruction	100 per school	99.59	37%
		200 per school	71.50	26%
		1 000 per school	26.81	10%
Barbados, Chile, Egypt, Turkey, Egypt, South Africa, Zimbabwe	Computers in schools		In range $9 to $646	n/a

Source: Chapter 3 except where shown.
a. Calculated from UNESCO *Statistical year book* except for Chile; b. Adkins 1999: 40–1; c. Potashnik 1996: 19–21.

generally declined over the years and demonstrate the possible economies of scale: South African unit costs roughly halved as numbers went from about 25 000 to nearly 700 000. But there is another way of looking at this: the fixed salary bill often makes up around 90 per cent of the total schooling budget so that these figures need to be seen against the one-tenth of that budget which may be available for curricular support and materials. The evidence suggests that the costs have often not been seen as sustainable by ministries of education, once external funding was withdrawn.

Computers have been introduced into classrooms for a variety of different reasons discussed in chapter 3. As with radio, they make for add-on costs and do not replace teachers. One report from Latin America found that 'computer projects are generally expensive educational inputs which can cost, on a per student basis, 50 per cent or more of what countries are currently spending on all education inputs' (Potashnik 1996: 10). A more detailed study in Chile found that costs per student varied with the size of the school, as larger schools could allow more students to use each computer. Total costs, in 1995 currency, varied from $21 (*$26*) in a school of 1000 students to $78 (*$99*) in a school of seventy-five students. These figures are between 5 and 18 per cent of national recurrent expenditure per student at secondary level and between 10 and 37 per cent at primary level (*ibid*: 14–16). An overview of costs in six countries (Barbados, Chile, Egypt, South Africa, Turkey and Zimbabwe) found a bewildering range of annual costs from *$955* to *$2048* (*$1079* to *$2313*, taking these as 2000 figures) per computer; annual cost per student was as high as *$646* (*$730*); in four of the six countries it was in the range $8 to $56 (*$9* to *$68*) (Cawthera 2001). All in all the figures suggest that one would need to budget at least $50 per student for expenditure on computers – a quite different order of figure from that shown for radio-based education.

We can summarise that open and distance learning methods can offer secondary education at lower unit costs than the conventional but that it is rarer for them to achieve competitive costs per successful student. Where educational technology has been used to enhance education rather than to provide an alternative, its costs are additional to those of regular schools. If these technologies are to be used, they need to demonstrate an educational value that justifies the extra cost.

Teacher education

As we saw in chapter 4, a number of distance-education projects have shown economies as compared with the costs of conventional education. The data from a set of projects, where costs were analysed in a standard form, are shown in table 7.4. They confirm that, with the relatively high completion rates often achieved in teacher education, costs per successful student tend to compare favourably with those of conventional education. This differential holds true both for projects with quite modest costs per

Table 7.4 Costs and effects of some teacher education projects

(currency: 2005 US$)

Country, Project, date[a]	GNP per capita at time of study		Student numbers	Average cost	Educational and cost impact
	Current US$	Constant 2005 US$			
Tanzania TTD 1979–84	1982: 310	625	15 000 p.a. 45 000 total	$2223 per student p.a. $8730 per graduate	Effects comparable to conventional education. Cost about half conventional education.
Brazil Logos II 1976–81	1978: 450	4 922	24 400	$252 per student p.a. $884 per graduate	80% pass rate. Costs lower than alternative
Sri Lanka Inservice programme 1984–8	1986: 410	728	c5000	$138 per student p.a.	Cost 1/6 –1/3 of alternative. More effective than alternative for some subjects but less effective for others
Indonesia Inservice programme 1985–8	1986: 530	788	c5000	$961 per student p.a.	Cost about 60% of equivalent. More effective than alternative in languages but less so in mathematics
Nepal RETT Basic teacher training course 1978–80	1979: 130	348	3 000	$234 per student p.a.	Cost slightly lower than alternative; completion rate 57%; no evidence that less effective than alternative

Nigeria National Teachers Institute 1978–89	1984: 730	1 366	20 327	$94 per student p.a.	Cost probably lower than regular colleges; completion rate estimated 42%, pass rate estimated 27%, both rates higher than those of regular colleges
COSIT University of Lagos 1980–8	1984: 730	1 366	2 000	$412 per full-time student equivalent $1556 per graduate.	If opportunity costs are omitted then cost per graduate slightly lower than residential campus cost
Pakistan Primary Teacher Orientation Course 1976–86	1981: 330	706	83 658 total enrolment 31 674 completed	$128–178 per successful completer	Cost per AIOU graduate 45–70% of conventional University
Kenya Inservice Teacher Training 1968–77	1972: 180	789	790	$962 per subject equivalent p.a.	Cost relatively high; favourable effect on access
University of Nairobi BEd 1986–90	1988: 370	609	515	$1308 per student p.a.	Cost thought to be lower than cost of residential equivalent
Uganda MITEP 1991–5	1995: 240	307	900	$4843 per successful student	Equivalent conventional cost was $3384
NITEP 1993–7			2 750	$2387 per successful student	Lower cost than equivalent
Malawi MIITEP 1997–2000[b]	1999: 190	222	2 500 per cohort	$654 per student	Alternative estimated at 2 to 4 ½ times cost of residential alternative
South Africa Shoma,1998–[c]	2000: 3020	3 411	13 500	$218 per teacher	Cost for 24 week course: no direct comparison

Source: Chapter 4 and Perraton 1993 except where shown.

Notes

a. The end date in column one refers to the period reported, not necessarily the project end date; b. Lewin and Stuart 2003: 154–7; c. Capper 2002a: 46.

student, reflecting limited student support, as in Pakistan, and those with relatively high costs incurred for extensive student support and supervision of classroom practice, as in Tanzania.

Some projects were probably too small to show economies of scale. With enrolments between 500 and 3000, the record of the Universities of Lagos and Nairobi is equivocal about the economic advantages of using distance education. In Uganda the Mubende Integrated Teacher Education Project with 900 enrolments probably had higher costs than a notional alternative – but had the merit of keeping the teachers in the schools – while the later Northern Integrated Teacher Education Project, with 3000 students, had costs that compared favourably. Costings in Malawi showed that conventional teacher training would have costs between two and four-and-a-half times the cost of the system in which trainees spent some time in school while studying at a distance (Lewin and Stuart 2003: 154–7).

Most of this experience was with print and broadcasting together with face-to-face tutorials and support. The Shoma project in South Africa demonstrated the feasibility of using a computer-based approach for professional development but at significantly higher costs: a 24-week course cost $198 (*$218*) per teacher and required capital investment for each school of $37 500 (*$40 543*) (Capper 2002a).

Two factors other than the costs of technology are significant in affecting costs. One is the extent of student support and in particular of supervising teaching practice. This was a major component in the early Tanzania programme, for example, which meant that the variable cost was relatively high. In contrast, the National Teachers' Institute in Nigeria provided rather less support to students and showed much lower variable costs per student. The second factor concerns opportunity costs; degree students in Kenya and Nigeria reported that, as well as paying university fees, their income also declined once they enrolled as they had less time to earn from part-time employment. There may therefore be a point at which the opportunity cost, as perceived by a student, combined with the actual cost of fees, will outweigh the uncertain and future increase in income to be expected on graduation.

With these qualifications, we can treat the economic case for using open and distance learning in teacher education as fairly robust, with projects achieving costs per successful student at between a half and two-thirds of those in conventional education.

Higher education

We have surprisingly few rigorous cost studies of open and distance learning in higher education. Where data are available, they tend to be for recurrent expenditure only. While this means that they tend to understate the cost advantage of a non-residential university, many reports give us costs per student rather than per graduate, which may therefore overstate the cost advantages, at least if we are measuring effectiveness in terms of producing graduates.

Reports on open universities tend to show that they have lower costs per student than conventional universities. (See table 7.5.) The Chinese television universities are the supreme, and largest, example. Their recurrent cost per student was between 25 and 40 per cent of that for conventional universities (Ding 1994: 159–61). The reduced cost reflected both a less generous staffing ratio and lower costs for building space. The universities were operating at a scale that justified the necessarily heavy costs of broadcasting over 5500 hours of television a year.

Other Asian open universities have reported costs per head that compare favourably with those of the conventional sector. In Korea the cost to the government of the (then) Korean Air and Correspondence University in 1990 was US$93. Student fees made up half the income of the university, which suggests an annual cost per student of $186 ($277). The cost of a conventional university place was then $2880 ($4285) (Kim 1992: 38). Early figures from Sukhothai Thammathirat Open University (STOU) suggested that the annual cost per head was between 21 and 30 per cent of the cost of conventional universities (between US$152 and $221 at STOU in 1986 prices ($270–$393) and between $589 and $1010 ($1527–$1792) at conventional universities) (Wichit and Tong-In 1985: tables 14 and 15).[3] Later figures from India show that Dr B. R. Ambedkar Open University – the longest established open university in India – was operating at about 15 per cent of the cost of conventional universities while the, then smaller, Indira Gandhi National Open University had costs of around 40 per cent of the conventional sector (Ansari 1994: 83).

Recent evidence from South Africa is more difficult to interpret. A detailed study of ten university courses found recurrent costs in 2003 of R181 to R9350 ($25–$1307) per student and R432 to R10 703 ($60–$1496) per course completer, identifying courses but not institutions. It did not make comparisons with the costs of conventional universities. Costs are shown for three large-scale courses, in business, psychology and law, which appear to be from institutions now forming part of the University of South Africa. (Higher figures were for small programmes, some of them using e-learning.) These three courses, which required 120, 172 and 255 learning hours respectively, had costs per student in the range R181 to R719 ($25–$100) and per completer of R432 to R1073 ($60–$150). (CHE 2004: 38ff. and 132; see also Mays 2005). Full degree programmes generally require 3600 learning hours which suggests that the cost per student for a full degree based on similar courses might be in the range R5430 to R13 772 ($759–$1924) which would compare favourably with the average annual expenditure per full-time equivalent student in conventional universities of R29 686 ($4148).[4] The shortage of detailed figures on graduation rates prevents the calculation of robust costs per graduate.

Where they are available, figures from dual-mode universities also show costs per student lower than in the conventional system. In India, a study of the costs for correspondence departments in 1980 suggested that their

Table 7.5 University costs

(currency: 2005 US$)

| Country, Institution, date | GNP per capita at date of study | | Approx annual enrolment at date of report | Cost per student graduate$$ | Comparative cost |
	Current US$	Constant 2005 US$			
Costa Rica Universidad Estatal Distancia 1980[a]	1 900	4 484	8 150	$1877 (1980$795) per full-time student equivalent	Cost per student lower; later data suggest cost per graduate may not be
Thailand STOU 1980[b]	670	1 581		Cost per student for bachelor's degree $270-393 (1985$152–221)	Cost in conventional university $1045–1792 (1986$589–1010) Comparative cost per graduate not known
Nigeria University of Lagos education and business degrees 1987-8[c]	440	753		Cost per graduate assuming students work for 8 years BSc Ed $2091 (1981N4910) BSc Bus $3346 (1987N7856)	University regular programme costs are: $2144 $2353

China CRTVU 1988/89[d]	380	625	417 400	Cost per student p.a. for equiv junior college in economics: $373 (844RMBy) humanities: $291 (650RMBy) science and technology: $456 (1032RMBy)	$1 081 (2445RMBy) $1020 (2309RMBy) $1118 (2350RMBy)
India 1991/92f IGNOU YCMOU BRAOU	330	471		$119 (Rs2046) $128 (Rs2214) $55 (Rs 947) per student p.a.	Conventional university costs in range $291–1456 (Rs5000–2.5 000) but graduation rates there reported as in range 55–60% and in OUs 22–34%
IONOU 2003/4[g]	620	638	334 315	$102 (Rs4500) per student on post- graduate diploma; enrolment of 150	
South Korea Air Correspondence University 1990[h]	5 450	8 111	148 650	Cost per student p.a. on 2- year and 5-year degree $277 (1990$186)	Cost of conventional alternative $4825 (1990$2880)

Continued

Table 7.5 University costs—cont'd

| Country, Institution, date | GNP per capita at date of study | | Approx annual enrolment at date of report | Cost per student graduate$$ | Comparative cost |
	Current US$	Constant 2005 US$			
South Africa UNISA 2003[i]	2 750	2 907		Cost per student per course for under-graduate degree/diploma business: $25 (R181) per student $60 (R432) per student; enrolment of 16 139 psychology $92 (R658) $121 (R866) per completer; enrolment of 1110 law $100 (R719) per student $150 (R1073) per completer; enrolment of 1400	Direct comparisons not available; UNISA funded on lower full-time student equivalent basis but completion rates lower than at conventional universities

Notes

a. Rumble 1981: 398; b. Wichit and Tong In 1985 tables 14 and 15; c. Cumming and Olaloku 1993: 375; d. Ding 1994: 160; e. CRTVU 1993; f. Ansari 1994: 83; g. Naidu 2005: 15; h. Kim 1992: 25, 38 (Kim shows a cost per student of $93 which has to be doubled to include student as well as government expenditure); i. CHE 2004: 122.

costs were only 15 per cent of conventional departments while a review in 1988–9 found a range of figures from as low as 1–2 per cent to 23 per cent (Ansari 1994: 81). Many dual-mode universities in other countries have smaller student numbers than the Indian correspondence departments, but costs per student still tend to be lower than those of conventional departments. At the University of Nairobi, for example, the cost per head of a residential BEd (neglecting opportunity costs) was nearly three times the cost of the course offered at a distance, with a cost per head, in 1988 currency, of $808 (*$1328*) as compared with $3000 (*$4933*) (Makau 1993: 331).

But this is only half the story, and low completion rates can erode the cost advantage if we compare costs per graduate rather than costs per student.

Again, the evidence from China is clear and positive about the strengths of distance education. The high completion rates there suggest that costs per graduate for the television universities remain below those of conventional universities. Successful completion rates in the late 1980s were more than 80 per cent so that costs per graduate were reported as being 35 per cent of the cost for conventional universities in economics, 29 per cent in humanities and 41 per cent in science and engineering (Ding 1994: 160).

Evidence from other countries is more equivocal. As noted in chapter 5, we are short of data from India on graduation rates, which makes it difficult to interpret the available data. If we neglect dropout rates, then, between 1989 and 1992, it would cost about Rs6000 (*$498* at 1990 exchange rates) for IGNOU to produce a graduate with a bachelor's degree as compared with Rs15 000 to 18 000 (*$1243–1493*) in the conventional system (Kulandai Swami and Pillai 1994: 80). (Recent figures, showing an annual cost for a postgraduate diploma course at $100 in 2004, suggest that IGNOU has been successful in holding down its unit costs [Naidu 2005].) In a further analysis Naidu went on to consider the effect of differential dropout rates on the cost per graduate at IGNOU. Assuming no dropout in conventional universities, then IGNOU's cost per graduate would still be lower than the alternative even if only 40 per cent of its students graduated. But Naidu goes on to caution 'that there is a possibility that distance education may prove to be costlier than conventional education [because of] high wastage rates' (Naidu 1994: 65–6). It looks a real possibility: using Naidu's averaged cost of Rs16 428 per graduate in the conventional system, if the wastage rate there was 20 per cent, and that in IGNOU 71 per cent, the distance-education cost would be higher. And, from the figures in chapter 5, it seems that wastage rates for degree courses of between 80 and 90 per cent can often be expected.

Figures from Korea are consistent with this pattern. Following Kim's analysis (1992), if KACU students took eight years to graduate, with a graduation rate of 12 per cent, the cost per graduate would be some *$18 137*, a higher figure than the cost of three years at conventional university if we assume that it achieved a graduation rate of 80 per cent, giving a total cost of *$15 814*. An estimate of the costs per graduate at the University of Lagos was more optimistic than this. Provided there was an 80 per cent graduation rate for students in education or 50 per cent in business studies, and students completed their courses within the minimum period, then costs would be lower than for regular study. If students took eight years to complete, then costs in education would remain slightly below those of the alternative but would be 40 per cent higher in the case of business (Cumming and Olaloku 1993: 375).

The subsequent history of two open universities, where we have detailed early cost studies, confirm that it has been difficult to achieve planned savings in the cost of producing graduates. At the Universidad Estatal a Distancia of Costa Rica, the cost per student in 1980 was lower than that of conventional universities while the cost per credit, on the basis of which one could calculate an eventual cost per graduate, was roughly comparable. A cost study forecast that student enrolments might reach 15 000 to 17 000 and that, subject to containing the dropout rate, the university had the 'potential for achieving greater economies of scale' (Rumble 1981: 379 and 399). A later study suggested that both forecasts were over-optimistic. Enrolments stabilised at around 10 000 while the dropout rate reached-at least 84 per cent (Ramirez 1994: 69–72); the cost per graduate probably rose to about that of the conventional system. There is the same contrast between early hope and later achievement in Israel. Here, an early study forecast that Everyman University (now the Open University of Israel) would have about 6700 studying in any one year, once it had reached a steady state, and a graduation rate of 37.5 per cent, giving a cost per graduate of $3600 ($11 555). Degrees from universities with a comparable mix of subjects had a cost of $6000 to $8000 ($19 259–$25 679) (Melmed *et al.* 1982: 236–7). While by 1992–3 the university was bigger than forecast, with 19 000 students, graduation rates appear to have been much lower than forecast with only 405 graduates that year so that cost per graduate may have exceeded that in conventional universities.[5]

The simple conclusion is that, while open and dual-mode universities are achieving lower costs per student than conventional ones, they may not always have favourable costs per graduate. If we regard their function as being to expand the production of graduates, then the economic case for using distance education would be strengthened if they could increase the efficiency of their teaching systems and raise their graduation rate. On the present figures, a strong economic case for investing in open and distance learning as a means of producing graduates needs more robust data than appear to have been published.

And e-learning?

Most of this discussion has been about programmes that use print and broadcasting. All this is beginning to change but we are short of studies that show clearly how it will do so. The figures on computers in schools and from the

Shoma project suggest that moves into more sophisticated technologies will require major increases in expenditure. In an overview in 2002 Fielden reviewed both the data and the costing methodologies that were being used, necessarily drawing evidence from the industrialised rather than the developing world. Given the costs and the fee levels currently being charged in east Asia, he warned industrialised-country institutions considering crossborder e-learning that, 'creative product and pricing models may be required for institutions with high overheads' (Fielden 2002: 7).

Conclusion

We began with a puzzle, asking whether there was an economic case for open and distance learning that would justify its remarkable expansion.

The evidence is mixed. Basic education for adults, on a large scale and in a poor country, may be possible only by using mass media linked with some kind of student support, perhaps provided by unpaid volunteers. Even so, its costs tend to be higher than those of primary schools and it is difficult to see how governments could afford to expand it to reach large, national audiences. Distance education has particular strengths where it is used to support extension agents so that a multiplier effect comes into play. Education out of school, whether for adults or through alternative secondary schools, has lower costs than conventional education and would probably not exist unless it did so. In many cases its modest costs are matched by modest success; poor completion and pass rates mean that its costs per successful student tend to compare much less favourably with conventional alternatives. Teacher education, with its multiplier effect, has been marked by high success rates, with competitive costs per graduate, especially where teachers have been motivated by the hope of promotion. In higher education, so far as we can tell, there are many examples of costs per student being kept quite modest while costs per graduate may rise to equal or exceed those of the conventional sector.

8 Technology: after Gutenberg and Turing

Soon, if we are not more prudent, millions of people will be watching each other starve to death through expensive television sets.

Aneurin Bevan 1952

Communication technology has shaped and reshaped our world as radio followed the telegraph, television followed radio, satellites and computers followed in their turn. Broadcasting and the internet have, in different generations, been heralded as forces that can transform education. Two ideas have been at play: about combining media to increase their effectiveness and about the role of particular technologies in driving the development of open and distance learning. Three questions follow: how have the technologies shaped open and distance learning? What have they been used for? Is it all now changing?

How have the technologies shaped open and distance learning?

Previous chapters have shown that, at every level of education, some projects have depended heavily on electronic communication, either for open broadcasting or for teleconferencing so that the technology can be seen as driving the programme. The radio colleges of Latin America saw it as the principal means of communication with peasant families. Interactive radio instruction is about using radio to raise school quality and sometimes to widen access to it. In Nepal, the project 'Radio Education for Teacher Training' was explicitly designed to exploit and experiment with the power of radio. The Chinese radio and television university system is on a scale that justifies the use of a dedicated broadcasting service. In all these cases, the choice of medium has been the starting point for the design of the project.

Broadcasting has often looked attractive because of its immediacy and its unique capacity to attract attention from potential students, from the general public and from decision-makers. Presence on a national radio or television service legitimises distance education. Ram Reddy, the founding vice-chancellor, told the story of his attempt to persuade a new chief minister in Andhra Pradesh that the planned open university needed to be based in Hyderabad and not in a remote town with no facilities or infrastructure. It was the proposed use of television that surprised the chief minister, a former film actor, and swung the argument (Reddy 1997: 115–16).

In exploiting the technologies, educators have been constrained by scale, cost and politics. Broadcast television, for example, was feasible and appropriate to respond to the scale of demand at secondary level in Mexico and tertiary in China. Central control of education and the use of a single language over a large geographical area, common to both systems, together with their status as government programmes, made the continuing use of television possible.

In a very different political context, radio was central to nonformal education in Latin America. Except in Colombia numbers were smaller but, with radio costing perhaps one-tenth of television, the economics worked out reasonably well. The political context was one in which the radio schools of Latin America have had continuing access to radio because it is not centrally controlled, as it was for more than a generation after independence in the former British and French colonies. Individual, often church-based, nongovernment organisations were free to run radio stations. The choice of radio as an appropriate technology was determined by the need to overcome isolation in reaching peasant learners and facilitated by the political context.

The Interactive Radio Instruction projects, discussed in chapter 3, were different again. Radio made sense for the large numbers of schoolchildren potentially or actually involved. The projects generally used national radio stations by agreement with the relevant ministry of education. The original projects can be seen as technology-driven in the sense that the funding agency set out to demonstrate the value of radio, rather than neutrally seeking the most appropriate means to an educational end.

Issues of scale and isolation have also led to experiments with satellite communication and teleconferencing. As seen in chapter 5, teleconference links have been used on a sustained basis by both the University of the South Pacific and the University of the West Indies in order to reach students in small islands. In both cases the imperative was to reach audiences who could not be expected to move to the campus for the whole of their education and who were living in territories that were funding the university. The costs of telecommunication technology – borne in significant part by external funding agencies – were justified by geography.

We can sum up that in a number of cases the nature of a distance-education programme has been determined by a particular communication technology, usually broadcasting, sometimes teleconferencing. Access to broadcasting has been a function of political control. The choice of technology has, in turn, been driven by numbers or geography, the need to reach many students or to overcome severe problems of distance and isolation.

What have the technologies been used for?

In many cases there has been an eclectic choice of technologies. Many, if not most, distance-teaching institutions have set out with the intention of using a variety of media. Broadcasting alone is seldom enough. In China, for example, despite the dependence on television, textbooks and tutors were needed to cover some of the ground: even with a dedicated channel there were, in 1990, over 500 courses available, with 294 options to be fitted into 22 teaching hours by microwave link and 84 hours by satellite broadcast (NIME 1993: 41). Guides for teachers and students are a necessary part of the teaching system. A combination of media is likely to be more effective, perhaps by keeping up motivation, perhaps because some aspects of a subject lend themselves to a particular medium, perhaps because the timing imposed by regular broadcasts or seminars keeps students working.[1] A combination of media may be necessary, too, because many programmes require them for two contrasted purposes: as distribution media, to carry teaching materials to students, and as interactive media for two-way communication with them.

In practice it has often been difficult to combine the media and many institutions, at all levels of education, are now making minimal use of any medium other than print. Chapter 2 showed that there was an early expectation that combinations of media, including broadcasting, would be used on a wide scale to support rural development and nonformal education. But the expectations of an expansion of public service broadcasting and communications, epitomised by Schramm's 1964 title *Mass media for national development*, were not upheld. INADES-formation, for example, has moved away from the use of radio. Secondary equivalence programmes – with the obvious exception of the broadcasting-based projects, such as Telesecundaria and Interactive Radio – have made limited use of broadcasting. The open schools of India and Indonesia have not seen radio or television as a priority. Teacher education has not generally been able to attract broadcasters, and those running distance-education programmes have seen the organisation of the practicum as more important than seeking broadcast time. At tertiary level there have been more sustained attempts at using a mixed-media approach so that some of the Asian open universities have limited access to open-circuit broadcasting (Latchem *et al.* 1999). The national open universities in India and Pakistan alike built their own studios and have explored the possibility of developing dedicated educational broadcasting channels. Others make extensive use of tape recordings. Universiti Sains Malaysia, for example, has used teleconference facilities and has made some use of videocassettes and audiocassettes, although it notes that, 'Print is the principal teaching material used by the Centre' (NIME 1993: 179). Many dual-mode universities lack access to airtime and use audio or videocassettes on a limited scale with little or no broadcasting.[2]

Print dominates. The idea of combining media, and the potential and publicity of broadcasting, gave distance education an impetus as it has expanded since the 1970s. But, with important exceptions where broadcasting technology has driven the process, there has been a tendency for institutions to retreat to the use of print with only limited electronic support and often restricted opportunities for face-to-face learning. Table 8.1 sets out some illustrations of the use of the technologies and the domination of print.

Is it all now changing?

Concerns about the digital divide, between and within countries, have brought a new attention and sense of urgency to questions about the effect on society of changes in communication technology. In 2000 a UN panel warned that, with 276 million internet users growing at 150 000 a day:

> These are astonishing figures, unprecedented by any measure, but they reflect activity by less than 5 per cent of the world's population. The gross disparity in the spread of the Internet and thus the economic and social benefits derived from it is a matter of profound concern. ... The formidable and urgent challenge before national governments and the development community is to bridge this divide and connect the remainder of the world's population whose livelihoods can be enhanced through ICT. As each day passes the task becomes more difficult.
>
> (ECOSOC 2000: 3)

And yet the world has not been universally convinced and effects on education have been limited. The Commission for Africa claimed that: 'The benefits of ICT are far-reaching – connecting schools to the internet; enabling remote rural communities to get urgent medical advice by phone; giving farmers access to market price information; potentially halving the cost of sending remittances'. But it noted that the share of resources allocated by governments and funding agencies had reduced over the 1990s (Commission for Africa 2005: 233). Even in Asia a review in 2004 found that in spite of 'burgeoning and often innovative developments, access to ICT appliances such as computers, communication networks, and Internet connectivity remains low or nonexistent for the vast majority of educators in all but the most developed of the Asia-Pacific countries' (Farrell and Wachholz 2004: 268).

Both the public and private sectors have reason for their caution in embracing the new technologies. A review carried out for the World Bank's 'Information for development programme' (infoDev) warned that:

> The history of development assistance is riddled with 'gaps' (the infrastructure gap, the financing gap, etc.), the 'filling' of which was seen as

Table 8.1 Use of technologies at some distance-teaching institutions

Institution	Use of					
	Print	Radio and television	Audio and videocassettes	Internet	Face-to-face study
INADES-formation 1994–5[a]	14 147 learners on correspondence courses				13 049 attending seminars
National Open School, India 1998–9[b]	6.5 million copies of publications	Half-hour programme weekly	35 audio programmes 56 video programmes		1000 study centres
Interactive radio instruction	Printed materials generally produced	Regular radio programmes central to methodology	Sometimes available as alternative		Designed for classroom use
JKUAT, Nairobi and Sunderland University[c]	Printed copies of course materials available to students	None	None	Used both for distribution of material and for tutoring	Regular face-to-face sessions in Nairobi
Indira Gandhi National Open University[d]	260 000 dispatches to students 2100 books printed(cumulative total to 1996)	Some satellite broadcasts being developed	645 audio and 554 video programmes produced to 1996	Experimental and trial use of internet	1068 study centres (2003) but thin attendance

Notes
a. INADES-formation 1996: 7; b. National Open School 1999; c. chapter 6; d. IGNOU 1996, *IGNOU Profile 2003*, Manjulika and Reddy 1996: 124.

key to solving the conundrum of sustainable development. The digital divide risks serving as another unicausal explanation of development success and failure that diverts attention from the much more complex and context-specific challenges of development.

(McNamara 2003: 31)

Looking beyond education to the more general case, reviews of developing-country experience confirm that there is little empirical evidence of relationships between investment in the technologies and economic growth (Bedi 1999: 49; Qiang and Pitt 2004: 23). Even in the industrialised world a review in 2000 found little 'evidence of important economy-wide effects linked to the widespread diffusion of these technologies' (OECD 2000: 4).

Despite these cautions, computer-based information and communication technologies are ubiquitous and have been influencing education in several different ways: by providing new access to information, in changing the curriculum, through changing educational methods, and by offering new opportunities especially to remote and scattered learners.

New access to information

The simplest use of the new technologies may be at the edge of open and distance learning, or of formal education, but none the less important.

> Harnessing, adapting and using knowledge is vital not only to growth and competitiveness in an increasingly global economy but also to addressing the needs of the poor and the root causes of persistent poverty. ... The capacity of ICTs to enable global, rapid and efficient exchange of information and knowledge, and to facilitate instantaneous communication across distance, seems to hold out vast opportunities to address the crucial information, knowledge and communications dimensions of persistent poverty and low growth in developing countries.
>
> (McNamara 2003: 28)

There are examples from the south and the north of projects designed principally to make information more abundantly available. The UNESCO International Institute for Capacity Building in Africa developed a cd-rom of resources for teachers' colleges throughout Africa; the institute saw that this was a manageable number of institutions, most of whom would have at least one computer, even if they had no internet access. From the north, services have been developed to reduce the cost of distributing literature by using cd-roms and the internet. Cornell university, for example, has created 'The essential electronic agricultural library' consisting of text from 140 journals and made available to developing countries at a fraction of the cost of the regular journal subscriptions (World Bank 2002: 38).

Sharing information in this way is still constrained by costs and by the practical availability of technology. And we have, as yet, few accounts of the development of electronic resources to empower intermediaries, such as the extension agents and health workers discussed in chapter 2, who are otherwise inevitably working on their own. But the unstructured distribution of information through the internet may be transforming society more rapidly than changes in education.

Curriculum

The fact that the new technologies create new jobs and demand new skills has stimulated changes in the curriculum at tertiary, secondary, and even in some cases primary education (see also chapter 3). Distance-teaching institutions have played their part in introducing courses to teach computer skills of various kinds. Indian examples can tell the story. Despite the false start with the CLASS project (see p. 54), the growth of communication-related jobs has created a demand for relevant courses. By 2002 the National Open School had introduced certificate courses in computer applications, wordprocessing and DTP together with computer science as a subject at senior-secondary level and a hardware-oriented computer technician programme. It had recruited more than 50 000 students on to these courses and was going on to introduce its first web-based course, a certificate in computer applications (National Open School 2002: 4). At tertiary level IGNOU, too, was responding to similar demands. It offers certificate, bachelor's, master's and advanced diploma courses in computing, computer applications and information technology. By 2005 it had provided master's level courses to 150 000 students and saw this as a significant contribution to the development of the national workforce (Dikshit 2006: 65). There are proposals for all – all? – schools to be computerised and for distance education to play a major role in training the teachers who will implement this policy (Baggaley 2004). The story could be replicated across many institutions and all continents. Open and distance learning has been used to provide education about the technologies to teachers in the *Enlaces* project in Chile (see pp 54–5) for example, to raise internet skills among teachers and students in Armenia, and to be a mainstay of the burgeoning corporate universities.

Curricula, like educational methodology, can be driven by technology.

Changing educational methods

Distance-teaching institutions have been quick to explore new technologies as they became available. Faxes came first and helped to internationalise distance education. Once students could communicate with tutors by fax, it was quick and easy for universities in the north to teach, and keep in close contact with, students in the south, especially in major cities.

Newer technologies have come in to play: the University of Pretoria uses mobile phone messages, for example, to keep in touch with students and remind them when assignments are becoming due.

The internet has brought more profound changes for materials development, distribution and communication. Internet-based courses can in principle include film-clips, animations, and interactive exercises. High-quality and sophisticated materials can be used for learners on or off campus although they make heavy demands in terms of the time and expertise needed to develop them. A simpler possibility is to use the internet for distribution, allowing institutions to distribute teaching material electronically rather than physically. This can save time and reduce postage and – for the institution – printing costs, with the last of these passed on to the students. But there are disadvantages. An outline plan for distance education at the University of the West Indies, for example, suggested that material should be developed centrally but then downloaded electronically to the resident tutors in the university's fourteen territories (Renwick *et al.* 1992: 66). This proved impracticable; resident tutors did not have the staff to print, collate, staple and store the set of units needed even for a modest range of courses, even if they had the reprographic equipment needed to produce it to the necessary quality.

Moving from distribution to interaction, the internet allows for communication between tutors and students, or among groups of students, either through email or through more complex software. Virtual classrooms become possible. They demand specialist software; some institutions have developed their own while others have used either proprietary or open-source programs. The most serious constraint, other than cost, is likely to be the bandwidth available to students.

The prospect of widening their recruitment, and recouping the heavy investment needed for sophisticated, computer-based, courses has led many institutions in both developing and industrialised countries into exploring e-learning, usually using the technologies for these three purposes of production, distribution and student contact. It is difficult to assess the significance of this, in terms of the proportion of courses and students it affects. Even at university level, recent surveys of Commonwealth experience found that, for responding institutions, there was little or no 'online presence' in 81 per cent of programmes or courses in 2002 and 75 per cent in 2004 (Garrett and Verbik 2004: 2). At the same time the collapse of the British e-university (see p. 114) offers a warning from the north.

Despite these warnings there are positive reports from the south. The Shoma project in South Africa demonstrated one use of computer and satellite technologies for the continuing professional development of teachers (see pp 70–1). Universities have made wider use of the technologies although many accounts are of trials, often of courses about computers. At the Open University Malaysia, for example, the faculty of information technology and multimedia communication used an online course to teach computer programming. Students were required to work collaboratively on a programming assignment and to do so using the online environment made available by the university. Tutors provided online feedback. The results showed that there was a relationship between the frequency of postings by students and the grade they obtained. (Kaur and Lee 2005). In a course of this kind, the distinction between distributing teaching material and encouraging interaction with students becomes blurred.

Alongside experimental courses of this kind there are some bolder plans. The ministry of science and technology in Pakistan, for example, has set up a Virtual University on the campus of a conventional university with the intention of using television courses with student support by the internet. In 2004 it was reported to have 2000 active students (Baggaley 2004: 30). But institutions of this kind look like the exception. Universitas Terbuka in Indonesia concluded that web-based course delivery was impractical, especially for students who were using cybercafes to log on, and was considering restricting online methods to tutorial support (*ibid*: 8). At Indira Gandhi National Open University there was similar scepticism about 'stressing online delivery to the exclusion of other media' (*ibid*: 19). Students at Jomo Kenyatta University of Arts and Technology in Kenya found it was unrealistic to download materials and print them out at cybercafes even where email exchanges were possible (see p. 119).

The tentative conclusion is that the costs to institutions of developing web-based courses, that go beyond simply making text available over the internet, are a major constraint on their development. Costs to individual learners may also be a constraint, except where they are working for employers allowing them free broadband access. Email contacts, allowing for the rapid submission and return of work, may be making inroads into more traditional means of communication. But for the most part open and distance learning still relies mainly on these older methods – broadcasting in a few, large, institutions and print more widely. A South African investigation found that, 'many submissions [in response to its enquiries] seemed to focus on beliefs about what technology could achieve in theory, rather than actual experience of introducing it into programmes' (CHE 2004: 26).

New opportunities for scattered learners

New technologies sometimes promote new organisational structures. While private entrepreneurs have responded to the demand for computer access by establishing cybercafes there have been public-sector and nonprofit attempts to set up multipurpose telecentres. Several international agencies, including UNDP and the Canadian International Development Research Centre (IDRC) have experimented with telecentres in order to explore how they can solve problems of rural communication. Typically they have provided public access to computers and to the internet, together with printers and copiers, and sometimes providing space for local community or business use.

In principle telecentres can bring educational resources into the village, provide key market information to farmers and support the work of extension agents.

In practice it is not yet clear whether this is a viable model for the south; early results suggest that they have to overcome several hurdles. One is financial: one international overview found that, 'there is no multipurpose telecentre in a developing country that has proved to be self-sustaining when all the financial factors are taken into account' (Oestmann and Dymond 2001: 9). Then technical problems still abound: developing-country users warn of the slowness of narrow-band internet connections; the IDRC project found that the last mile of interconnection still caused technical problems. They also stressed the importance and difficulty in mobilising support (Rose 1999). While access to international information solves some problems, others need something more local: a project in Uganda, for example, documented the demand for local-language material (O'Farrell 1999: 8).

Telecentres, if they become viable, provide technical possibilities but difficulties remain – especially in finding a way of linking them with the more ordinary processes of learning and teaching and of locating or developing appropriate software. Experience also suggests a familiar educational conclusion: that providing a technical facility is not enough to ensure results: one recent study of Latin America experience argued that 'For each $100 invested in telecenters, one is more likely to obtain high-impact results if *simultaneous* investments are made to improve access, use, and appropriation, than if the $100 is more broadly allocated to improve only access, while expecting use and social appropriation to increase on their own' (Capper 2002b: 49).

Satellites

Much satellite technology is hidden from us and demands no decisions from educators: the telephone company decides whether to route calls terrestrially or by satellite. But new satellite technologies, may offer educational opportunities and possibly lead to a reshaping of distance education and of broadcasting's role within it. In 1995 a consortium including the American Hughes Communication group and the Cisneros group in Brazil launched a Galaxy satellite with audio and television programmes direct to listeners in Latin America. Broadcasts were planned to be in the Ku band, requiring a separate receiver. Satellite capacity was offered both to the World Bank and to the University of the West Indies but it proved forbiddingly difficult to find actual uses common to whole regions. Similarly in Africa Worldspace has plans to provide direct broadcasting and has announced that it will make channels available for educational purposes. The commercial company has set up a separate charity to allocate time on the channels. Again, a new receiver would be necessary at a cost estimated in 1999 at between $250 and $500.

Satellite opportunities may be more important in countries large enough to launch their own so that educational decisions do not demand crossborder agreement. India, which has experimented with the educational use of satellites since 1975, launched a satellite dedicated to education in 2004. Its six transponders allow for both regional and national programmes, opening possibilities for two-way audio and video communication and the development of work at all levels of education (Dikshit 2006: 66–9).

It is difficult at this point to see how far satellite technology will be a new driver for open and distance learning although it is already clear that it is likely to be more significant for large countries than small. With imagination, the satellite opportunities may bring opportunities for an expansion of educational broadcasting and of mixed-media distance-education programmes. Without it, we may simply have a costly medium seeking a role. In either case, as with broadcasting in the past, questions of scale and politics are likely to shape decisions on the use of satellites for education.

Access and cost

Technology excites, opens some possibilities, closes others. In the mid-nineteenth century the advance of the telegraph to Constantinople meant that London could keep in daily touch with affairs in the Balkans and south-west Asia; it was not welcomed by the British ambassador, Stratford de Redcliffe, who immediately lost the freedom make up his own policy. Today, while the cost of much technology has been declining dramatically, many advances may restrict access, rather than widening it, by putting more costs on the user. In much of the south, courses available on computer will reach the rich, or those at work in the modern sector; they will cut out the poor, the remote, and those not employed in the modern sector. This process will hurt women more than men. The technologies raise familiar issues about access and costs.

Learners need access to the right equipment if they are to do anything more technologically demanding than read books. Appropriate receivers or computers, reliable power, and a service industry capable of maintaining equipment, are all prerequisites. Computer and internet costs are likely to be higher, in absolute terms as well as in relation to earnings, in the south than in the north. These requirements already restrict access. Courses that depend on computer-based technology may be appropriate for small audiences, and in specialised subjects, but cannot at present reach the large, often rural, audiences of many of the world's distance-teaching institutions.

Sound decisions about using new technologies need to take account of their costs. While few recent data are disaggregated in a way that enables us to compare the costs of teaching media, two studies, in Europe and America, looked at the costs of producing teaching material in various media with the results shown in table 8.2. Their significance is not so much in the actual figures as in the relationship between them.

Table 8.2 Comparative costs of some technologies

	European data			US data		
	Cost per learning hour		Ratio to basic cost	Cost per 3-unit course		Ratio to basic cost
	1998 £	2005 US$		1998 £	2005 US$	
Basic text as print	350	692	1	6 000	7 160	1
Text online	700	1 384	2	12 000	14 319	2
Text with reference material and images				37 500	44 747	6
Audio	1 700	3 360	5			
Video	35 000	69 178	100			
Audio and video				120 000	14 390	20
Television	121 000	239 157	346			
CD-rom	13 000	25 695	37			
Simulations				250 000	298 133	42
Virtual reality				1 000 000	1 193 252	167

Source: Hülsmann 2000: 17 and Arizona Learning Systems reported in Rumble 2001: 80.

The European study, found that, as a rough guide it was costing European tertiary level institutions about £350 (*$692*) to produce the text, or print version, of material that would occupy a student for one hour. Using audio or radio was likely to increase the cost 30 to 50 times, with television or video significantly more. If computer communication was used to distribute printed material, unchanged, then costs should be no higher than for conventionally printed material. But where producers took advantage of the possibility of including sound, and simulation, or the inclusion of filmclips, costs rose sharply. It was found that simply adding a small number of hyperlinks to printed materials would increase costs two to three times while a well-developed cd-rom, using a variety of visual material, was likely to increase costs 40 times. The American study found ratios that were broadly in line so that the costs of a three-unit internet course could vary between $12 000 and $1 000 000 according to the sophistication of the production (Hülsmann 2000: 17; Rumble 2001).

There are two warnings here. The first is that, while institutions may save time and money on distribution if they move from print to computer, any savings are likely to be overwhelmed by increased production costs if they seek to use the variety of opportunities that computer-based learning makes possible.

Second, there is a danger that the use of the internet will increase not only these fixed costs but also the variable costs of interaction with tutors. Once email contact becomes easy then the demands which students put on their tutors are also likely to increase (Rumble 2001: 81–3), unless the tutor limits student contact, which goes against the grain of good teaching, or the institution has to pay more, or the tutor is exploited. Evidence from the United States and Europe shows that this is happening so that 'the costs of Web based E-learning courses may sometimes be higher than the alternative' and tutors are spending longer tutoring online than they would face-to-face (Romiszowski 2004: 2). The real benefits of the newer technologies need to be set against these twin dangers, that they may increase both fixed and variable costs.

Conclusion

If educators are cautious in their embrace of the technologies, they are following a familiar path. For the most part, with the exceptions of the large programmes of secondary education in Latin America and tertiary education in China, open and distance learning has not been technologically driven. Rather, there has been a cautious and restricted use of any technology other than print, backed by limited opportunities for face-to-face study. The early television experiments and interactive radio seldom proved sustainable and offer a warning to the newer computer or satellite-based projects.

It may all have been too cautious. The powerful idea of distance education, when it was new, was to use a variety of approaches for out-of-school audiences, doing something more interesting and more effective than old-style correspondence education. The institutions now using open and distance learning have been producing teaching material of a new quality. At the same time, the near-abandonment of media other than print means that teaching is less varied, less interesting, perhaps less effective than we had hoped for in that dawn. Radio, to reiterate, remains underused. We know that it is a powerful tool for public education, with modest unit costs, but one that has largely slipped into the background. There may be a danger of grasping tomorrow's technology and neglecting yesterday's.

9 Globalisation: and culture follows trade

А между тем ВНУТРЕННИХ ДЕЛ вообще не осталось на нашей тесной Земле! И спасение человечества только в том, чтобы всем было дело до всего: людям Востока было бы сплошь небезразлично, что думают на Западе; людям Запада – сплошь небезразлично, что совершается на Востоке.

Meanwhile no such thing as INTERNAL AFFAIRS remains on our crowded Earth. Humanity's salvation lies exclusively in everyone making everything his business, in the people of the East being anything but indifferent to what is thought in the West, and in the people of the West being anything but indifferent to what is happening in the East.

Alexander Solzhenitsyn 1970

Haroun el Rashid sent Charlemagne an elephant, Abu 'l-Abbas, as a gift in 800. To his chagrin it died, ten years later, on the Lüneburg Heath (Hodges and Whitehouse 1983: 113). More than a millennium later Marx and Engels forecast that 'the need of a constantly expanding market for its products chases the bourgeoisie over the whole surface of the globe' (1955: 58). In the present century we have seen universities following heavy industry in joining the export trade, selling courses and recruiting internationally. The hyperglobalists argue that the internationalisation of economic processes, and of all that follows them, is the dominant force of our times. A more modest interpretation of the evidence still shows that global processes play a much increased role in all our economies and societies.

Globalisation can, of course, like language, be used to explain anything. In a sense, as all educational systems respond to labour market demands, themselves a function of global activity, so education is shaped by globalisation. But, more than this, there is a widespread perception that education – and especially higher education – is becoming an international activity (OECD 1996: 8). Bold claims are being made about the international potential of the new technologies touched on in chapters 6 and 8. We need, in consequence, to ask two kinds of question about global processes affecting distance education. First, can we report what is happening just within national frontiers or does an adequate report also demand some investigation of global activity? Second, to explain what has happened, do we need to look at agencies working internationally as well as nationally? The indirect answer to both questions is yes: where, for example, distance education is taking advantage of changes in communication technology, it is inevitably shaped by the global forces acting upon them. But there is a direct answer too: several groups of actors are working internationally to support or develop open and distance learning.

Four kinds of actors are at play. Finance comes first; international funding decisions have affected educational development at least since 1813 when the East India Act of the British parliament authorised the Governor General of India to spend 100 000 rupees (*$500 000*) a year on education.[1] The international funding agencies have played a major part in shaping the development of conventional education and have provided funds for open and distance learning at various levels of education. Then, second, several international agencies have been active in exploring, encouraging or promoting the use of open and distance learning. Third, as set out in chapter 6, universities have been seeking new students across national borders, helped by changes in communication technology. Fourth, we can trace the activities of several specialist agencies and of invisible colleges which have often worked in partnership with one or another of the global actors.

The funding agencies

Funding agencies pay the piper and sometimes call the tune. By the 1980s, many countries in Africa and the Caribbean were mainly dependent on external finance for capital expenditure in education, while retaining responsibility for recurrent expenditure. The bilateral donors, the regional development banks, and above all the World Bank have all brought their influence to bear on national plans for education. The changing policies of the World Bank have played a major role in shaping educational policy in much of the south since the 1970s. They are set out in a series of policy papers but also to be inferred from its practice.

The 1974 *Education sector working paper* barely discussed distance education and had only a passing reference to broadcasting, in noticing the importance of attracting a big enough audience to bring down the cost of television in Côte d'Ivoire from $115 for 21 000 students to $6 for 700 000 students (*$453* to *$24*) (World Bank 1974: 40). Neither broadcasting nor distance education featured in the short list of measures identified as leading to higher educational achievement and low costs (*ibid* 56). By 1980 the reference to Côte d'Ivoire television had disappeared in embarrassment and the *Education sector policy paper* had a discussion of the use of mass media and distance learning within a chapter on measures to increase internal efficiency. Distance learning was seen as having the potential to improve quality, widen access, and reduce costs, provided the numbers reached were high enough, with a particular emphasis given to radio (World Bank 1980: 35–6). The bank saw distance education as relevant to schooling as well as to higher education. By the time of the 1995 review of *Priorities and strategies* the bank's emphasis had shifted and distance education is discussed only in the context of open universities and of teacher training. The review confirmed that distance teaching was likely to be more cost effective than residential teacher education (World Bank 1995: 83). It was concerned that while open university unit costs were generally lower than those of conventional universities, high dropout might erode economies (*ibid*: 62). The review is also interesting for what it did not say: it did not discuss the use of distance education at other levels of education, and did not include distance education among the six key reforms to which it gave priority.

The bank's lending, over this period, reflected its policy documents and their scepticism about nonconventional education. The Côte d'Ivoire collapse (see chapter 3) led to the reaction that the bank had tried distance education and it did not work. While it supported research in the area, distance education was tarred by its association with nonformal education, where the research of this same period, discussed in chapter 2, had failed to deliver the hard evidence on costs per student needed to convince economists and bankers.

Perhaps more important, bank policy was reflecting the demands of borrowing countries. For the most part they wanted funds to build schools and colleges and most bank lending was spent on that. There were some exceptions. In the late 1970s, when ideas of community education still had some appeal, the bank funded some buildings for distance education, within the framework of educational loans that were mainly for school buildings, in both Botswana and Lesotho. But, generally, projects

> included distance education as a relatively minor component, with the important exception of China III (for the Chinese television universities). The peak period was 1974–78, when about 19 per cent of education projects included this component. Overall, only 32 projects out of 302 (10.6 per cent) have incorporated distance education.
>
> (Hawkridge 1987: 1)

While the China loan was significant, at $60 million (*$109 million*, assuming 1985 prices) it was in fact a modest proportion of the total bank lending to China for higher education where the total loans and credits in place in 1985 amounted to $2140 million (*$3869 million*) (Hayhoe 1989: 162).

World Bank policy changed in the 1990s with the arrival of James Wolfensohn as its president. He talked of the bank as a 'knowledge institution', gave a new emphasis to the role of education in attacking poverty, and was excited by the potential of applying the new technologies. In 1997, with Wolfensohn's strong personal involvement it hosted a 'Global Knowledge' forum in Canada to demonstrate its concern with learning and with the application of technology to it. In the same year, too, it put an initial invest-ment of $1 million into its exploration of the African Virtual University (see chapter 6). The 1999 *Education sector strategy* reflected the changes in thinking. In the run-up to the Dakar conference the bank's first concern was basic education, particularly for girls and for the poorest. These were the first priorities in the new strategy, but were followed by three others: early interventions in child health and education; 'innovative delivery: distance education, open learning and the use of new technologies'; and systems reform with an emphasis on curriculum, governance and new funding strategies (World Bank 1999). A bank educational strategy paper for Africa gave some prominence to distance education with boxes on the African Virtual University and external programmes at the University of Namibia together with a commitment to increase support for educational technology (World Bank 2001: 70).

In its expanded role as a knowledge institution the bank put new energies into informing the world about information and communication technologies. It set up a task force on the digital divide, launched a journal, *Education and technology notes series*, started revisiting distance-education policy for subsaharan Africa, and funded a series of initiatives using or reporting on open and distance learning. In order to reach the scattered professional audiences who had been the main clients of its training arm, the World Bank Institute, it created the 'Global Distance Learning Network' (GDLN) in 2000. This consists of a network of learning centres, equipped with videoconferencing and high-speed internet resources. The network is now used both by the bank and by affiliate partners including governments and other funding agencies. Confusingly, the bank has also set up a quite sepa-rate 'Global Distance EducationNet' or 'Global DistEdNet' using its website to inform the world about the strengths and weaknesses of distance educa-tion. To widen understanding of the technologies, in partnership with other international development agencies, it has also supported and housed the secretariat of an information and research service, infoDev, which works on the role of information technologies in development. And, adding to this tangle of networks each with its typographically inept acronym, the bank also supported a 'World Links for Development' (WorLD) programme designed to link secondary schools internationally through the internet.

This set of activities is a marked change of direction for the bank and a tribute to technological excitement and the power of World Bank presi-dents. Distance education, under the information and communication tech-nology flag, is more visible than ever before on the World Bank stage. It is more difficult to assess how far this has influenced the bank's lending, which has probably varied by region: certainly subsaharan Africa has made the running in documentation (Saint 1999, Murphy *et al.* 2002). A work-ing paper reported that 22 out of 27 educational projects in subsaharan Africa over the previous four years had technology components with an expenditure of up to $203 million (*$229 million* assuming these are on average 2000$$) or 25 per cent. But the figure needs to be treated with caution: some nontechnology components were included in the technology figure (Murphy *et al.* 2002: 2); infoDev have found that 'it is extremely difficult to identify where donor-supported education initiatives, including those funded by the World Bank, utilize ICT components, and, where such components *are* identifiable, it is quite difficult to identify the size of such investments' (infoDev 2005: 2). There are often no standard methods of defining the use of technologies, or disaggregating costs.

The World Bank story is therefore complicated. It contributed to the intellectual debate about distance education in the 1970s and 1980s and, even after Côte d'Ivoire, funded a small number of projects. It then had little involvement in the two decades of institution-building as open universities were being established. It lacked specialist staff, or a location for them (cf. Woods 1993: 42). All this has changed: the bank is now deeply involved in the debates about information and communication technologies and about distance education if not yet a major driver of development.

The regional development banks have sometimes seemed more enthusiastic than the World Bank. The Asian Development Bank agreed to fund 80 per cent of the costs of the first five years of the Bangladesh Open University, investing $43 million (*$60 million* assuming 1992 values).[2] In contrast, too, with the emphasis in the bank's earlier papers on distance education's role in higher education, a major feature of the Bangladesh development was work at secondary levels, in nonformal education and for teacher training. Back in higher education, the Caribbean Development Bank made a loan and grant of some $12 million (*$16 million*) in 1993 to the University of the West Indies to expand its work off-campus (see chapter 5). While it is reported that the proposals for both loans encountered opposition within the banks concerned, they may be indications of potentially increased regional support. So too may a decision by the African Development Bank in 2006 to appraise a loan to strengthen distance education across subsaharan Africa.

The bilateral donors have pursued varied policies but ones that reflect the World Bank's view of distance education as existing some way from the mainstream of educational development. The Swedish International Development Agency (SIDA) funded early developments in distance education in Tanzania and Zambia. France has supported educational broadcasting, and some distance-education projects, in francophone west Africa. Britain and the United States, two of the other major actors, provide contrasting examples in the development of policy.

Like the World Bank, the British Overseas Development Administration (now the Department for International Development – DfID) produced a series of educational policy statements, in 1984, 1990, and 1993. Although there are important changes of direction after the new government in 1997, with new statements in 1998 and 2001, the documents tend to be more pragmatic than the World Bank, long on priorities and short on choosing between them.

Distance teaching was identified as one of ten areas of major importance in 1984 (Overseas Development Administration 1984: 3–4). The 1990 and 1994 papers referred to British comparative advantage in distance education, reasonably enough in the light of the size and reputation of the Open University (Overseas Development Administration 1990; Education Division ODA 1994). For the most part British funding in the period covered by these documents went to support existing institutions or programmes rather than to start new ones; Britain did not fund institution building on the grand scale of the Chinese television universities or the Bangladesh Open University. Funding went to projects at all levels of education with support for distance education at secondary level going to Malawi, for example, in the early 1990s and Botswana in the late 1990s and intermittently for its use in teacher education in, for example, Botswana, Swaziland and Ghana. This kind of funding for institutional development has been cautious and limited, and probably biased if anything towards higher education. Of ten programmes launched or supported by the International Extension College between 1971 and 1992 and at lower levels of education, for example, only one was funded principally by the Overseas Development Administration, the Functional Education Project in Rural Areas in Pakistan (see chapter 2).

There appears to have been more activity in higher education although, as with the World Bank, it is difficult to disaggregate data by level or type of education. Britain provided significant funding to Allama Iqbal Open University for ten years from 1976 and provided consultancy support to open universities in Costa Rica, India, Indonesia, Iran under the Shah, and Sri Lanka. Probably its largest programme of support was for Indira Gandhi National Open University with a total expenditure of £3.7 million between 1986 and 1993 (*$10.1 million* assuming 1988 prices). There were 54 visits by British staff to India and 53 visits and 'trainee placements' in the other direction so that consultancies, visits and training took up 28 per cent of the total, with 51 per cent going on equipment (Fielden *et al.* n.d.). We can look at these costs from two angles. From the British end, the expenditure was modest when compared either with total aid to India – £79.4 million (*$160.3 million*) in 1993–4 or total aid to education of £86.6 million (*$174.8 million*) (Department for International Development 1998: tables 7.3 and 22). But it may look different from Delhi where IGNOU's total income for the period 1985–92, excluding international grants, was Rs 668.7 million (*$75.9 million* assuming 1988 prices) (Manjulika and Reddy 1996: 139). Funding at a level equivalent to 14 per cent of local expenditure gives the potential for leverage: we come back to its significance below in looking at the influence of the British Open University which provided and advised on much of this investment.

The 1997 government brought a series of policy changes. Aid was now the responsibility of a department, represented at cabinet level, with policy set out in policy documents, three white papers and an act of parliament.

In the dotcom era it was inevitable that the information and communication technologies and the digital divide would get a new prominence. But two other policy developments had a major bearing on expenditure, on the technologies or on distance education. First, the commitment to education for all by 2015 has increasingly dominated British policy. There was interest in alternative approaches to education if – and only if – they could help basic education. Second, in the same period, British policy favoured sector-wide approaches to aid and providing budgetary support rather than funding individual educational activities.

A 1998 policy framework referred to information and communication technologies and saw them as relevant to education sector management, widening access to post-primary education and raising quality in secondary, tertiary and vocational education, but did not set out specific policies (Department for International Development n.d.: 35–6). By 2001 a strategy paper was more nuanced with a heading 'Technology – yes but' followed by a warning on costs and concern to look for multiplier effects when applying technologies to basic education (Department for International Development 2001: 19). Reflecting work the department had commissioned for the Dakar conference, the department reminded the world of the existence of radio and books and warned against enthusiasm for expensive and untried technologies (*ibid*: 27). A white paper on *Eliminating world poverty: Making globalisation work for the poor* in 2000 devoted only a couple of pages to the digital divide including a statement that: 'We believe new technologies can play an important role in improving education in developing countries' from primary through to tertiary levels' (Department for International Development 2000: 41).

The white paper also referred to:

> The Prime Minister's initiative on technology in teacher training, known as Imfundo (Ndebele for education) is a new kind of public/private partnership dedicated to finding new ways to enhance educational opportunity in developing countries, with a particular focus on sub-Saharan Africa. The initiative has been developed in partnership with Cisco, Marconi and Virgin.
>
> Imfundo will use information and communication technologies such as radio, satellite, computers and the internet to support teacher training, professional development and support, and the management of education systems.
>
> (*ibid*: 38)

It all started grandly enough with an advisory committee meeting in Downing Street to endorse the plans and a civil servant despatched from the prime minister's office to get it started within the Department for International Development. Imfundo was to stimulate and encourage distance learning for teachers, collect and publish guides to good practice, and create a resource bank of pledges, mainly from the private sector, that could be used for the benefit of subsaharan Africa.

But difficulties soon emerged. Imfundo was created as a project just at the point when its host department was moving away from supporting projects. It had a budget of only £7 million (*$11.1 million* assuming 2001 prices) over six years – enough to explore and to prime some pumps but not enough to implement. Funds for major activities within Africa would have to come from other budgets. It proved difficult to get pledges of any size into the resource bank: a review halfway through Imfundo's life recorded only £18 000 (*$31 100*) in hard cash; some contributions were no more than a reduced rate for consultancy and the hosting of a dinner (Harrison *et al.* 2003: 26). The private sector proved to be neither wise, in its assumptions about easy effects on education, nor generous. At least as serious, 'Imfundo had a high-level sending off, but a bumpy landing almost immediately. DFID, with its devolved offices is not structured to accept what it calls "central initiatives" (i.e. policy or activities emanating from London)' (*ibid*: 4).

> This has led to the bizarre situation of Imfundo staff (who are also DFID staff) receiving a "hostile" reception in some offices ... Imfundo thus exists within a somewhat strange reality: established and supported at the highest level (Prime Ministerial); developed by various parts of DFID in London concerned with policy, poverty and education, as well as ICTs; its work focussed on an area of great need – Africa; and yet finding itself unwanted in most of DFID's Africa offices.
>
> (*ibid*: 7)

It is hardly surprising that, some two years before it was due to end, its 36th newsletter of October 2004 was the last. Nor that its achievements were modest; despite multiple visits to eleven countries Imfundo seems to have supported some uses of technologies in South Africa, encouraged the use of distance education within the framework of a larger educational grant in Kenya, experimented with computers for the education of out-of-school children in Ethiopia and helped Ghana develop a policy for the use of the technologies. Less than had been hoped for but more than the achievements of the e-university (p. 114) which cost seven times as much.

With the decline of Imfundo British policy has moved back to its eclectic and pragmatic self, seeking to integrate policy about the technologies into its aid programme more generally. Two conclusions; first, the British are reluctant to drive policy. If Imfundo had had a funeral, one of the ghosts present would have been the Centre for Educational Development Overseas, created by government in 1971, and embracing specialisms in educational broadcasting, only to be absorbed into the British Council and out of sight in 1974. From then until Imfundo there has been no nationally funded agency with expertise in the international use of distance education. Where government aid has been used to fund projects, and provide technical assistance to them, decisions have been affected not so much by a consistent policy about distance education, as by the values and activities of the major British professional actors in providing consultancy and training like those involved in the 107 visits between IGNOU and Britain.

Second, we have gone beyond the age of imperialism. Britain had by 2000 so far devolved decision making to its partners and its overseas agents that, even with the highest level support, it could not make Imfundo work.

The United States offers a contrast. Its policy has been more focused and, from the 1960s on, its support for distance education has been dominated by projects, often closely similar in structure, mainly based on the use of broadcasting and telecommunications. In Kenya, for example, as early as 1967, it worked with the University of Nairobi in establishing a Correspondence Course Unit. It provided expertise, buildings, a radio studio and recurrent funding. The next wave of projects (see chapter 3) used television to be followed by the first educational projects to use satellite communication. The United States Agency for International Development (USAID) enabled the early satellite ATS–3 to be used for the Indian SITE project, ran a rural satellite programme and, as seen in chapter 5, provided communications services to the University of the South Pacific and the University of the West Indies.

More recent USAID funding for distance education has been concentrated on the series of Interactive Radio Instruction projects (see chapter 3). These were conceived as curriculum projects but were at the same time technology-led, designed as a series of demonstrations for the world about how radio might be used as well as being aid projects designed to strengthen education in the countries where they were operating. The same style of operation continues today. A recent American aid project, LearnLink, supports 'the development of tools and methods to establish programs for the effective use of communication and learning systems for sustainable development' (USAID 1998). This series of activities forms a more coherent whole than British aid projects: the various interactive radio projects, for example, learned from each other, followed a similar pattern, and resulted in a steady building up of expertise within the agencies concerned. It seems reasonable to assume, too, that one of the purposes of demonstrating the potential of communication technology was to seek markets for American industry. The rural satellite programme which ran from 1979 to 1986, for example, with expenditure of $8.4 million (*$16.5 million* if we average this at 1983 prices), had as one of its stated purposes 'providing evidence to communication carriers of the existence of a market in ldc rural services' (Farren 1999). Leaving aside questions of appropriateness, one difficulty of the approach lies in sustainability. It led aid officials to design projects and then look for locations, many of which proved not to be sustainable when American funding was withdrawn.

Despite the strength of the British tradition of educational broadcasting, Britain has twice closed down specialist development agencies in this area while American support for open and distance learning has continued to emphasise broadcasting, primarily for schools. The limited American capacity in what the rest of the world sees as distance education, and the absence of an American open university, means that little American aid has flowed to open universities.

The work of three major international actors suggests that, for different reasons, the funding agencies have played only a minor role in shaping the development of open and distance learning. The World Bank's policy agenda has driven its lending – although its actual portfolio of loans is more diverse than that might suggest – and it has rarely been convinced of the value of distance education, though this may now be changing. The British have generally eschewed policy. If they have influenced distance education it has been as a result of pressure from the invisible colleges of consultants whom they employed rather than a consequence of government policy. The Americans have had policies of promoting technological solutions to educational problems, but have had difficulty in ensuring that their demonstration projects are sustainable. We can interpret some of the evidence as being a manifestation of globalisation; British funding helped the near-global process of founding open universities, while the American drive for communication markets led distance-education projects into a selected group of countries. But, despite this, the funding agencies have not been driving the expansion of open and distance learning; rather they have been influencing it at the margins.

The international institutions

International institutions have a paradoxical relationship with the process of globalisation, at once forerunner and outsider. The European Commission, UNESCO, the International Telecommunications Union and OECD have all had a stab at writing policies for education or communication but, bound by the policies of national member states that control them, do not look like major actors. The European Commission has developed policies, and created budgets, to support open and distance learning within Europe. But its education staff, responsible for activities within the European Union, are physically and ideologically a long way from those controlling its development expenditure, where there has been no consistent policy of favouring – or opposing – support for distance education.

UNESCO has a long interest in the use of distance education in the south. After its project with UNRWA for Palestinian teachers (chapter 3; cf. Lyle 1967) it went on to publish some of the key early works about the international use of distance education (e.g. Schramm 1967; MacKenzie *et al.* 1975). But, with its budget savaged by the small-minded withdrawal of Britain and the United States, its influence inevitably declined. It ran a conference on distance education in Africa in 1990, and has retained an active interest in the use of computers in education. In the mid-1990s it explored the possibility of developing cooperative projects in distance education for the nine high-population countries (Bangladesh, Brazil, China, Egypt, India, Indonesia, Mexico, Nigeria and Pakistan), gained expressions of goodwill but was not able to get much further with this heterogeneous group. It commissioned a series of case studies on distance education for teachers in the late 1990s and has a growing interest in the application of technologies to education. UNESCO now has a specialist Institute for Information Technologies in Education in Moscow and has produced guides on using the technologies in education, with the main emphasis on their use within institutions rather than for students outside (UNESCO 2002c, 2002d).[3] Open and distance learning is not a main theme of its medium-term plan – even in relation to a major series of activities to strengthen teacher education in Africa. Its policy documents generally summarise the state of play but without offering clear guidance either to the rest of the world or to UNESCO itself (UNESCO 1997, 2002b, UNESCO IITE 2000).

UNESCO has been more vigorous, however, in exploring quality standards and accreditation for crossborder enrolment. With OECD it has produced draft guidelines on crossborder enrolment and may therefore, begin to play a more active role in encouraging – it cannot enforce – good standards internationally (see p. 124). On open and distance learning more generally, however, it has not been able to give the intellectual, research or policy guidance to the world which one would have hoped for from the United Nations agency with the education portfolio.

There has been more vigorous activity by Commonwealth and francophone agencies. Educational cooperation within the Commonwealth predates the establishment of the Commonwealth Secretariat, with the first Commonwealth education conference taking place in Oxford in 1959. The Secretariat took over responsibility for educational cooperation and soon showed an interest in distance education with its publication of a series of guides to correspondence education in the Commonwealth and with support for distance education projects for Namibian and South African exiles. Threats to Commonwealth student mobility led it in 1986 to establish an 'Expert group on Commonwealth cooperation in distance education and open learning' chaired by the British historian Asa Briggs. The group reviewed the development of open and distance learning within the Commonwealth and recommended creating a new agency 'to widen access to opportunities for learning and to co-operate with Commonwealth institutions of higher education in extending the range and raising the quality of their work' (Briggs *et al.* 1987: 63). Like the United Nations University, this would not enrol individual students but would work in cooperation with other universities. It would work

> in three broad areas. The first is for materials and course development, where materials can be shared, or new materials created, to meet widespread and significant educational needs. The second is in supporting

individual learners by arranging for mutual accreditation procedures...
The third is in institutional development... in staff training, in the use of
communications technology for two-way links for teaching and research,
in information and in common programmes of research and evaluation.

(*ibid*: 3)

The proposal got a mixed reception. Britain was lukewarm, doubting
whether we really needed a new institution, but pledged support especially
where it meant using and strengthening British resources. Commonwealth
developing countries were more enthusiastic. The Jamaican minister of
education epitomised their approach by quoting Demosthenes: 'No man can
tell what the future holds. But great ends often follow from small beginnings'.
Sonny Ramphal, the Commonwealth Secretary General, put his considerable authority behind the ideas. Later that year Commonwealth heads of
government agreed to support a modest start. Further work on the nuts and
bolts of the new agency shifted its priorities: cooperative activities, which
came first in the Briggs report, moved down the list of functions in the next
report, while institutional development, information and training moved up
(Daniel *et al.* 1988). The new agency, now called the Commonwealth of
Learning (COL), was launched, with champagne and a speech from Ramphal,
on 1 September 1988.

Brunei, India and Nigeria, along with Britain and Canada pledged most
of the funds. Canada offered a headquarters. But there was not much
money. The Briggs group had suggested an annual budget rising from
£895 000 (*$2.3 million*) in the first year to £2.5 million (*$6.5 million*) in
the fifth. By 1988 there was about £14 million (*$40.9*) committed, some of
it in kind rather than cash for the first five years work (*ibid*: 22). At this
time the budget of a medium-sized university in Britain was around
£65 million (*$190 million*).[4] Nor has the Commonwealth of Learning been
able to maintain its funding even at this level. Commonwealth heads of
governments have endorsed – which does not mean paid – Cdn$9 million
(*$7.3 million*) as its minimum core funding but the actual figures for the
years from 2001 to 2004 fell below this level (Commonwealth of Learning
2006a: 14). The evidence suggests that governments can see the case for
global activity in education, but are not willing to contemplate funding
global activities in education on anything like the same scale that they see
as reasonable at home.

In its first years, the Commonwealth of Learning wanted to demonstrate
its relevance to education in as many corners of the Commonwealth as
possible and to claim the status that went with its constitution as an
intergovernmental agency. Perhaps inevitably its *Compendium of activities*
in 1993 reads like a catalogue of meetings, consultancies and reports. Pan-
Commonwealth and regional activity got little attention. The agency looked
as if it were moving even further towards being a technical assistance body
and away from being a body concerned with an international approach

to education. In doing so it was following a precedent long set by UNESCO in giving priority to aid to development rather than confronting the more difficult job of being 'awkwardly in the middle of quarrelling States, trying to persuade them to agree on a line of action in a contentious area.' (Hoggart 1978: 92).

Over the last decade COL's activities have become more varied, mainly concentrated on information, training, advocacy and field work. It has given some support to research designed to guide policy. Through this, through its publications and website, by supporting the first six volumes of the *World review of distance education and open learning*, and by working with the World Bank on its Global Distance EducationNet, COL has ensured that the world is better informed about open and distance learning. Its draft plan for 2006–9 claims with some justification that its greatest achievements are in south–south exchanges of knowledge and experience (Commonwealth of Learning: 2006b: 11). From the outset it has seen the training of professionals in distance education as one of its concerns, leading it to support for courses, the running of seminars and the development of training materials. Advocacy has probably increased in importance in COL's work. In 2000 COL initiated a biennial Pan-Commonwealth Forum on Open Learning in Brunei to be followed by forums in South Africa, New Zealand and Jamaica; they have been unusual in attracting educational decision makers – chief education officers and permanent secretaries – from outside the distance-education ghetto alongside the specialists. All these activities have been informed by COL's own field work where it has responded to requests for help from governments moving into, or adapting, open and distance learning. It has, for example, worked with Mozambique in setting up a secondary-equivalence programme, with Nigeria on the development of its open university and with the Caribbean Examinations Council in strengthening secondary education.

The Commonwealth of Learning has also sought to develop cooperative work both with its Commonwealth partners and with other agencies. It has promoted pan-Commonwealth work on legislative drafting and the development of materials for science education in southern Africa. Using existing teaching materials it has supported a Commonwealth Executive MBA. At the request of ministers of education it explored plans for a Virtual University for Small States which looks as if it will become a mechanism for the sharing, and perhaps collaborative development, of course material.[5]

In recent years COL has had to resolve the dilemma of responding to the demands of over fifty Commonwealth governments and to the pressures of the main funding agencies, especially in Britain and Canada. After the Dakar conference, British and Canadian aid policy to stress the millennium development goals, and in particular the educational goal of education for all, did not sit easily with requests from member governments to COL, especially where these related to other levels of education. The aid agencies were also pressing COL 'to "move upstream" to support the development of national and institutional policy' (Commonwealth of Learning 2006b: 12). COL has responded to this partly by a new concentration on the relationship between its work and poverty reduction, partly by careful presentation of its work in relation to development goals.

The Commonwealth of Learning has now been working long enough to make an assessment of what it has done for Commonwealth education. The simple fact of its existence has some significance. Its presence at meetings of Commonwealth ministers of education and heads of government amounts to a political demonstration of legitimacy for open and distance learning. By providing a mechanism for the documenting and exchange of experience, especially south-to-south, it has probably made for better decision-making internationally. It is possible that there are distance-education projects or institutions that would not exist without COL; more often, and probably as important, its existence has shaped decisions about how things are done. While questions of international funding, intellectual property, and the new competitiveness among universities still inhibit the free sharing of resources, there are the beginnings of international cooperation, and the potential for more.

The francophone story is shorter and sadder. The Canadian government supported the creation of a Consortium International Francophone de Formation à Distance (CIFFAD) in 1987 in parallel with its support for COL. It had a difficult beginning as it was transplanted from Quebec Province to France where it became part of the Agence de la Francophonie. As with the Commonwealth of Learning, CIFFAD devoted considerable resources to technical assistance, much of it designed to raise the capacity of those working in francophone countries in the techniques of open and distance learning. It also funded and supported one-off technical assistance projects; examples range from a project for electronic technicians in Vietnam to training for small and medium enterprises in Tunisia. (The restricted development of open and distance learning within francophone countries meant that it devoted more resources to running its own projects, rather than supporting national institutions, in marked contrast with COL's practice.) By 1999 CIFFAD had four main programmes: support for basic education, French language teaching, technical and professional education and training, and the development of tools and mechanisms to support distance education (Agence de la Francophonie 1999). But absorption into the Agence proved fatal: in the same year managers decided to close down distance-education programmes and CIFFAD came to an end.

In contrast, the Commonwealth was wise – and lucky – to ensure that the Commonwealth of Learning should be an independent agency, well away from London. Open and distance learning in Africa, where it is easiest to compare anglophone and francophone experience, was already more vigorous in Commonwealth countries in 1987 and the difference has probably become more marked. COL can take some credit.

Universities and invisible colleges

The remaining two groups of institutions with global influence are the universities and the invisible colleges. As argued in chapter 6, it is early to assess the global impact of universities' new international activities. But despite the ending of the dotcom extravaganza, and the collapse of e-universities, they may yet have a major effect on open and distance learning in the south.

Alongside them are the invisible colleges, each an informal nexus of people with shared experience and a common commitment to the perceived advantages of open and distance learning. Their stories weave in and out of those of the other agencies.

Here we can distinguish a number of families of institutions that have learned from each other. In Latin America, and as far as the Canary Islands, there are similarities of philosophy and of method among the radio schools which go back to the foundation of Acción Cultural Popular in Colombia in 1947. In Africa, the various branches of INADES-formation use the same methods, and in some cases the same material. They are linked by a more formal structure than the radio schools and have moved out of francophone, Roman Catholic, Africa into Ethiopia, Kenya and Tanzania. (Curiously, and to the disappointment of conspiracy theorists, though there have been Jesuits running both sets of institutions, there has been little contact between them.)

The biggest family of institutions are the open universities. At one level it is easy enough to illustrate how the legitimacy of this new kind of institution helped to diffuse the idea. Countries of the south had not picked up the – quite viable – models of distance education developed in France, Australia, or the Soviet Union with the sudden enthusiasm shown for the British approach in the 1970s. Ram Reddy, founding vice-chancellor of two of India's open universities, explained how his minister in Andhra Pradesh urged him to visit the Open University while in Britain on academic business:

> I spent two days at Milton Keynes, met a number of people and visited various offices and work places of the university and collected the relevant literature. Based on the discussions with the people in the Open University and my own study of the literature given to me, I prepared a report on the UKOU and sent it to the minister. He showed keen interest in the report and became a great enthusiast for the open university idea.
>
> (Reddy 1997: 111)

Consultants from Britain helped draw up plans for the Andhra Pradesh Open University while Walter Perry, founding vice-chancellor in Britain, provided continuing support and advice to Indira Gandhi Open University in the first phase of the British assistance project (Perry 1997: 122).

Across the subcontinent, Allama Iqbal Open University had already been established in 1974, as the People's Open University, the first open university outside Britain:

> The establishment of the UKOU helped to remove the scepticism of the educational authorities in Pakistan, which had hitherto been suspicious of such new methods of teaching. As the UKOU became successful and demonstrated the effectiveness of its methods in reaching large number of people, it came to be seen in Pakistan as a model for a new institution there.
>
> (Zaki 1997: 26)

Again, the British Open University was heavily involved, with a team of three people (including a pro-vice-chancellor and the university's most senior administrative officer) working as consultants for a year in its early days to be followed by further support over the next decade.

Accounts like this can be multiplied; the Open University was a dramatic demonstration of an educational innovation and a legion came to visit. But at a different level, it is more difficult to weigh the significance of the global movement to start open universities against national pressure to expand tertiary education. The British model had four unusual features: a free-standing institution, open to students regardless of their educational background, that had a regional structure to support students, and employed a course team to develop multi-media and high-quality teaching materials. Three of these features can be found in many of the wave of new open universities whose planning and establishment owed something to the British influence. One did not transplant; there are few examples outside Europe of access being opened to students without regular university entrance requirements. In other areas, too, British experience was of limited relevance. Ram Reddy again noted that the Andhra Pradesh Open University 'was not only a new university but also a new type of university. Therefore the government did not know how to finance it. There were no models in the country and the UKOU was not of much help in this respect' (Reddy 1997: 118). Similarly, 'it soon came to be seen that hypotheses and methods that had proved workable in the United Kingdom were largely inapplicable in Pakistan. A Pakistani university had to evolve its own system that was at once economical and capable of operating within the resources, services and technologies available in Pakistan' (Zaki 1997: 26–7). Over the years, the differences between the universities has grown as they have each adapted to national demands. Global exchanges may have been more significant in helping suspend disbelief than in reproducing blueprints.

There is one small piece of evidence that suggests that limited and informal contact is as powerful a way of shaping an institution as generously funded programmes of cooperation. As noted above, ideas from Britain were important in legitimising the notion of an open university for Andhra Pradesh. But it got under way, rapidly, and by 1998 had a quarter-million enrolment and a solid reputation for the quality of its work. In contrast with Indira Gandhi National Open University, Dr B. R. Ambedkar Open University gained very little from the Overseas Development Administration project (Fielden *et al.* n.d.). Its success demonstrates a local capacity to pick up an idea from global sources even without external funding and an extensive programme of consultation.

One consequence of the expansion of the open universities has been a widening of the boundaries of the invisible college, once limited to those with air tickets to fly from Milton Keynes. Today, the existence of open universities, and of considerable managerial capacity within them, means that there is the beginning of south–south cooperation. When the African National Congress decided to review the potential of distance education for the new South Africa it set up an international commission chaired by the head of the Open Learning Institute of Hong Kong and advised by Ram Reddy of India, who later advised the team establishing the Bangladesh Open University (SAIDE 1995). When Tanzania came to plan its open university in 1993 it was able to send a team to look at relevant experience in Asia as well as in Europe and north America.

All this means that open colleges may be moving south. Indira Gandhi National Open University has become an intellectual power house and has, for example, been advising Ethiopia on the use of open and distance learning. Its staff have built up experience, expertise and contacts that are beginning to shape practices outside India as well as within. The South African Institute for Distance Education, whose work developed from the ANC-backed commission, is now itself providing consultancy and advice within Africa.

We can track a set of activities belonging to a second invisible college. Wilbur Schramm, who put together the set of UNESCO studies on *New educational media in action*, set up the Institute of Communication Research at Stanford. Its former students and staff members were involved in planning, managing and evaluating a series of projects using broadcasting. Schramm worked on the use of educational television in Samoa and documented its rise and fall. Staff members and students were involved in the American-funded projects to support educational television in Colombia and in El Salvador. As the glamour of television faded, members of the institute were involved in evaluation of some of the early work on radio mathematics and with the subsequent interactive radio projects and with a slightly different radio education project in Nepal (Holmes *et al.* 1993). There was American support for the initial work of OLSET in South Africa (chapter 3).

The work of this group contrasts with that of those concerned with open universities in several ways. It has been mainly concerned with education within school and has been dominated by technology, with a search for appropriate uses moving from television on to radio and to computers. Then, its influence is more concentrated both geographically, with a traditional concentration on Latin America, and thematically, with support for a series of related projects, many of them funded by the Agency for International Development, and with careful sharing of experience and even materials between them. All this work has been strengthened by a rigorous tradition of research so that the group's influence is better documented than much work in the field.[6]

There is one further contrast, significant in assessing the power of globalising forces. The idea of an open university spread through the normal channels of academic discourse, gossip and straight news. There was no planned strategy of diffusion. Once established, open universities have generally managed to find recurrent funding to keep in business. In contrast, while claiming an interest in the diffusion of ideas – as it happens, one of the themes of a line of Stanford research – the work of this college has essentially been within an aid paradigm and has had only moderate success in getting its projects institutionalised.

A third college, now invisible in another sense, deserves a requiem. The International Extension College was based in Britain from 1971 to 2006 when it appears to have suffered a funding crisis, not for the first but for the last time, and was closed down. In its time it ran training courses in distance education from 1977 with the University of London Institute of Education; over 400 students, virtually all working in distance-teaching institutions in the south, attended an annual short course. Alongside its training it set up or supported some eleven projects or institutions in Africa and Asia. The main emphasis of its work was on out-of-school education for adults and on nonformal education. This is an unglamorous area, addressing the needs of people who generally cannot afford to pay much for education or put much political pressure on governments. An appraisal of the International Extension College's work, ten years before its collapse, was muted in its conclusions:

> All the programmes in this study have... survived for at least six years. Some are now more than twenty years old. During that time they have pioneered the use of distance education in their countries, in varying combinations, with groups of students for whom such methods had not been used before. They have all, therefore, contributed programmes of educational innovation. In some cases those innovations are now established elements in the educational system. Those programmes that survive are now managed by local staff.... Several of the refugee programmes have not survived due to the return home of the refugees for whom they catered....
>
> One poignant plea to IEC from one institution participating in the study reflected an all-too-common sense of frustration at the lack of continuing political support; 'Help us with our governments'. Many of the

institutions were launched with a blaze of political support that went with it, though often with external funds. That political priority, or at least the overt political support that went with it, has not usually survived the passage of time and the assumption of local funding responsibility.

(Dodds and Mayo 1996: 148–9)

International activity, in this example, had a modest influence in a dozen countries and led to the existence of projects or programmes with some hope of institutionalisation. The college's former students are to be found, influencing the practice of distance education, across the south. But its concern for a low-technology approach – and ironically for basic education at a time when the international agencies were unanimous in its support – were not enough for its survival as an institution.

These three invisible colleges are not, of course, the only actors. Professional associations of those working in distance education have played a role in exchanging ideas and experience. An African Association of Correspondence Education, set up in 1973, barely got off the ground though there are now more active subregional associations such as the Distance Education Association of Southern Africa. The Asian Association of Open Universities is active and vibrant. There is a Pacific Islands Region Association of Distance Education and an Asociación Iberoamericana de Educación Superior a Distancia. The International Council for open and Distance Education, and regional bodies in north America and Australasia, may be significant for some institutions in the north but are of less relevance to the south. As in any discipline, journals with an international circulation help the flow of ideas. But the invisible colleges, which also operate through these other mechanisms, look more significant actors.

An examination of their influence makes two conclusions possible. First, the exchange of ideas about the operation of open and distance learning, through formal and informal contact between practitioners, has influenced the initial design of projects and institutions. This may have been at its most effective where it has been generously lubricated with money but modest global flows have also been extremely influential. The idea of an open university, to take the most dramatic example, has had a potent and near-global influence. But, second, subsequent institutional development has been much more heavily dependent on national demands and on the availability of funding, generally from local sources, than on external pressure or external funding or an attempt to replicate an international model. Where, as with the American technology-based projects, there has been a centrally developed and diffused model, it has seldom been institutionalised.

Conclusion

Globalisation looks as if it is more significant in higher education than at other levels. While there are significant regional groups of activities, like the radio schools and INADES-formation, the global actors have not played a major part in distance education at school level, or for school equivalency. (In contrast, when we look at conventional basic education, world policy since Jomtien and Dakar is significant.)

Indeed, the major funding agencies have played a modest part in our story. The World Bank moved in the late 1990s towards a policy of backing the use of technologies in education, and of stimulating the flow of information, but it is less clear how far this has pushed the practice of open and distance learning. The British have generally avoided having a policy. In three, very different, cases, where agencies have been policy-driven they have had difficulty in ensuring the effective implementation of their policy. USAID has pushed its model of interactive radio instruction but achieved quite limited success in institutionalising it. The International Extension College's policy of supporting non-university projects, aiming at educationally disadvantaged groups, and with a bias towards nonformal education left its projects at the margins of ministry of education concern and chronically underfunded. Imfundo came and went in six years with its staff unable to persuade even their own colleagues of the merits of the policies it was promoting. In two of these cases – and in the earlier case of educational television in Côte d'Ivoire – technology seems to have come first and turned out to be an inappropriate driver of development.

The contrasting stories of the Commonwealth of Learning and CIFFAD show how specialist agencies may be able to use the processes of globalisation to support educational sharing internationally, but illustrate the political and funding risks they face as they do so.

It looks as if the invisible colleges, whose working is facilitated by cheap air travel and modern communication technology, may be the most important instrument of globalisation. This suggests that globalisation's main effect has not been in the development of international policy for open and distance learning, or the establishment of specialised agencies, or the development of common courses, or in international enrolment, but in accelerating and easing the diffusion of innovations. At the same time international cooperation, competition and exchange in distance education have been on a relatively modest scale. International forces and agencies do not seem to be operating with the intensity and extent, or with the speed and level of impact, that would mark a fully globalised system.[7] National policies, and national perceptions of the strengths or weakness of open and distance learning remain the main determinants of its shape.

10 Political economy: who benefits, who pays?

A Nation under a well-regulated Government should permit none to remain uninstructed. It is monarchical and aristocratical Government only that requires ignorance for its support.

Thomas Paine 1791

All governments – and indeed many charities, companies and individuals – support education. In 2002 public expenditure on education amounted to 4.6 per cent of world GNP and, in most countries, took between 10 and 20 per cent of government budgets. Governments fund and manage education for a mixture of reasons: because education is a human right, because it brings social and economic benefits, because of public demand. The weight given to the different purposes of education, and the balance of expenditure within budgets, respond to national priorities and expectations. At the same time, the process of globalisation means that there is a homogeneity about educational policy; many countries are pursuing similar educational ends, for their citizens and their economies (Ramirez 1997: 49).

In the same way, we can find international similarities in government policy towards open and distance learning and, within any one country or at any one institution, find it being justified on a number of different grounds. Thus we can distinguish ideological arguments, often to do with equity or empowerment, economic arguments, often about equipping the workforce, and political arguments, about meeting demand, and then find appeals to all of them in relation to a single institution (see chapter 5). The act establishing Indira Gandhi National Open University, for example, starts with a broad ideological and cultural aim, requiring the university 'to play a positive role in the development of the country and, based on the rich heritage of the country, to promote and advance the culture of the people of India and its human resources'. It moves on to economics in specifying that the university will run 'courses related to the needs of employment and necessary for building the economy of the society' and to a political agenda of providing 'access to higher education for large segments of the population and in particular the disadvantaged groups' (Manjulika and Reddy 1996: 78–9).

Educational purposes: ideology, economy, politics

We can assess and contrast educational policy by looking at the weight given to different educational purposes and go on to ask why there has been investment in open and distance learning and for what purpose. For there is a conundrum here: given that all educational budgets are stretched, why should a government, or a church or a funding agency, choose to invest in an unconventional method of education?

Some governments have done so for explicit ideological reasons, most often in pursuit of equity or, in a stronger formulation, with the intention of empowering poor, remote and disadvantaged people. Because of its technology, distance education was seen as something that could narrow the distance between privilege and poverty. The founding vice-chancellor of the People's Open University (now Allama Iqbal Open University), for example, gave the political reason for its establishment by the Pakistan People's Party: 'Being a socialist party, the main thrust of its manifesto was the socio-economic uplift of the masses, an idea that obviously included education' (Zaki 1997: 29). There is a similar appeal to equity in the documents about many open universities.

Some nongovernment organisations have seen distance education as a way of empowering, and changing the lives of, rural people. This was a mainspring of the more radical radio schools in Latin America. They grew out of a Roman Catholic, libertarian, concern to provide education as a key at the minimum to individual self-improvement and at the maximum to community transformation. The schools faced a dilemma between being irrelevant, if their aims were too modest, and being closed down if they came into direct conflict with government. The Movimento de Educaçao de Base in Brazil, for example, ran into political danger once it moved into community development because its aims threatened the status quo. (International Extension College 1978: 15) while the collapse of Acción Cultural Popular in Colombia was to follow (see p. 21).

With the possible exception of South Africa, where the SACHED trust ran distance-education programmes during the apartheid regime aimed at empowerment, few other distance-teaching institutions have had as direct and radical ideological agenda. Statements by INADES-formation, for example, suggest that their aim is one of increasing participants' control over their own lives, and supporting community institutions, but remaining well short of social transformation. In the early years of independence, some African governments – notably Tanzania and Zimbabwe – emphasised the ideological case for adult education, as a means of equipping its people for citizenship. The Zambian National Correspondence College was founded as one response to this kind of concern (Siaciwena 1994: 103–4). But this is no longer the language of educational planning.

In tertiary education at least, economic statements about workforce training are more prominent than ideological ones. Chapter 5 demonstrated how China, Iran and Sri Lanka among others have highlighted the economic case for using distance education. In Sri Lanka the vice-chancellor of the open university commented that, while most higher education concentrated on traditional non-vocational courses, the open university programmes were planned in the light of advice 'from those, especially in industry, who are the prospective employers' of its graduates (Wijeyesekara 1994: 107).

At other levels of education, too, labour-market needs have been quoted as a reason for using distance education. Almost by definition, the programmes of teacher education discussed in chapter 4 were set up in response to the needs of the state as employer. And at secondary level, some of the investment in distance education has been a response to the needs for a better-educated workforce. Thailand and Indonesia have used distance education to increase the number of workers with secondary qualifications.

Government investment in distance education has most often, however, been justified in terms of public demand rather than of ideology or economics. Distance-teaching institutions have been set up where it did not seem possible to meet demand conventionally. The study centres of central Africa, for example, were set up and continued to get government support because they were meeting a demand from those excluded from regular school. More recently the open-school system in India was seen as having 'an important role in the universalisation of educational opportunities ... while reducing pressure on the formal system' (Mukhopadhyay 1994: 30). Bangladesh set up its open university in part as a response to unmet demand for education at secondary level.

Public demand, which governments cannot readily meet through the conventional system, has been a major justification for the expansion of open and distance learning at tertiary level and especially for the creation of open universities, in rich and poor countries alike. In Hong Kong, alongside the expansion of the existing universities, the colonial government supported the establishment of an Open Learning Institute that was to become an open university (Swift 1997: 129). In India, at the other extreme of wealth, a national education commission in 1964–5 'perceived correspondence education as an answer to the increasing pressure of numbers as well as the growing financial pressure on universities'; in its turn the open-university system became a way of widening opportunities for education where the conventional system could not meet the scale of demand (Manjulika and Reddy 1996: 19, 78–9). The Sri Lanka open university 'is regarded as an alternative route to provide access to higher education' for the 92 per cent of qualified students who cannot enter conventional universities (Jayatilleke 2002: 141). Similarly, the Sukhothai Thammathirat Open University in Thailand specifically refers to secondary-school leavers, who cannot get to college or university, in the first of its objectives (NIME 1993: 416).

We need to qualify the statement that governments have adopted open and distance learning largely in response to demand, by examining the audiences it has in fact attracted.

Audiences

New forms of education may provide an alternative for existing groups of students and potential students, or reach out to quite new audiences. As we have seen, many open university charters talk of reaching out to new, most often deprived, groups of students, often in the interests of democratisation. But other institutions have been set up mainly to provide an alternative route to education for students comparable to those in the conventional system.

We can, therefore, identify two main groups among the audience for distance education. One group is the young men, and usually fewer women, who, if they are seeking tertiary education, have missed out on the good university life but still want to get a degree. From rural black South Africans enrolling with the University of South Africa to Chinese students at the radio and television universities, these were not the most successful or more privileged school leavers but the ones who had failed to get into conventional universities. For this first group, the merit of open and distance learning is not that it is available in remote spots, or without attendance, but that it offers an alternative to the conventional education they would have preferred. The other group consists of older students trying to get back on to an educational ladder some years after leaving school. In a few, exceptional, cases, these audiences are of economic significance to governments: this looks like being the case in China and may be in Iran where large numbers are enrolled on job-related courses. The age pattern (see table 5.2 above) suggests that, at least in many open universities, this group is smaller than the first.

The audiences for open and distance learning, from either group, have generally been at a disadvantage when compared with those for conventional education. The audiences for the secondary-level distance-education programmes discussed in chapter 3 were predominantly rural. Even in the countryside, and even more in the towns where enrolment ratios tend to be higher, the children who did best on finishing their primary education went to conventional schools and the distance-education programmes were for those who had not made the grade.

Beyond school the picture is more complicated. Some vocational education – and especially teacher education – has been aimed at very broad audiences and there is little evidence to suggest that its audiences share the disadvantage that is common at secondary level. The nurses offered upgrading at Anadolu University in Turkey, or those following the open-university course in Sri Lanka which was the only one open to the profession, or the teachers taking higher degrees at Lagos or Nairobi are probably not deprived groups as compared with others working in health or education. But most students at tertiary level come from socially, educationally or geographically disadvantaged groups: more favoured students have pursued a conventional education.

This provokes a question about the purposes which governments most want to serve by providing open and distance learning programmes. If we are to take at face value statements about democratisation then we might expect to find policies to give particular support to the relatively disadvantaged students studying at a distance as compared with those studying conventionally. But there is an alternative explanation of government investment, especially in open universities: that it provides a safety valve, apparently reducing unsatisfied demand for education, with the minimum of resources and little concern for the effectiveness of that education. Open and distance learning may be there to satisfy a demand or to contain it.

We can try to assess government policy and intentions, and to see how far open and distance learning is meeting the political and economic objectives claimed for it, by looking at formal government statements about education generally and by examining the funding of distance-teaching institutions.

Policy statements

In a handful of cases, formal government documents on education have explicit statements about open and distance learning. India and South Africa, the world's largest and newest democracies, provide contrasting examples.

India produced a *National policy on education* in 1986, accompanied by a *Programme of action*, which was followed by a revised programme in 1992 (Ministry of Human Resource Development 1986, 1992). Both refer to distance education as do the sequence of Five Year Plans.

Plans for the open-school system were relatively modest and, as time has gone on, have been scaled down. While the 1992 action plan proposed to increase numbers by 600 000 over the next five years, with the establishment of state open schools operating in a number of languages, by 2002 the *Tenth Five Year Plan* reported that the National Open School had 200 000 enrolments a year which would grow at 20 per cent per annum. At this time there were some 28 million children in secondary schools. The National Open School, in contrast with state open schools, was funded mainly by student fees and plans to refund fees for girls and students from scheduled castes and scheduled tribes were only 'on the anvil' (Planning Commission 2002, vol. 2: 44). With a history of benign neglect of their predecessor state departments of correspondence education, secondary education at a distance does not look a high government priority.

Higher education is different. The starting point, set out in the *Eighth Five Year Plan* was an intention to expand higher education 'in an equitable and cost effective manner mainly by large-scale expansion of distance education system and increased involvement of voluntary and private agencies'. Enrolment through open and dual-mode universities was 'expected to increase from about 11.5 per cent of the total enrolment in higher education to about 16.5 per cent' (Planning Commission 1992, vol. 1: 11). In practice, and in part because of the expansion of conventional universities, this figure was not achieved. Ten years later open and distance learning students amounted to only 13 per cent of the total enrolment in higher education, which still meant 7.7 million (Planning Commission 2002, vol. 2: 56).

Why invest in distance education at this level? The 1986 and 1992 policy documents do not make much play of economic arguments. The overview of policy for higher education in the tenth plan begins by referring to the need to raise quality of higher education and meet the needs of the knowledge economy but does not refer to open universities in this context (*ibid*: 21). Only in the more detailed discussion of higher education do they make an appearance, in the context of expanding enrolment from 6 per cent to 10 per cent of the 18–23 age cohort (*ibid* 54–6). There are, of course, references to issues of access; in 1992, for example, for 'learners from disadvantaged groups like women, people living in backward regions and hilly areas'; in 2002 for 'backward regions, remote and inaccessible tribal areas of the northeast and some of the eastern states' (Planning Commission 1992, vol 2: 294; Planning Commission 2002, vol. 2: 56). But the plan did not pick up a proposal from the Distance Education Council to change the funding of open universities and correspondence departments, and reduce the dependence on student fees, in the interest of quality as well as equity (DEC 2001c: 83–5).

The main tenor of the various documents seems to be that, despite serious concerns about its quality, higher education is expanding in response to demand and that distance education offers one way of meeting that demand without a commensurate increase in the budget. Government concerns for the quality and relevance of higher education have not deflected it from the wish to use distance education mainly to expand numbers. But concern for quality may grow: in 2005 the governor of the state of Uttar Pradesh was so disturbed by the quality of the distance-education programmes offered by state universities that he closed them all down (Sharma 2005: 239–40).

South Africa produced a white paper on education in 1995, a report of a National Commission on Higher Education in 1996, and a white paper on higher education in 1997; there are reports on distance education by an international commission in 1994 and from the statutory Council for Higher Education in 2004 (SAIDE 1995; CHE 2004). The documents are of particular interest as statements from a country in transition, with a mature system of open and distance learning, which has been exploring its relevance for the new society. And they are of interest both for what they include and for what they leave out.

The first white paper set out the values and principles that would inform the new South Africa's education and training policy: human rights, access, redress, equity and quality all carried more weight than arguments about economics. Much of the discussion in the paper was general, setting policy rather than writing a shopping list of activities. Beyond a recommendation – since abandoned – to establish a National Open Learning Agency as a co-ordinating body there were only isolated references to open and distance learning (Department of Education 1995: 25). The white paper suggested that as much teacher education as possible should use distance education linked with professional support; it was seen as having a potential role in expanding further education; adult basic education and training might be facilitated by the use of electronics and associated support systems (*ibid*: 28–31).

To discern government policy, what the white paper did not say is perhaps more revealing. It identified, for example, that the poor quality of education in science and mathematics available to black South Africans, which meant few were going on to study these subjects at university level, was 'catastrophic from the perspective of national developmental needs' (*ibid*: 29), but did not suggest an open-learning approach to help solve the problem. The international commission's case for its use in adult basic education (SAIDE 1995: 147–62) was hardly noticed in the white paper. Open and distance learning was not to be given a major role in redressing the educational wrongs of the previous era. The implicit message of the document was that open and distance learning had a significant part to play in teacher education but was of quite limited relevance to South Africa's other basic, secondary and further education needs.

The National Commission on Higher Education in 1996 saw a transformed system of higher education as widening access, responding to the needs of the economy, running programmes 'conducive to a critically constructive civil society' and advancing scholarship (NCHE 1996: 4). Its report reviewed apartheid's legacy and made proposals for an expansion and restructuring of higher education, for changes in governance, and for a new funding regime. At the time of the report, distance education was already playing a major part in higher education, at least in terms of enrolments, with 40 per cent of university and technikon students studying at a distance. The report saw an important future for flexible learning, with the same materials being used on and off campus. At the same time it recognised that much existing distance education was neither of adequate quality nor cost effective. It also set out proposals for growth rates in the various sectors of tertiary education with distance education to grow at 5 per cent per annum from 1995 to 2005 in universities and 8 per cent in technikons, higher than the rates proposed for face-to-face study. The fastest rate of growth, at 9.8 per cent, was reserved for community colleges, further education, and private institutions.

It has not worked out quite as planned. By 2001 university distance education was expanding more rapidly and face-to-face education more slowly than had been proposed. In part this reflected the growth of distance-education courses for teachers that had been called for in the white paper. Sadly this was expansion without quality: these were 'low-cost, low quality, and high profit teacher education diploma programmes which constitute over 65% of distance education FTEs at predominantly face-to-face universities' (CHE 2004: 183). Furthermore, with the exception of the programmes for teachers, the growth has not been in the areas identified as most important for the country with enrolments heavily weighted against health, science and technology; the commission does not identify a strategy to address this.

In terms of organisation, government has made two key decisions on which the planning documents were less certain: to merge UNISA and Technikon SA to provide one, large, dedicated, multi-purpose open university and to restrict the development of distance education in conventional universities in the interests of cost effectiveness.

The 2004 report recognised that distance education could widen access to higher education, increase participation, and achieve economies of scale. The numbers were significant at 29 per cent of full-time equivalent students or 43 per cent of the total. Distance education had a higher proportion of female students and a higher proportion of African students than face-to-face (CHE 2004: 174–5). The document, and we may infer government, clearly assume that these numbers will stay high; distance education is here to stay, not a temporary fix until the country is rich enough for face-to-face institutions to displace it. Government's commitment is demonstrated in two ways. First, the report, like its predecessors, is concerned about the poor quality of much distance education and sets out proposals to monitor and improve it, and to move away from its over-dependence on under-supported correspondence courses. Second, by international standards, distance education is generously supported. Universities are funded for undergraduate distance students in terms of full-time equivalence at 50 per cent of the amount for full-time students; despite comments from universities, who wanted more, the report proposes to continue this level of funding but for it to be exceeded in come cases such as advanced postgraduate courses and ones for which there is a clear demand but for which there will only be low enrolments (*ibid*: 179–81).

Despite their enormous differences, there are policy similarities between India and South Africa. In both cases, government support for distance education is quite restricted at secondary level. Like many other countries, South Africa recognises its potential value for teacher education though it is unhappy about its achievements. At tertiary level both countries see that the expansion of distance education can play a major role in the growth of higher education; there are concerns in both countries with issues of quality. Neither country gives particular prominence to the use of open and distance learning as a way of expanding the trained workforce in order to meet specific needs of the economy as contrasted with responding to a more general concern for access and expansion. There is one major contrast: South Africa is relatively more generous in funding tertiary-level distance education while India has been requiring students to meet an increasing proportion of the costs through their fees.

To fill out the picture of government policy we can move on to ask who is paying for open and distance learning.

Finding the money

Distance-education programmes have often drawn their funding from several different sources: mainly government grants, student fees, foundations, the private sector, and international funding agencies. There are trade-offs between them. Government money may bring stability, but does not necessarily grow in line with increasing demand or with inflation. Student fees may give a manager freedom that would otherwise be lacking but limit enrolment to those who can afford them. Foundations, the private sector, and international funding agencies tend to change their funding policies not because of the success or failure of what they are funding but for exogenous social and political reasons. The balance between these different sources of funding varies between different levels of education and different parts of the world, as set out in table 10.1.

With the important exception of agricultural extension, government funding for nonformal and adult education is usually minimal. Agencies like INADES-formation have charged nominal fees to students but relied heavily on external support, mainly from foundations. The University of South Africa literacy project, which closed down when it lost British aid funding, demonstrates the risks of relying on external funding (see chapter 2).

At secondary level there is a continuum of approaches from heavy reliance on student fees to full government subsidy. In India, although the National Institute of Open Schooling is described as a means of democratising education, 90 per cent of its income comes from student fees while pupils in government secondary schools get free or subsidised education. Other secondary-level projects have been less generously funded than regular schools: Malawi met 77 per cent of the costs of day secondary schools but 50 per cent of distance-education centres when it was running the two systems in parallel. In contrast the Botswana and Namibia open colleges charge only nominal fees and draw most of their funding from government, though their grant per head is lower than that for regular schools. Further along the continuum, Telesecundaria has become such a well-established part of the structure, that by 1972 government was meeting more of their costs than those of regular schools – 75 per cent rather than 64 per cent. As a result of funding through the Roberto Marinho Foundation and the Federation of Industries in the State of São Paolo Telecurso in Brazil was able to limit the costs falling on students to those of books and of testing (Guibert 1999). At the far end of the spectrum the open school in Andhra Pradesh, funded by the state rather than the national government, charged no fees.

Teacher education also provides a mixed picture. Although teacher-education projects are generally designed to raise teachers' skills and qualifications a review of ten projects found an unexpected diversity of funding. Five projects, in Chile, China, India, Nigeria and South Africa, drew some of their funding from students; no funding came from government in Brazil, Burkina Faso or Chile; external funding agencies played a significant role in four of the cases while government met the total bill only in the richest country reported, Britain (Perraton *et al.* 2001: 36–7; Perraton 2004b: 103–5). The evidence suggests that government support for distance education even to upgrade its own employees is sometimes muted.

At the tertiary level there are occasional examples of open universities being treated and funded on much the same basis as the rest of higher education. At the radio and television universities in China, for example, student fees have in the past amounted to only 5 per cent of their income, with central and regional government and employers meeting most of the rest of the cost, although students in China are now generally being required to meet an increased proportion of the cost of higher education. In Latin America, where conventional university education is often free, fees tend to be low. In South Africa, funding in terms of full-time-student equivalents helps keep down fees.

But these are the exceptions. Much more often, government policy, especially in Asia, is something like that articulated in Hong Kong: 'Adult higher education is not seen as a government responsibility – it is regarded as an individual responsibility and government's role is only to provide an environment in which an adult educational enterprise can function through its own efforts' (Hope and Dhanarajan 1994: 44). This probably goes further than most countries and is certainly more explicit. In India, for example, a former vice-chancellor of Indira Gandhi National Open University has repeatedly argued that 'neither at the time of IGNOU's foundation nor since has the government of India articulated any funding policy for the open university' and that 'there is no clear-cut and criteria-based funding policy at any level for distance education programmes' (Kulandai Swamy and Pillai 1994: 72; Kulandai Swami quoted in Sharma 2005: 237).

We can, however, infer a policy that seems to be widely followed and has three elements. First, governments have been more willing to find start-up funds for open universities than to increase them as student numbers rise. Thus the annual grant to IGNOU which was at $5.95 million (*$10.4 million*) in 1986–7 and was only $6.59 million (*$7 million*) in 2002–3 despite an increase in student numbers from 4400 to 316 500 (Perraton and Naidu 2006: 160). Student fees have in consequence been rising from as low as 2.4 per cent of annual operating costs to 66 per cent (Panda 2005: 217).

Second, most distance-education students are expected to pay fees that meet a significant proportion of the costs of their study. There are big differences in the size of this proportion. In the early 1990s South Korea and Sri Lanka governments were meeting more than 60 per cent of open-university costs. Other figures are much higher; the planning document of the Bangladesh Open University assumed that the university would be funded by means of cost recovery by 2002–3 while SNDT Women's University in India met 92 per cent of its recurring expenditure from student fees. In contrast, much conventional higher education is still heavily subsidised in many countries. In India, for example, student fees meet only 5 to 10 per cent of conventional university income; they are between 3 and 15 per cent in Indonesia. Students also have to meet costs over and above their fees – mainly for books, stationery, communications and travel – which can easily outweigh the actual fee. One study of four programmes at IGNOU found

Table 10.1 Sources of income for some distance-teaching institutions

Country, institution, date	Funding percentage			Comment and comparison with conventional institutions
	State	Student fees	Other	
SECONDARY				
India National Open School 1998[a]	1	90	9	Conventional secondary education is subsidised or free for many students
Malawi College of Distance Education 1984–5[b]	50	38	12	Government meets 77% of costs of day secondary schools
Mexico Telesecundaria 1972–[c]	75	24	1	Government meets only 64% costs of conventional schools, whose unit costs are higher
Namibia NAMCOL 2002[d]	80	20		Government subsidy calculated by reference to costs of conventional schools
TEACHER EDUCATION				
Brazil A Plus 2001[e]	0	0	100	Entirely funded by 16 sponsors
Chile Universidad de la Frontera 1997–2000[f]	0	100	0	
TERTIARY				
Bangladesh Open University 1995[g]	n/a	75–114	n/a	Cost recovery by 2002/3 was aim; conventional university fees are 15–10% of total
China RTVUs 1988–89[h]	52	5	43	Employers and other agencies separate from central government are significant sources of funding. Proportion from student fees thought to have increased

India				
8 distance-education institutions in dual-mode universities 1988–9[j]	n/a	63	n/a	Much higher proportion of costs met from students in d.e. institutions
3 dual-mode institutions 1999–2000[j]	0	>100	0	Distance-teaching departments show surplus
IGNOU 1986–7[k]	97	3	n/a	Conventional universities derive only 5–10% income from student fees
IGNOU 1996–7	67	33	n/a	
IGNOU 2002–3	17	83	n/a	
BRAOU 1999–2000[i]	n/a	69	n/a	
YCMOU 1999–2000[i]	n/a	88	n/a	
Indonesia				
Universitas Terbuka 1992–3[l]	41	38	21	Student fees at conventional university are 3–15%
South Korea				
Air Correspondence University 1993[m]	62	38	0	Government subsidy is $1/30$ of that for conventional universities[n]
Pakistan				
AIOU 2003–4[o]	11	88	1	Conventional state universities have been funded mainly by government grants. Students funded at 2/3 rate of full-time equivalents in conventional university
Sri Lanka				
Open University 1991–3[p]	67	33		
Thailand				
STOU 1993[q]	23	49	28	

Notes

a. Sujiatha 2002: 129; b. Murphy 1992: 83–9; c. UNESCO 1977:120; d. Personal communication; e. Perraton *et al.* 2001: 8; f. *ibid*: 12; g. Ali *et al.* 1997: 23–5; h. Ding 1994: 161–5; i. Ansari 1994: 78; j. DEC 2001c: 26; k. Naidu 2005:5 with other sources included with fees; l. Djalil *et al.* 1994: 22–9; m. Insung Jung 1994:119; n. Kim 1992:38; o. *Vice Chancellor's Annual report 2004–5*; p. Wijeyesekara 1994: 112–13; q. Iam Chaya-Ngam 1994: 54–61.

that the fee represented only from 24 to 45 per cent of the total costs falling on students (Naidu 2001: 44).

Third, the fees charged to students are often higher than those charged in conventional universities. In Andhra Pradesh, for example, open university students were charged a fee of Rs700 (*$41*) in 1991 while the fee for a conventional university was Rs150 (*$8*). In India generally the distance-education departments of conventional universities were charging higher fees than the open universities, and using these to cross-subsidise conventional departments (Manjulika and Reddy 1996: 141).

In short, students – though not universally – have been expected to pay more, and governments willing to pay less, for an education that both will regard as inferior and which tends to have a lower unit cost than its comparators. There are a number of possible explanations of this policy: that governments had a naive faith in technology that would make distance education cheap as well as effective, that it was unlikely to achieve significant results and therefore did not merit more funding, or that it was reaching audiences that were of little political consequence. There is probably some truth in the first, while the modest completion rates at many distance-teaching institutions make the second look plausible. The third has obvious strength even if it is too simplistic to be the whole truth.

Conclusion

The last four chapters have tried to assess how far open and distance learning has developed as a consequence of its economic strengths, or of technology, or of globalisation, or of national politics. Of course economics, technology and globalisation affect national policy; the conviction that distance education had economic strengths, the homogenisation of world educational policy, and the availability of communications technology have all influenced national political decisions. Using broad brush strokes we can sum up 25 years of educational politics.

Distance education's first appeal was partly ideological, partly economic. It looked as if it might help democratise education, even empower the poorest. Many early statements, and policy documents, referred to its capacity to reach audiences who could not get to conventional school or college. And it was sold as being cost effective, with the promise of economies following from the magic of technology. Occasionally, it has provided a cheap way of expanding secondary education but, in most countries, the expansion of conventional secondary education has limited the demand for a nonconventional alternative. Acclaimed by educators, it has been used in their own backyard, for the inservice training of teachers. In some cases it has, modestly but significantly, expanded the production of graduates and brought consequent economic benefits. And it has now expanded to the point that there may be new government recognition of the need to raise its quality; changes here will have repercussions on funding and perhaps on its status.

More often, it became a way of responding to demand, offering higher education on the cheap. It suggested a way out of the dilemma of either bolting the doors of the university or starving the rest of the educational system in order to provide the funds to build more campuses. It has had the advantage of looking different enough from conventional education for it to be funded differently, but similar enough to be proclaimed as an alternative with parity of esteem. Where the ideology of widening access has run up against that of cost recovery, economics has usually triumphed.

One powerful critique of education suggests that its central role is to enable the reproduction of society, creating the educated labour force needed by society and reinforcing existing social roles. In doing so it is faced by a number of inherent contradictions: the free examination of ideas and pursuit of new knowledge may conflict with the values demanded by the market place while those running education – the large profession of educators – may develop interests and values at variance with those of the society that is seeking to mould the schools. On this analysis, schools and colleges allow for social mobility, offering access for the talented, on a meritocratic basis, to a small number of individuals while generally reinforcing the existing class structure.

If open and distance learning were offering a broad, new, path to education, outside the regular structure of conventional institutions and with a different set of values, it might seem to threaten the power structure of education. But, in fact, the evidence suggests that it reinforces the existing structure rather than threatens it. At secondary level, distance education has such little prestige that it is usually of no political significance. At tertiary level the conventional universities have an established place in the creation of an educated workforce: governments believe that their education is productive and the increased wages they command on graduation show that the market shares their faith. Universities also have long-standing social functions, of providing an enjoyable life-style for privileged adolescents and sometimes of providing social contacts that will be of continuing value (Stone 1983). Distance education cannot compete. While distance-teaching departments and universities remain a small proportion of the whole, they have little influence on the social outcomes of the larger and more privileged parts of the university system. Indeed, while distance education has lower prestige, and is less efficient in terms of its graduation rates, it may have no deeper political function than providing a safety valve, or a narrow route for educational advantage open to a small number of students whose rare success cannot threaten the status quo.

Part III
Evaluation

11 Legitimacy: a solution or a problem

Expansion can bring us higher standards more fairly shared. Education has changed society in that way and can do more. It does so slowly against the stubborn resistance of class and class-related culture. But it remains the friend of those who seek a more efficient, more open and more just society.

A. H. Halsey 1980

Education is contested. We can assess the value of changes in health practice by measuring morbidity and mortality. Few measures in education are as simple. The purposes of education may include the transmission of culture, individual enrichment, civic capacity, and empowerment, alongside job skills relevant to the individual and society.

Educators vary in the stress they give to individual and social ends. For Freire, 'the essence ... of the human species is its repeatedly demonstrated capacity for transcending what is merely given, what is purely determined' (da Veiga 1972: 9). Dialogue is therefore at the heart of education and 'the educator's role is to propose problems about the codified existential situations in order to help the learners arrive at an increasingly critical view of their reality' (Freire 1972: 36). From a different standpoint,[1]

> schooling has been justified as a way of increasing wealth, of improving industrial output, and of making management more effective. The schools' role has been to socialize economically desirable values and behavior, teach vocational skills, and provide education consistent with students' expected occupational attainment.
>
> (Cohen and Lazerson 1977: 373)

At least from the Faure commission report in 1972, lifelong learning has got increasing prominence in international dialogue (Faure *et al.* 1972). More recently the terms 'learning society' and 'knowledge society' have come into the dialogue; their achievement is perceived both as an educational end and as a means to national prosperity.

Dialogue in the interest of liberation, sustaining the economy, and creating the knowledge society may all be appropriate ends for education but they do not allow us to identify a single indicator of effectiveness. To assess the legitimacy of a nonconventional approach to education we would need to establish some consensus on the comparative importance of the different aims of education: another book. Short of that, we can gather and organise the evidence about open and distance learning under headings that will enable different users to reach different conclusions. The American researcher Emile McAnany suggested an approach which is of double value for us, both as a structure for assessment and for his conclusions on Latin American experience a generation back.

> The evaluation literature suggests a useful paradigm for an assessment of the radio schools under the category of effort, performance, adequacy, efficiency and process. How have radio schools performed on each of these criteria? In *effort*, or the amount of work done the evidence is impressive: radio schools exist in all Latin-American countries and reach an estimated 250 000 people in organized listening groups, plus a much greater but unorganised audience among rural people. The *performance* criterion asks what effect radio schools have had on their audiences, and here the evidence is much less clear cut, although an increasing number of evaluations have attempted to measure their impact. The *adequacy* question is whether radio schools have had an impact relative to the nonformal education needs of the rural audience; there is little data but, looking at needs, radio schools are a long way from meeting them. *Efficiency* asks a comparative question: Are radio schools the best (most cost-effective) way of meeting rural education needs? Again, no cost and little effectiveness data leave this question open. Finally, *process* calls for an understanding of why radio schools succeed or fail and we are getting more answers to this question with more studies and self-evaluations.
>
> (McAnany 1975: 238)

By looking at what open and distance learning has achieved and might achieve against each of these criteria we should be able to reach some conclusion about its legitimacy.

Effort

This is the easiest criterion for the evaluator, judged by the simple indicator of student numbers. McAnany found impressive numbers in Latin America, although social, economic and political changes have since cut these back. Outside Latin America, programmes to extend basic education have not been reaching large audiences. The experience of AMREF, INADES-formation and ABET suggests that open and distance learning will have more impact when it has a multiplier effect, through courses for field agents rather than for individual learners. At secondary level, we found large absolute numbers in Mexico, while teacher education programmes from Pakistan to Tanzania reached students in their tens of thousands. And in higher education, distance-education programmes have achieved their most dramatic numbers with several of the Asian open universities enrolling over 100 000 students.

Mass media can reach mass audiences.

Performance

Here it gets more tricky, both because it is hard to agree a set of indicators and because we have less data than we would like. Different indicators may be needed for different kinds of course: an acclaimed radio project in Tanzania was judged a success by the number of latrines built by study group members. And the choice of indicator may have a subtle and complex effect on our view of success. If, for example, we improve tutoring and support then we may raise completion rates but, at the same time, by encouraging marginal students to take their examinations, lower the proportion of good grades awarded. Here, too, there are particular difficulties in comparing open and distance learning with conventional education; even when their aims are similar, they often reach different groups of students.

Several indicators are possible. For nonformal programmes, such as those aimed at improving health or agriculture, the most appropriate indicator will be evidence of a change in health or agricultural productivity. Data of this kind have been collected for conventional approaches to agricultural extension and we could in principle look for them in relation to distance education (Orivel 1983). Similarly, where programmes have had a vocational orientation, it is sometimes possible to see if learners' work practices change. Unfortunately we have few data although occasional studies have looked at the classroom behaviour of teachers (chapter 4). Within formal education, learning gains have been measured in relation to interactive radio instruction and some programmes of teacher education. We have more data, although less than we would like, on two simpler indicators – successful completion, or dropout, rates and examination performance.

The evidence is mixed. Generally, distance-education programmes have suffered from low completion rates, at both secondary and tertiary level. Some programmes of teacher education have dramatically better figures, achieved most often where increased pay on completion kept up motivation. Examination results tend to compare more favourably with the conventional alternative than completion rates; it looks as if keeping on to the end of the course is more demanding than passing examinations. As noted in chapters 3 and 5 we need to look at these figures in the context of the efficiency achieved in conventional education. Conventional secondary and tertiary education also have low internal efficiency in many developing countries. Within conventional institutions at tertiary level in sub-saharan

Africa, for example, noncompletion rates of between one-third and two-thirds are reported (Neave and van Vught 1994: 2).

There are two conclusions. First, the evidence from teacher education shows that distance-education methods can be relatively effective in terms of completion and pass rates. But, second, the record of many other programmes is that distance education is not particularly effective when measured in terms of examination performance – the objective for many students. Most abandon study long before they get that far.

Adequacy

How adequately is open and distance learning meeting educational needs? We need to look at adequacy not only in relation to the numbers offered an education but also in relation to its quality in terms of its curricular, social and economic ends.

In basic and nonformal education, the evidence quoted in chapter 2 suggests that it is making an extremely small contribution. The tiny numbers reached by exciting projects, and the difficulty of institutionalising their success, demonstrates at best potential rather than achievement. Earlier hopes even for the radio schools of Latin America have fallen away. This judgment may be harsh. Nonformal education tends to be uncoordinated and under-reported. But the evidence suggests that, in basic and nonformal education as a whole, McAnany's 1975 verdict on the radio schools can stand for the sector.

Within formal education, only a handful of institutions, like Telecurso in Brazil and Telesecundaria in Mexico, are addressing large audiences at secondary level. Perhaps with reason: many students want a formal secondary school and not a substitute. For the most part the evidence at secondary level is of institutions that may be adequate in response to the evident demand for an alternative form of secondary education but are puny in relation to the numbers of adults who never completed secondary education. In teacher education, the scale of some distance-education projects has demonstrated that the methods have reached significant proportions of their target populations and may meet the criterion of adequacy. At the same time, distance education has seldom been fully integrated into the structure of teacher education. More often it has been an add-on, or a response to an emergency, as if decision makers were unconvinced of its potential. 'Could be adequate' sounds a miserable but fair judgement.

The big numbers, reported in chapter 5, are in higher education. With the large proportions of higher-education enrolments at the open universities in China, Thailand, Turkey and India, distance education is regarded as adequate to a significant educational task. Although the expansion of distance education has usually been part of a more general expansion of higher education, its growth has made a marked contribution to that process, itself a response to the increased output of secondary education.

Most distance-education programmes have had limited ambitions in terms of curriculum. Some teacher-education programmes, such as the Primary Teacher Orientation Course in Pakistan, had curriculum innovation as an aim. In nonformal education, there have been attempts to create a curriculum that matched rural needs more closely than the conventional and formal curriculum of school, but with only modest success. Radio and computer technologies have done something to change school curricula. But formal programmes have, by and large, been addressed to disadvantaged groups of students whose demand is for something that matches the formal curriculum as closely as possible. If we think that the world's curricula need radical change, there is only limited experience to suggest that open and distance learning is adequate to the task.

We have few studies that tell us how far open and distance learning is adequately meeting the social needs that led students to enrol. The anecdotal evidence is more encouraging than the statistical; individual students tell warming stories about what they have gained. But we lack tracer studies to tell us how many of those who complete their studies through nonconventional channels achieve their ambition in terms of jobs or status. The odds are against them. They tend to be older than students studying conventionally and, almost by definition, have used distance education because of social, educational or geographical disadvantage. Structures may restrict them; it is not generally possible, for example, for students to move from one of the Indian open universities into a conventional university. Social mobility through distance education is possible but there is no evidence to suggest that it is easy.

We have stronger evidence of distance education's capacity to respond adequately to economic demand. The scale at which the China radio and television universities have produced graduates suggests that distance education can be organised so that it contributes to workforce training. South Asian universities, as reported in chapter 5, are making a significant contribution to the production of graduates.

We have just enough evidence to conclude that open and distance learning can respond adequately to educational demands. The extent to which it actually satisfies them is conditioned by its efficiency.

Efficiency

We have two possible measures of efficiency: the cost per student and the cost per successful student. Both lend themselves to comparisons with conventional education.

As argued in chapter 7, distance education may have economic advantages because it allows economies of scale. Upfront costs in course development and in setting up an administrative system are balanced by reduced recurrent costs. The level of these upfront costs is, in good measure, unaffected by the level of education: you need to pay writers and editors, and fund the management of student records, whether students are at basic or tertiary level. It follows that, the higher the level of education, the more likely we are to find that distance education has economic advantages.

The evidence confirms this. Chapter 3 showed that programmes of basic education at a distance have rarely compared favourably with conventional primary schooling. In contrast, at secondary and tertiary level, distance education tends to have lower costs per student. If, however, we use the tougher criterion of cost per successful student then the evidence is more equivocal. Dropout rates so reduce the efficiency of distance education in terms of successful completers or graduates that efficient programmes seem to be the exception rather than the rule.

We can approach questions of efficiency from a different angle, asking how far distance-teaching institutions are deploying their resources in the ways they believe will maximise their efficiency or effectiveness. This takes us into questions of process.

Process

While McAnany proposed searching for reasons for success or failure we need also to ask qualitative questions about the process of open and distance learning if we are to establish its educational legitimacy.

The practice of open and distance learning, and the heuristics that have been derived from it, suggest that its professionals know how to make it effective. The best-run programmes are probably better, more effective, and more interesting for their students than they were a generation back. There is a reasonable consensus on good practice which will include using a combination of media, ensuring that there is effective tutoring and student support, having an efficient administrative system, and developing clear and well-produced teaching material. There is a reasonable understanding of good practice, even in relation to nonformal education (Hornik 1988: 158) and an even fuller record of good practice to guide us within formal educa-tion. And yet many institutions are a long way from achieving and imple-menting what they know to be good practice. Chapter 8 showed how, despite lip-service to the use of a combination of media, most distance education remains dominated by print; we have not moved all that far from correspondence education. The annual reports from many institutions are a litany of lacking resources which show that their administration cannot meet the demands put upon it. In a counterpoint to the papers acclaiming the scale on which open universities are recruiting students, there is a rich and sad literature on open and distance learning demonstrating that practi-tioners know how to run programmes but lack the resources to do so (e.g. Fagbamiye 1995: 75; Murphy and Zhiri 1992: 140; Arger 1990).[2] The sad conclusion is that while we know enough about the process of open and distance learning to design and run programmes that will maximise their effectiveness, few institutions can actually do so. For the reasons examined in chapter 10, most lack the political strength to acquire the funds or allies they would need to work as well as they know how.

One further set of doubts remain. Many conventional educators remain sceptical about the process of open and distance learning. They were epitomised by the chief education officer in Botswana, who greeted the New Zealand consultant, who had just arrived to launch their teacher upgrading project, with the mournful words, 'It won't work, you know' (personal communication). Even within the distance-education literature there is a continuing dialectic. On the one hand its protagonists, from the ideologues of the 1960s to the technophiles of the 2000s, argue that it is transforming education, widening access, and offering a future that is both richer and more equitable. On the other, its critics from H. G. Wells, once a correspondence-college tutor, who denounced its encouragement of the rote learning of trivia to the sceptical ministers of education who constrict its budgets, see it as a poor substitute for the real thing (Wells 1934: 343–52). The case against it is easily made. It may, indeed, foster rote learning. If students have to rely on pre-prepared text, then they may come to regard the word – rather than critical dialogue – as sacred. It is an unsocial form of learning, lacking or restricting the opportunities for interaction among students and tutors that is at the heart of much lively and rewarding education. While arrangements for two-way communication are built into most programmes, it is more difficult to structure open and distance learning so that it becomes a shared experience between teacher and learner, with the possibility of moving into areas of study that were not envisaged at the outset, and with the potential of generating knowledge that is new to both parties. When these inherent weaknesses are put alongside the evidence of its inefficiency, an elegant and simple conclusion is that it is an inherently second-rate form of education, lacking full educational legitimacy.

But this is too stark. Much conventional education is also substandard. Many teachers do not seek this grand vision, many students want to pass their examinations, learning by rote if need be, more than they want unfettered dialogue. And education is multi-faceted. If we distinguish between training, concerned with skills, instruction, concerned with information, initiation into social norms and induction, in which students are introduced to thought systems enabling judgment (Stenhouse 1975), then we may conclude that open and distance learning lends itself more readily to some aspects of education than others. A working hypothesis might then be that open and distance learning has to face severe difficulties if it is to match the best of conventional education but, if well-designed, may often match the best of what is available.

Two consequences flow, one political and one educational. If different forms of education have different strengths and weaknesses, but one of them is widely perceived to be superior, then there is an argument on grounds of equity to share them out and ensure that all students spend some of their time working in one mode and some in another. The adoption of flexible learning, at least by a handful of universities, suggests that they are moving in this direction. Many are not, and few governments or universities would willingly impose a mixture of on and off-campus study on all learners. The educational challenge may be easier. If open and distance learning is to move away from instruction and training it needs to promote induction, in Stenhouse's terminology or, at least within higher education, to develop courses that promote high levels of understanding, encourage problem-solving, and move towards the development of high-order concepts with increased explanatory power. In order to establish our intellectual legitimacy we therefore need to develop courses that encourage the development of these higher-order capacities so that 'the quality student should be able to challenge and extend and even *transform* the knowledge he is given' (Lewis 1973: 203). Transformation is as necessary a part of adult basic education as of higher education. Much conventional agricultural extension, for example, has been criticised because it takes too little account of indigenous farming knowledge; if distance education is to be applied to basic farming it needs not merely to provide information but also to enable the learner to challenge the information and develop a new synthesis of knowledge that combines the new, and generally applicable, knowledge from the field station with the old and particular of the individual farm. This in turn demands the production of teaching materials that encourage questioning and dialogue and a teaching system in which there are enough opportunities for interaction among students and between tutor and student.

Are we moving in these directions? The record of the twenty-first century, available for this second edition, suggests that we do so only with difficulty; changes in ideology, a retreat from equity, a neglect of theory and a misplaced faith in technology all make the development of good practice and process more difficult. Respect for the market, and a rising expectation that users and learners should pay, have seen Indian students, for example, meeting 80 per cent of their course costs, rather than the 20 per cent of their luckier elder siblings. Pressures to constrain variable costs – those that bear on the interaction that is at the heart of good process – are a natural response by institutions needing to keep down fees. Good practice is constrained, too, where neglect of theory allows practitioners to forget the multistep theory of communication or the case for multimedia approaches in the interest of effective education. Meanwhile, though many programmes lack resources, they have been lavished more generously on occasional and improbable technology-led inspirations like the British e-university.

Conclusion

The conclusions are contested as well. The evidence shows that open and distance learning has been used for many different purposes, at various levels of education, and with a measure of success. It has done something to transmit cultural values, to empower students, to learn job skills, to help students get better jobs and to improve their life chances. At the same time, the evidence is of achievement falling far below hope.

The contest is between two views. We can interpret the growth of open and distance learning as something that has provided education to thousands, even millions, for whom it would not otherwise have been available. Many have been disappointed by what was on offer. But others have benefited and we can interpret this widening of education as a move towards equity. The alternative view is harsher. Open and distance learning is regarded, by students and ministries of education alike, as a second-rate system, used to offer a shadow of education while withholding its substance. It is an inefficient but cheap way of containing educational demand without meeting it. Through its existence it helps insulate the elite system from pressures that might otherwise threaten its status or its ways of working.

The evidence will fit either interpretation. But probably only hard-line maoists, working on 'the worse the better' principle that incremental reforms should be resisted as delaying the revolution that will put everything right, will take the harsher view and argue that nothing should be done about it. For the rest of us, the evidence suggests that open and distance learning can bring social and educational benefits to its students.

But there is an economic, ethical and social dimension to all this. Secondary and higher education are continuing to expand, and are doing so at a time when dependency ratios remain unfavourable. Debt servicing, the low costs of primary products, military expenditure, and current widespread reluctance to raise taxes are all holding back funds for education. Programmes of distance education have become established, here and there at secondary level, on a large but probably insufficient scale for teacher education, and for large numbers of students in tertiary education. They have demonstrated potential for nonformal education, the poor relation. It would be at least churlish, at most irresponsible, simply to denounce all this as an inferior kind of education and hope for it to go away so that, come the next millennium everyone would have the ideal face-to-face education dreamt of in the groves of Athens or the shades of Oxbridge. (And even then it might not suit everyone, or their circumstances.) There is, then, a case both for looking critically at how open and distance learning is working and for trying to make it better. Distance-education students deserve that. The alternative, to say that it cannot be more than second best and so is not worth improving, is close to arguing that we can have food standards for caviare but not for bread.

Paraphrasing Gandhi, my answer to the question 'can we make open and distance learning as good as conventional education?' remains, as in the previous edition, 'I think it would be a good idea'.

Annex
Currency values

Inflation, and the variety of currencies in which the costs of education are reported, bedevil comparative analysis. In order to facilitate comparison, costs throughout the book have been converted to constant United States dollars, shown in *$italic* using a two-stage process. First, costs have been converted to US$ for the date on which they were incurred or reported. Exchange rates from World Bank *World tables* and IMF *Financial statistics* have been used for this conversion. Then, costs have been converted to 2005US$ using the US consumer price index, and taking the June 2005 figure for that year. Where figures were included in the first edition of this book, they have simply been updated by converting the US$ figure shown from the 1998 value shown then to the 2005 value. Table A1 shows the US consumer price index; table A2 shows the values of the currencies for the years relevant to data quoted.

Table A1 US Consumer price index

Date	Index	Date	Index	Date	Index
1965	31.5	1982	96.5	1994	148.2
1970	38.8	1983	99.6	1995	152.4
1972	41.8	1984	103.9	1996	156.9
1973	44.4	1985	107.6	1997	160.5
1974	49.3	1986	109.6	1998	163.0
1975	53.8	1987	113.6	1999	166.6
1976	56.9	1988	118.3	2000	172.2
1977	60.6	1989	124.0	2001	177.0
1978	65.2	1990	130.7	2002	179.9
1979	72.6	1991	136.2	2003	184.0
1980	82.4	1992	140.3	2004	188.9
1981	90.9	1993	144.5	2005	194.5

Table A2 Currency values

Country	Currency	Date	Equivalent to US$1.00
Bolivia	bolivaro	1990	3.173
Botswana	pula	2004	4.6929
Brazil	cruzeiro	1977	14.144
Canada	dollar	2000	1.4851
		2005	1.2388
China	RMB yuan	1988	3.720
Côte d'Ivoire	CFA franc	1996	511.55
		2004	528.28
Honduras	lempira	1986	2.00
India	rupee	1988	14.447
		1990	17.949
		1991	24.519
		1997	36.313
		1998	41.259
		2004	45.316
Israel	shekel	1992	2.4591
Kenya	shilling	1985	16.432
		1989[a]	20.57
		1996	57.115
Lesotho	maloti	1984	1.475
Malawi	kwacha	1978[a]	0.83
		1980[a]	1.20
		1985	1.719
Namibia	dollar	1998	5.5828
Pakistan	rupee	1985	15.160
South Africa	rand	1994	3.5508
		2002	10.5408
		2003	7.5648
United Kingdom	pound	1985	0.779
		1987	0.612
		1988	0.562
		1993	0.667
		1998	0.604
		2001	0.694
		2003	0.612

Note
a. This value is taken from original project report.

Notes

Chapter 1

1 The sources for quotations at chapter headings are as follows. 1: Macmillan 1938: 125; 2: proverb quoted by T. Riseley Griffith 1882, *Proceedings of the Royal Colonial Institute* 23: 78 and minute by W. W. F. Ward quoted in Morgan (1980: 75); 3: Tawney 1964: 146; 4: Arnove 1994: 209 and former student quoted by Buley-Meissner 1991: 42; 5: Young 1962; 6: plaque on wall of Sabarmati ashram, Ahmedabad; 7: Durrell 1954: 102; 8: Bevan 1952: 164; 9: Solzhenitsyn on receiving Nobel prize, quoted in *Oxford dictionary of modern quotations*; 10: Paine 1906: 252; 11: Halsey, Heath and Rudge 1980: 219.

2 The UNESCO-UIS cd-rom does not include total figures for tertiary education. These figures for 2000 are therefore taken from those shown by UNESCO-UIS on their website for individual countries, with the figure for the nearest available year included where no data are shown in the table for 2000/01. The tertiary enrolment figure is probably an underestimate.

3 In Uganda in 1985 current expenditure per pupil as a proportion of GNP per capita was 8 per cent at primary and 499 per cent at tertiary level (UNESCO 1998: table 11). Differences have narrowed but remain large: in 2002 the comparable figures for Lesotho were 24 per cent and 693 per cent. (UNESCO-Institute for Statistics 2005: table 12.)

4 Here, and throughout the book, figures have been converted to constant 2005 US$ in order to facilitate comparison. Where figures are shown in another currency, they are converted to 2005 US$ with the constant $ value shown in italics. For more detail see annex A.

5 The book had four authors, all then at the International Extension College. This one, like its previous edition, is a successor in the sense that it takes the story on 25 years but it moves in a different direction and has a single author.

Chapter 2

1 The review (Coombs with Ahmed 1974) was accompanied by two academic studies of adult education (Coombs *et al.* 1973; Ahmed and Coombs 1975).

2 New figures may be showing that large-scale literacy projects are now being run at costs something like that of primary schooling. Oxenham (2004: 16) estimated annual costs per enrolled learner at $20 in south Asia and $50 in west Africa, between 30 and 70 per cent of the cost of primary schooling.

3 See chapter 1 note 4.

Chapter 3

1 One reviewer of the first edition apparently did not recognise Churchill's description of the naval tradition but it is his phrase, alas, not mine.
2 The major sources for this account are Dewal 1994, Mukhopadhyay 1994, Mukhopadhyay 1995, Gaba 1997a, Mitra 2004 and NIOS 2004.
3 The main sources here are Sadiman *et al.* 1995 and Sadiman and Rahardjo 1997, with useful shorter accounts in Sadiman 1994 and Sadiman 1995.
4 Three papers in Murphy and Zhiri 1992 are a major source. Others are Murphy 1993 and Siaciwena 1994. Laymaman 1999 gives some later data on Malawi.
5 The projects are well documented. The literature includes a detailed study of the Nicaragua project in Friend, Searle and Suppes 1980. A series of reports on individual projects has been produced by the Learning Technologies for Basic Education project (LearnTech case study series). Overviews include Radio Learning Project (n.d.) (about 1991), Bosch 1997, Tilson 1991 and Dock and Helwig 1999.
6 These calculations can only be approximate. They are based on data in UNESCO *Statistical yearbook 1989* which show total expenditure on education in local currency, the proportion allocated to primary education, and the total number of students.

Chapter 4

1 We are short of developing-country evidence. But one American study comparing student achievement and teacher policy within the 50 states found that student achievements were highest 'in the states that have the most highly qualified teachers and that have made consistent investments in teachers' professional development' (Russell and McPherson 2001: 8).
2 The African experience has been well documented and for that reason dominates the next part of this chapter.
3 The main sources on Tanzania are Chale 1993 and Mählck and Temu 1989 and on Zimbabwe Chivore 1993 and Gatawa 1986.
4 The main source on the University of Lagos is Cumming and Olaloku 1993. On the University of Nairobi there is Odumbe 1988, Makau 1993 and Dodds and Mayo 1996.
5 Strategies for integrating supervised teaching practice with distance education are discussed in Creed 2001: 29 and Perraton *et al.* 2002: 53–6.

Chapter 5

1 Statistics that are not individually referenced are generally taken from the relevant volume of UNESCO *Statistical yearbook*, the UNESCO *World education report* or the EFA *Global monitoring report*. Economic data are from World Bank *World development report* or *World tables*.
2 Data about them are sometimes difficult to interpret. Some institutions use the term 'enrolments' to refer to the number of new students in a year or a semester while others use the same term for the total number of students registered. Total figures in some cases include large numbers of inactive students, while some totals published include all students who have ever been enrolled since the institution was established. Comparative tables needed to be treated with care.
3 There is a useful discussion of the problem of using indicators in Shale and Gomes 1998. The British Open University has allowed a period of provisional registration for students who find, early on, that enrolment was a mistake. This is

probably good for potential students, who can ease their way out of the situation but it also improves their satisfactory completion rate. But, in the absence of universal policies of this kind, we can make sense of comparative statistics only by taking a tough line and looking at available figures on graduations set against enrolments.

Chapter 6

1 Various agencies (e.g. the Committee of Vice-Chancellors and Principals in Britain in 1999) have tried to weigh up the significance of virtual enrolment. Figures are hard to come by, partly because they seldom disaggregate between different modes of crossborder activity such as franchising and e-learning.

Chapter 7

1 Chu and Schramm 1968 summarised the evidence in the heyday of educational television. More recent reviews are by Clark 1983 and 1993.
2 Costs are quoted in Perraton 1984 with minor corrections from those in Perraton 1983a. In the latter figures are also quoted from Radio ECCA; these are based on a more partial analysis but, so far as they go, they confirm the general findings quoted.
3 See also Perraton 1987. Wilson (1991: 256) also uses these figures but appears to overestimate the cost advantage of the STOU by omitting from the costs those borne by the individual student.
4 South African performance indicators for 2003 show average recurrent expenditure per weighted full-time equivalent student as R29 686 (*$4148*) across conventional universities and R19 073 (*$2665*) for UNISA (http://www.education. gov.za.content/documents/662.xls).
5 The earlier study proposed a simple calculation of the cost per graduate–dividing the annual budget by the forecast number of graduates–which would give a cost, in 1977 prices, of $5330 (*$14 338*) but went on to argue that this left out of account the value of a partially completed degree for dropouts and suggested the real figure should be two-thirds of this at $3600 (*$9684*) (Melmed *et al.* 1982: 236–7). By 1992–3 the university had 19 039 students and a budget of NIS79.3 million giving a cost per student of NIS4164 (*$1968*). But, using the original formulae and the number of graduates at 405, this suggests upper and lower costs per graduate of NIS195 728 (*$92 487*) and NIS87 862 (*$41 517*), greater than the cost of conventional universities (Herskovic 1995: tables 3.13, 5.11).

Chapter 8

1 We are curiously short of research evidence to confirm that mixtures of media teach more effectively than a single medium. As noted in chapter 2, the multi-step theory of communication justifies the use of group discussion along with broadcasts if we are seeking to change attitudes. It is probably safe to say that we know that combining media helps to maintain motivation. If the biggest problem with distance education is that people get bored out and drop out, then this may be justification enough.
2 There are trade-offs for the institution between broadcasting programmes and distributing cassettes which go beyond cost comparisons. Cassettes have no public presence. They have sometimes been available for use only in study centres and not by individuals. And, while the discipline of filling a regular broadcasting slot forces radio or television on to the agenda of course developers and managers, it is always possible to treat the making of recordings as an add-on.

Chapter 9

1 Currency conversions across the centuries are somewhat arbitrary. This one is complicated by the effect of inflation on the value of the pound in 1813. It is based on the following decisions: sterling is used as the international currency to 1946 and the US dollar since then; an exchange rate of 10 rupees to the pound is taken for 1813; British price indices are 203 for 1813 and 106 for 1914 (Mitchell 1988: 722–7); rebased UK retail price index gives us 1914 and 1946 values of 2.8 and 7.4; 1946 £1.00 = $4.03; US CPI for 1946 is 19.5. This then gives us the equation:

$$\left(\frac{1813\text{Rs}100\,000}{10}\times\frac{106}{203}\times\frac{7.4}{2.8}\right)\times4.03\times\frac{194.5}{19.5}=2005\$554\,720$$

If expenditure in India had been a few years later, or the decision-makers had in mind the more usual value of sterling, then the calculation would give an answer closer to *$1 000 000*.

2 The Asian Development Bank had previously shown its interest in the application of distance education by holding a regional conference on Asian experience in 1987; it held a further meeting in 1997 on its potential for teacher training within the largest Asian countries.

3 Curiously, these documents are much more prescriptive than the policy documents UNESCO produced around the same time. At the same time they are more dominated by rich-country experience. One bit of advice, for example, comments that a unit could be omitted if students had sufficient practical experience with computers in primary school (UNESCO 2002b: 64).

4 University Funding Council statistics for 1988–9 show the total income of Warwick, Southampton and Nottingham universities, all around the mean in size, as £56.4 million, £67.7 million and £65.5 million.

5 The main sources for COL are its own publications and this has drawn in particular on its 3-year report for 2000–3, its plan for 2003–6, its report to Commonwealth Heads of Government in 2005 and its draft plan for 2006–9. At the time of writing all of these were on its website www.col.org.

6 The best critics have come out of this invisible college. Good examples are Hornik's (1988) analysis of development support communication and Klees' (1995) critical examination of the economics of educational technology.

7 Held *et al.* (1999: 16) have defined globalisation as 'a process (or set of processes) which embodies a transformation in the spatial organization of social relations and transaction–assessed in terms of their extensity, intensity, velocity and impact–generating transcontinental or interregional flows and networks of activity, interaction, and the exercise of power.'

Chapter 11

1 Cohen and Lazerson's quotation may read like an account of education today but is in fact a critique of the narrowness which market values imposed on American education in the late 19th and early 20th century.

2 Arger appears to conclude not just that distance education is not working but that it cannot work: Papua New Guinea is operating on too small a scale, Malaysia in too elite a way, and Thailand with too high attrition rates. Whether or not one goes as far as his pessimism takes him, the paper has a useful summary of the problems afflicting much distance education in the south.

References

Abbas, R., Hughes, B. and Dodds, T. 1985 *An evaluation of FEPRA* (mimeo), Cambridge: International Extension College

Aderinoye, R. A. 1995 'Teacher training by distance: the Nigerian experience' in Sewart 1995

—— 2006 'An alternative route to primary-teacher qualifications, Nigeria' in Perraton, Robinson and Creed 2006

Adkins, D. 1999 'Cost and finance' in Dock and Helwig 1999

African Virtual University 2004 *DfID seminar: 29 March 2004*, Nairobi (power-point presentation)

—— 2006, available at http://www.avu.org (accessed 12 April 2006)

Agence de la Francophonie 1999 *Formation à distance*, Bordeaux. Online, Available: http://ciffad.francophonie.org (accessed 29 April 1999)

Aguti, J. N. 1999a 'The first graduates of the Makerere University external degree programme in Uganda: a case study', paper presented at the Pan-Commonwealth Forum on Open Learning *Empowerment through knowledge and technology* Bandar Seri Begawan, Brunei Darussalam: 1–5 March

—— 1999b 'One year of Virtual University experience at Makerere University in Uganda', paper presented at Pan-Commonwealth Forum on Open Learning *Empowerment through knowledge and technology* Bandar Seri Begawan, Brunei Darussalam: 1–5 March

Ahmed, M. and Coombs, P. H. 1975 *Education for rural development: case studies for planners*, New York: Praeger

Ajayi, J. F. A., Goma, L. K. H. and Johnson, G. A. 1996 *The African experience with higher education*, Accra: Association of African Universities

Ali, M. S., Haque, A. K. E. and Rumble, G. 1997 'The Bangladesh Open University: mission and promise' *Open learning* 12 (2): 12–28

Allama Iqbal Open University 1999 *25 Years of AIOU 1974–1999*, Islamabad

Alvarez, M. I. *et al.* 1998 'Computers in schools: A qualitative study of Chile and Costa Rica' *Education and technology series* Special issue

AMREF 2003 *Annual report*, Nairobi

Ansari, M. M. 1994 'Economics of distance education in India' in Dhanararjan *et al.* 1994

Anzalone, S. 1991 'Educational technology and the improvement of general education in developing countries' in Lockheed *et al.* 1991

Arger, G. 1990 'Distance education in the third world: critical analysis on the promise and the reality' *Open learning* 5 (2): 9–18

Arnove, R. F. (ed.) 1976 *Educational television: a policy critique and guide for developing countries*, New York: Praeger

—— 1994 *Education as contested terrain: Nicaragua 1979–93*, Boulder: Westview

Ashton, D. and Green, F. 1996 *Education, training and the global economy*, Cheltenham: Edward Elgar

Asian Development Bank 1987 *Distance education in Asia and the Pacific*, Manila

—— 1997 *Distance education for primary school teachers*, Manila

Avalos, B. 1991 *Approaches to teacher education: Initial teacher training*, London: Commonwealth Secretariat

Avalos, B. and Haddad, W. 1978 *A review of teacher effectiveness research*, Ottawa: IDRC

Baggaley, J. P. 2004 *Distance learning technologies: deploying Canadian and southern technology engines to build an Asian research network (Consultant's report)*. Ottawa: IDRC

Bako, C. I. and Rumble, G. 1993 'The National Teachers' Institute, Nigeria' in Perraton 1993

Baranshamaje, E. n.d. *The African Virtual University: knowledge is power*, Washington DC: World Bank

Bates, A. W. and Escamilla de los Santos, J. G. 1997 'Crossing boundaries: making global distance education a reality' *Journal of distance education* 12 (1/2): 49–66

Bbuye, J. 2000 'Uganda: Distance education programmes of the ministry of health' in Siaciwena 2000

Bedi, A. S. 1999 *The role of information and communication technologies in economic development – a partial survey*, Bonn: Center for Development Research, Universität Bonn

Belawati, T. 1998 'Increasing student persistence in Indonesian post-secondary distance education' *Distance education* 19 (1): 81–100

—— 2001 'Indonesia' in O. Jegede and G. Shire *Open and distance education in the Asia Pacific Region*, Hong Kong: Open University of Hong Kong Press

—— 2004 'Malaysia: ICT use in education' in Farrell and Wachholz 2004

Bellamy, C. 1996 *State of the world's children 1996*, Oxford: Oxford University Press

Bennell, P. with Furlong, D. 1997 *Has Jomtien made any difference? Trends in donor funding for education and basic education since the late 1980s* (IDS Working Paper 51), Brighton: Institute of Development Studies

Bevan. A. 1952 *In place of fear*, London: Heinemann

Blight, D., Davis, D. and Olsen, A. 1999 'The internationalisation of higher education' in Harry 1999

Blunkett, D. 2000 'Higher education' speech delivered at Greenwich University, 15 February, available at http://cms1.gre.ac.uk/dfee/#speech (accessed 21 December 2005)

Bosch, A. 1997 'Interactive radio instruction: twenty-three years of improving educational quality' *Education and technology notes* 1 (1): 1–11

Bradley, J. (ed.) 2003 *The open classroom: Distance learning in and out of schools*, London: Kogan Page

Brahmawong, C. 1993 'Teacher education through distance education: the case of Sukhothai Thammathirat Open University in Thailand' *Educational media international* 30 (2): 69–73

Briggs, A. *et al.* 1987 *Towards a Commonwealth of Learning: Commonwealth cooperation in distance education and open learning*, London: Commonwealth Secretariat

Buley-Meisner, M. L. 1991 'Teachers and teacher education: a view from the People's Republic of China' *International Journal of Educational Development* 11 (1): 41–53

Calderoni, J. 1998 'Telesecundaria: using TV to bring education to rural Mexico' *Education and technology technical notes series* 3 (1)

Capper, J. 2002a 'Shoma: A multimedia approach to South Africa's teacher development', *TechKnowLogia* 4 (4): 44–8

—— 2002b 'A review of telecenter effectiveness in Latin America', *TechKnowLogia* 4 (3): 49–50

Carnoy, M. 1976 'The economic costs and returns to educational television' in Arnove 1976

Carnoy, M. and Levin, H. M. 1975 'Evaluation of educational media: some issues' *Instructional Science* 4: 385–406

Casas Armengol, M. 1995 'Distance education universities in Latin America: expectations and disappointments' in Sewart 1995 vol. 1

Cawthera, A. 2001 *Computers in secondary schools in developing countries: costs and other issues*, London: Department for International Development

Chale, E. M. 1993 'Tanzania's distance-teaching programme' in Perraton 1993

CHE (Council on Higher Education) 2004 *Enhancing the contribution of distance higher education in South Africa*, Pretoria

Chivore, B. R. S. 1993 'The Zimbabwe Integrated Teacher Education Course' in Perraton 1993

Chu, G. C. and Schramm, W. 1968 *Learning from television: what the research says*, Stanford: ERIC

Clark, R. 1983 'Reconsidering research on learning from media', *Review of educational research* 53 (4): 445–59

—— 1993 'Media will never influence learning' *Educational technology* 31 (2)

Cobbe, J. 1995 *Economics of interactive instruction: the case of South Africa*, Washington DC: Education Development Center

Cohen, D. K. and Lazerson, M. 1977 'Education and the corporate order' in J. Karabel and A. H. Halsey (ed.) *Power and ideology in education*, New York: Oxford University Press

Colle, R. D. and Roman, R. 2004 'ICT4D: A future for higher education in developing countries', in N'D. T. Assié-Lumumba (ed.) *Cyberspace, distance learning, and higher education in developing countries*, Leiden: Brill

Commission for Africa 2005 *Our common interest* n.p.

Commission of the European Communities 1991 *Memorandum on open distance learning in the European Community*, Brussels

Commonwealth of Learning 1993 *Compendium of activities 1993*, Vancouver

—— 1996 *Summary report 1994–6*, Vancouver

—— 1998 *Summary report 1996–8*, Vancouver

—— 2006a *Networking learning communities for development (Report to Commonwealth Heads of Government meeting, Valletta)*, Vancouver

—— 2006b *Draft three-year plan: Learning for development*, Vancouver

Coombs, P. H. 1968 *The world educational crisis: a systems analysis*, New York: Oxford University Press

—— 1985 *The world crisis in education: the view from the eighties*, New York: Oxford University Press

Coombs, P. H. with Ahmed, A. 1974 *Attacking rural poverty*, Baltimore: Johns Hopkins

Coombs, P. H. with Prosser, R. C. and Ahmed, M. 1973 *New paths to learning for rural children and youth*, New York: International Council for Educational Development

Creed, C. 2001 *The use of distance education for teachers (Report to the Department for International Development)*, Cambridge: International Research Foundation for Open Learning

CRTVU 1993 *Education statistics yearbook of Radio and TV University in China 1992–3*, Beijing

Cumming, C. and Olaloku, F. A. 1993 'The Correspondence and Open Studies Institute, University of Lagos' in Perraton 1993

Curran, C. and Murphy, P. 1992 'Distance education at the second level and for teacher education in six African countries' in Murphy and Zhiri 1992

CVCP (Committee of Vice-Chancellors and Principals) 2000 *The business of borderless education: UK perspectives (Case studies and annexes)*, London: CVCP/HEFCE

da Veiga Coutinho, J. 1972 'Preface' in P. Freire 1972 *Cultural action for freedom*, Harmondsworth: Penguin

Daniel, J. S. 1996 *Mega-universities and knowledge media: technology strategies for higher education*, London: Kogan Page

Daniel, J. S. *et al.* 1988 *The Commonwealth of Learning: institutional arrangements for Commonwealth cooperation in distance education*, London: Commonwealth Secretariat

DEC (Distance Education Council) 2001a *Open universities in India*, New Delhi: IGNOU

—— 2001b *Distance education in central universities*, New Delhi: IGNOU

—— 2001c *Tenth five-year plan perspectives on distance higher education*, New Delhi: IGNOU

Demiray, U. 1995 *Distance education versus classroom*, Eskişehir: Turkuaz

Department for International Development 1998 *Statistics on international development 1993/4 – 1997/8*, London: Government Statistical Service

—— n.d. (1998?) *Learning opportunities for all: A policy framework for education*, London

—— 2000 *Eliminating world poverty: Making globalisation work for the poor (White paper on international development)* (Cm5006), London

—— 2001 *Education strategy paper: The challenge of universal primary education*, London

Department of Education 1995 *Education and training in a democratic South Africa: first steps to develop a new system*, Pretoria

Department of Foreign Affairs and International Trade n.d. *Canada–Caribbean distance education scholarship programme* (Powerpoint presentation at Commonwealth of Learning)

Dewal, O. S. 1994 'Open learning in Indian school education' in Mukhopadhyay and Phillips 1994

Dhanarajan, G., Ip. P. K., Yuen, K. S. and Swales, C. (ed.) 1994 *Economics of distance education: recent experience*, Hong Kong: Open Learning Institute Press

Dikshit, H. P. 2006 'Re-engineering social transformation through ICT-enabled education: IGNOU perspective' in Garg, Panda, Murthy and Mishra 2006

Ding, X. 1994 'Economic analysis of Radio and TV Universities' education in China' in Dhanarajan *et al.* 1994

—— 1999 'Distance education in China' in Harry 1999

Ding, X., Gu, X., and Zhu, Z. 2005 'The Chinese approach', in C. McIntosh and Z. Varoglu *Lifelong learning and distance higher education*, Vancouver: Commonwealth of Learning/Paris: UNESCO

Dirr, P. J. 2001 'The development of new organisational arrangements in virtual learning' in Farrell 2001

Djalil, A., Musa, I., Kesuma, R. and Damajanti, N. S. 1994 'The financing system of the Universitas Terbuka' in Mugridge 1994

Dock, A. and Helwig, J. (ed.) 1999 *Interactive radio instruction: impact, sustainability and future directions*, Washington DC: Education and Technology Team, World Bank

Dodds, T. 2003 'From government correspondence schools to parastatal colleges of open learning: out of school secondary education at a distance in central and southern Africa' in Bradley 2003

Dodds, T. and Mayo, J. 1996 *Distance education for development: promise and performance*, Cambridge: International Extension College

Dodds, T., Perraton, H. and Young, M. 1972 *One year's work: The International Extension College 1971–1972*, Cambridge: International Extension College

Durrell, L. 1958 *Mountolive*, London: Faber

Duque, F. J. C. 1999 'Distance education in Latin America at the technology cross-roads' in Mitter and Bastos 1999

Du Vivier, E. 1998 *NAMCOL fee structure*, Windhoek: NAMCOL

ECOSOC 2000 *Report of the high-level panel of experts on information and communication technology* (New York 17–20 April) New York

Education and Skills Committee 2005 *UK e-University Third report of session 2004–05*, London: House of Commons

Education Development Center 2004 *Final report: Zambia's Interactive Radio Instruction Program*, Washington DC, available at http://pdf.dec.org/pdf_docs/PNADB926.pdf (accessed 10 March 2006)

Education Division, Overseas Development Administration 1994 *Aid to education in 1993 and beyond*, London

Fagbamiye, E. 1995 'Survival of a distance education institute in a developing country' in Sewart 1995

Farrell, G. M. (ed.) 2001 *The changing faces of virtual education*, Vancouver: Commonwealth of Learning

Farrell, G. and Wachholz, C. (ed.) 2004 *Meta-survey on the use of technologies in education in Asia and the Pacific*, Bangkok: UNESCO

Farren, V. J. 1999 'Interactive radio instruction/rural satellite program/LearnTech'. Online. Email: vfarren@rrs.cdie.org

Faure, E. *et al.* 1972 *Learning to be: the world of education today and tomorrow*, Paris: UNESCO/London: Harrap

Fielden, J. 2002 *Costing e-learning: Is it worth trying or should we ignore the figures?* London: Observatory on Borderless Education

Fielden, J., Dodds, A., Somiah, M. and McLean-Ler, J. n.d. (?1995) *Evaluation of ODA assistance to Indira Gandhi National Open University* (*Evaluation report EV.579*) London: Evaluation Department, Overseas Development Administration

Forbes, B. 1996 *Quicksand*, London: Arrow

Fraser, C. and Restrepo-Estrada, S. 1998 *Communication for development: human change for survival*, London: Tauris

Freire, P. 1972 *Cultural action for freedom*, Harmondsworth: Penguin

Friend, J., Searle, B. and Suppes, P. 1980 *Radio mathematics in Nicaragua*, Stanford: Institute for Mathematical Studies in the Social Sciences, Stanford University

Fryer, M. L. 1995 *Ministry, union, the church and teachers: Bolivia's partners in innovation*, Washington DC: Education Development Center

Gaba, A. K. 1997a 'Open learning in India: development and effectiveness' *Open learning* 12 (3): 43–9

—— 1997b 'Is open schooling in India really cost effective?' in M. Mukhopadhyay and M. Parhar (ed.) *Open and distance education*, New Delhi: Jawahar

Garg, S., Panda, S., Murthy, C. R. K. and Mishra, S. (ed.) 2006 *Open and distance education in global environment: opportunities for collaboration*, New Delhi: Viva Books

Garrett, R. and Verbik, L. 2004 *Online learning in Commonwealth universities: selected data from the 2004 Observatory survey, part 2*, London: Observatory on Borderless Higher Education. Available at http://www.obhe.ac.uk (accessed 3 May 2006)

Gatawa, B. S. M. 1986 'The Zimbabwe Integrated National Teacher Education Course (ZINTEC)' in C. B. W. Treffgarne (ed.) *Education in Zimbabwe* (mimeo) London: Department of International and Comparative Education, University of London Institute of Education

Guibert, A. A. de P. 1999 'The Brazilian "Telecurso 2000"' in Mitter and Bastos 1999

Gultig, G. and Butcher, N. 1996 *Teacher education offered at a distance in South Africa*, Braamfontein: South African Institute for Distance Education

Guy, R. 1992 'Distance education in Papua New Guinea: reflections on reality' *Open learning* 7 (1): 28–39

Halsey, A. H., Heath, A. F. and Ridge, J. M. 1980 *Origins and destinations: family, class and education in modern Britain*, Oxford: Clarendon

Harrison, M. *et al.* 2003 *Imfundo DFID: Output-to-purpose review*, available at http://www.dfid.gov.uk/pubs/files/imfundo/Imfundo-OPR.pdf (accessed 22 March 2006)

Harry, K. (ed.) 1999 *Higher education through open and distance learning*, London: Routledge

Hawes, H. and Stephens, D. 1990 *Questions of quality: primary education and development*, Harlow: Longman

Hawkridge, D. 1987 *General operational review of distance education*, Washington DC: Education and Training Department, World Bank (mimeo)

Hawkridge, D., Kinyanjui, P., Nkinyangi, J, and Orivel, F. 'In-service teacher education in Kenya' in Perraton 1982

Hayhoe, R. 1989 *China's universities and the open door*, Armonk: Sharpe

Held, D., McGrew, A., Goldblatt, D. and Perraton, J. 1999 *Global transformations: politics, economics and culture*, Cambridge: Polity

Helwig, J., Dock, A. and Bosch, A. 1999 'Brief case studies of six IRI initiatives' in Dock and Helwig 1999

Herskovic, S. (ed.) 1995 *The higher education system in Israel: statistical abstract and analysis*, Jerusalem: Council for Higher Education Planning and Budgeting Committee

Hezel, R. T. and Mitchell, J. 2005 'Developing a global e-learning program: From conceptualization to implementation', available at http://www.hezel.com/globalreport (accessed 22 December 2005)

HMSO 1966 *A university of the air* (Cmnd. 2922), London

Hodges, R. and Whitehouse, D. 1983 *Mohammed, Charlemagne and the origins of Europe archaeology and the Pirenne thesis*, London: Duckworth

Hoggart, R. 1978 *An idea and its servants: UNESCO from within*, London: Chatto and Windus

Holmes, D. R., Karmacharya, D. M. and Mayo, J. K. 1993 'Radio education in Nepal' in Perraton 1993

Hope, A. and Dhanarajan, G. 1994 'Adult learning and the self-funding imperative – funding the Open Learning Institute of Hong Kong' in Mugridge 1994

Hornik, R. C. 1988 *Development communication*, New York: Longman

Hülsmann, T. 2000 *The costs of open learning: a handbook*, Oldenburg: BIS, University of Oldenburg

Husen, T., Saha, L. J. and Noonan, R. 1978 *Teacher training and student achievement in less developed countries* (Staff working paper 310), Washington DC: World Bank

Iam Chaya-Ngam 1987 'Distance education in Thailand' in Asian Development Bank 1987

—— 1994 'The funding of open universities: the case of STOU' in Mugridge 1994

ICDL (International Centre for Distance Learning) 1997 *Distance education database* (cd-rom), Milton Keynes

—— 1999 *Distance education database* (online), Milton Keynes, http://www-icdl.open.ac.uk/icdl (accessed various dates 1999)

IGNOU (Indira Gandhi National Open University) 1996 *A profile*, New Delhi

INADES-formation 1996 *Evaluation des activités des Bureaux nationaux et du Siège: exercise 1994–5*, Abidjan

INADES-formation 1997 *Rapport des activités 1996–7*, Abidjan

—— 1998 *Evaluation des activités des Bureaux nationaux et du Siége: exercise 1996–7*, Abidjan

—— 2004 *Rapport de synthése de l'auto évaluation des bureaux nationaux et du Secrétariat général: Exercise 2004*, Abidjan

infoDev 2005 *Knowledge map on information and communication technologies in education: Current projects and practices*, available at http://www.infodev.org/files/1158_file_KnowledgeMap_ICTsEducation_projects.pdf (accessed 22 March 2006)

Inkeles, A. and Smith, D. H. 1974 *Becoming modern: individual change in six developing countries*, London: Heinemann

Insung Jung 1994 'Improving the economics of budget allocation in distance education: a case study of Korea Air and Correspondence University' in Dhanarajan *et al.* 1994

International Extension College 1978 *Seeking the barefoot technologist*, Cambridge

Isaacs, F. 2004 'Africa' in Naidoo and Ramzy 2004

Jamison, D. T. and Lau, L. J. 1982 *Farmer education and farm efficiency*, Baltimore: Johns Hopkins

Jamison, D. T., Klees, S. J. and Wells, S. J. 1978 *The costs of educational media*, Beverly Hills: Sage

Jamison, D. T. and McAnany, E. G. 1978 *Radio for education and development*, Beverly Hills: Sage

Jayatilleke, B. G. 2002 'Asian students: Are they really different?' in H. P. Dikshit, S. Garg, S. Panda, and Vijayashri (ed.) *Access and equity: Challenges for open and distance learning*, New Delhi: Kogan Page

Jayatillike, B. G., Lekamge, G. D. and Weerasinghe, B. 1997 'Survey of student characteristics at the Open University: a comparison with conventional universities in Sri Lanka' *OUSL Journal* 1: 63–82

Jean-Louis, M. 2001 *Canada-Caribbean distance education scholarship programme: evaluation report*, Vancouver: Commonwealth of Learning

Jenkins, J. and Perraton, H. 1982 *Training farmers by correspondence in Cameroon*, Cambridge: International Extension College

Jenkins, J. and Sadiman, A. 2000 'Open schooling at basic level' in Yates and Bradley 2000

Jones, P. W. 1992 *World Bank financing of education*, London: Routledge

Kaur, J. and Lee, Y. L. 2005 'An analysis of frequency of online interaction and learners' achievement in distance education course' in Garg, Panda, Murthy and Mishra 2006

Kay, C. 1989 *Latin American theories of development and underdevelopment*, London: Routledge

Kaye, A. 1976 'The Ivory Coast educational television project' in Arnove 1976

Kim, S. 1992 *Distance education in Korea*, Seoul: Korea Air and Correspondence University

King, K. 1991 *Aid and education in the developing world: the role of donor agencies in educational analysis*, Harlow: Longman

Klees, S. 1995 'Economics of educational technology' in M. Carnoy (ed.) *International encyclopedia of economics of education*, Oxford: Pergamon

Komba, D. A. 2004 'The challenges to achieving relevant, cost-effective and quality distance education provision in Africa: The experience of the Open University of Tanzania' Cape Town conference paper, available at http://www.africaodl.org/conference/odl.htm (accessed 22 March 2006)

Kulandai Swamy, V. C. and Pillai, C. R. 1994 'Indira Gandhi National Open University: a case study' in Mugridge 1994

La Belle, T. J. 1986 *Nonformal education in Latin America: Stability, reform, or revolution*, New York: Praeger

Lakshmi Reddy, M. V. 2002a 'Students' pass rates: a case study of Indira Gandhi National Open University programmes', *Indian journal of open learning* 11 (1): 103–25

—— 2002b 'Development of formulae for studying students' pass rates of programmes of open universities', paper presented at Pan-Commonwealth Forum on Open Learning *Transforming education for development*, Durban: 29 July–2 August

Latchem, C. and Walker, D. (ed.) 2001 *Telecentres: Case studies and key issues*, Vancouver: Commonwealth of Learning

Latchem, C., Abdulla, S. and Ding, X. 1999 'Open and distance learning in Asian universities' *Performance improvement quarterly* 12 (2): 96–118

Laymaman, C. F. 1999 'Malawi College of Distance Education to move to resource-based open learning', paper presented at the Pan-Commonwealth Forum on Open Learning *Empowerment through knowledge and technology* Bandar Seri Begawan, Brunei Darussalam: 1–5 March

Lee, K-W., Futagami, S. and Braithwaite, B. 1982 'The Korean Air-Correspondence High School' in Perraton 1982

Leigh, S. 1995 *Changing times in South Africa: remodeling interactive learning*, Washington DC: Educational Development Center

Levin, H. M. and Lockheed, M. E. (ed.) 1993 *Effective schools in developing countries*, London: Falmer

Lewin, K. M. and Stuart, J. S. 2003 *Researching teacher education: New perspectives on practice, performance and policy (Multi-Site Teacher Education Project Synthesis report)*, London: Department for International Development

Lewis, B. N. 1973 'Educational technology at the Open University: an approach to the problem of quality' *British journal of educational technology* 3 (4): 188–204

Lewis, R. 1990 'Open learning and the misuse of language: a response to Greville Rumble' *Open learning* 5 (1): 3–18

Lockheed, M. E., Middleton, J. and Nettleton, G. S. (ed.) 1991 *Educational technology: sustainable and effective use*, Washington DC: Population and Human Resources Department, World Bank (mimeo)

Lockheed, M. E., and Verspoor, A. 1991 *Improving primary education in developing countries*, Oxford: Oxford University Press

Lyle, J. J. 1967 'The in-service training programme for UNRWA/Unesco teachers' in W. Schramm (ed.) *New educational media in action: case studies for planners*, Vol. 2, Paris: UNESCO/IIEP

McAnany, E. G. 1975 'Radio schools in nonformal education: an evaluation perspective' in T. A. La Belle (ed.) *Educational alternatives in Latin America*, Los Angeles: UCLA Latin America Center Publications, University of California

MacBride, S. *et al.* 1980 *Many voices, one world*, Paris: UNESCO

McKay, V. 2004 'Methods of distance education for training adult educators in South Africa' in M. Singh and V. McKay (ed.) *Enhancing adult basic learning: Training educators and unlocking the potential of distance and open learning*, Hamburg: UNESCO Institute for Education/Pretoria: UNISA Press

MacKenzie, N., Postgate, R. and Scupham, J. (ed.) 1975 *Open learning*, Paris: UNESCO Press

Macmillan, W. M. 1938 *Warning from the West Indies*, Harmondsworth: Penguin

McNamara, K. S. 2003 *Information and Communication Technologies, Poverty and Development: Learning from Experience*, background paper for the *InfoDev Annual Symposium*, Washington DC: World Bank

Mählck, L. and Temu, E. B. 1989 *Distance versus college trained primary school teachers: a case study from Tanzania*, Paris: International Institute for Educational Planning

Makau, B. 1993 'The external degree programme at the University of Nairobi' in Perraton 1993

Mandevu, E. 2006a *Analysis of 2005 junior certificate BOCODOL results*, Gaborone: BOCODOL

—— 2006b *BGCSE 2005 examination summary of results*, Gaborone: BOCODOL

Manjulika, S. and Reddy, V. V. 1996 *Distance education in India: a model for developing countries*, New Delhi: Vikas

Marx, K. and Engels, F. 1955 [1848] *Manifesto of the Communist Party*, Moscow: Foreign Languages Publishing House

Mason, R. 1998 *Globalising education: trends and applications*, London: Routledge

Matthewson, C. and Va'a, R. 1999 'The South Pacific: kakai mei tahi' in Harry 1999

Mays, T. 2005 'Costing distance education and open learning in sub-saharan Africa', *Open learning* 20 (3): 211–25

Melmed, A. S., Ellenbogen, B., Jamison, D. T. and Turniansky, U. 1982 'Everyman University in Israel: the first two years' in Perraton 1982

Mensah, F. J. 2005 *The establishment of the Namibian College of Open Learning: A case study*, available at http://www.col.org/worldreview/vol6_cases/Ch2_CS-Tau.pdf (accessed 10 February 2006)

Ministry of Human Resource Development 1986 *National policy on education: programme of action*, New Delhi: Government of India

—— 1992 *National policy on education: programme of action – revised*, New Delhi: Government of India

Mishra, S. 2004 'India' in Naidoo and Ramzy 2004

Mitchell, B. R. 1988 *British historical statistics*, Cambridge: Cambridge University Press

Mitra, S. 2004 *State open schools in India: a situational analysis*, New Delhi: National Institute of Open Schooling

Mitter, S. and Bastos, M.-I. (ed.) 1999 *Europe and developing countries in the globalised information economy: Employment and distance education*, London: Routledge

Mmari, G. 'The Open University of Tanzania' in Harry 1999

Morgan, D. J. 1980 *Developing British colonial resources 1945–51 (The official history of colonial development: vol. 2)*, London: Macmillan

Moulton, J. 1994 *Interactive radio instruction: broadening the definition*, Washington DC: Educational Development Center

Mugridge, I. (ed.) 1994 *The funding of open universities*, Vancouver: Commonwealth of Learning

—— (ed.) 1997 *Founding the open universities: essays in memory of G. Ram Reddy*, New Delhi: Sterling

Mukhopadhyay, M. 1994 'The unfolding of an open learning institution: the National Open School of India' in Mukhopadhyay and Phillips 1994

—— 1995 'Multichannel learning: the case of the National Open School, India' in S. Anzalone (ed.) *Multichannel learning: connecting all to education*, Washington DC: Education Development Center

Mukhopadhyay, M. and Phillips, S. (ed.) 1994 *Open learning: selected experiences*, Vancouver: Commonwealth of Learning

Murphy, D. and Fung, Y. 1999 'The Open University of Hong Kong' in Harry 1999

Murphy, P. 1992 'Costs of an alternative form of secondary-level education in Malawi' *Comparative education review* 37 (2): 107–22

—— 1993 'Effectiveness of full-time second-level distance teaching in three African countries' in Murphy and Zhiri 1992

Murphy, P., Anzalone, S., Bosch, A. and Moulton, J. 2002 *Enhancing learning opportunities in Africa: Distance education and information and communication technologies for education*, Washington DC: Africa Region, World Bank

Murphy, P. and Zhiri, A. (ed.) 1992 *Distance education in anglophone Africa: experience with secondary education and teacher training*, Washington DC: World Bank

Mwangi, A. P. 2000 'Kenya: The African Medical Research Foundation distance education project' in Siaciwena 2000

Naidoo, V. 2004 'Introduction' in Naidoo and Ramzy 2004

Naidoo, V. and Ramzy, H. (ed.) 2004 *Emerging trends in the development of school networking initiatives*, Vancouver: Commonwealth of Learning

Naidu, C. G. 1994 'Some economic aspects of conventional and distance education systems in India' in Dhanarajan *et al.* 1994

—— 2001 *Student costs in distance education: IGNOU*, New Delhi: Planning and Development Division, IGNOU

—— 2005 *Funding and management: a case study of Indira Gandhi National Open University*, available at http://www.col.org/worldreview/vol6_cases/Ch8_CS-Naidu.pdf (accessed 27 January 2006)

NAMCOL (Namibia College of Open Learning) 2005 *Statistical digest 2004*, Windhoek

National Open School 1999 *Profile 1999*, New Delhi

—— 2002 *E-learning – The NOS initiative*, New Delhi

National Steering Committee 1996 *Inservice education of primary teachers: national action plan of India*, New Delhi: Ministry of Human Resource Development

NCHE (National Commission on Higher Education) 1996 *A framework for transformation*, n.p.

Nduba, N. 1996 'AMREF distance education programme' in University of London course reader, MA in distance education, course 2, unit 6, reading 5

Neave, G. and van Vught, F. 1994 'Government and higher education in developing nations: a conceptual framework' in G. Neave and F. A. van Vught (ed.) *Government and higher education relationships across three continents: the winds of change*, Oxford: Elsevier

Nettleton, G. 1991 'Uses and costs of educational technology for distance education in developing countries: a review of the recent literature' in Lockheed, Middleton and Nettleton 1991

Nielsen, H. D. and Tatto, M. T. 1993 'Teacher upgrading in Sri Lanka and Indonesia' in Perraton 1993

NIME (National Institute of Multimedia Education) 1993 *Distance education in Asia and the Pacific: country papers*, Chiba

NIOS (National Institute of Open Schooling) 2004 *National Institute of Open Schooling at a glance*, available at http://www.nios.ac.in/glance.pdf (accessed 27 January 2006)

Nyerere, J. K. 1973 *Freedom and development*, Dar es Salaam: Oxford University Press

OBHE (Observatory on Borderless Higher Education) 2005 'Connecting "believers" or expanding awareness?' *Breaking news article*, 9 December, available at http://www.obhe.ac.uk (accessed 17 May 2006)

Odumbe, J. 1988 'The establishment and the development of the external degree programmes of the University of Nairobi' in D. Sewart and J. S. Daniel (ed.) *Developing distance education*, Oslo: International Council for Distance Education

OECD 1996 *Internationalisation of higher education*, Paris

—— 2000 *OECD Economic outlook* 67 (preliminary edition), available at http://www.oecd.org/eco/out/eo.htm (accessed 31 May 2000)

Oestmann, S. and Dymond, A. C. 2001 'Telecentres – experiences, lessons and trends' in Latchem and Walker 2001

O'Farrell, C. 1999 *Information and communication technologies for sustainable livelihoods: preliminary study April–November 1999*, available at http://www.rdg.ac.uk/AcaDepts/ea/AERDD/Csds.htm (accessed 20 August 2001)

Oliveira, J. B. 2006 'A-Plus Teacher Education Programme, Brazil' in Perraton, Robinson and Creed 2006

Oliveira, J. B. and Orivel, F. 1982a 'The Minerva project in Brazil' in Perraton 1982

—— 1982b 'A Madureza project in Brazil' in Perraton 1982

Oliveira, J. B., Castro, C. de M. and Verdisco, M. 2003 'Education by television' in Bradley 2003

Olsen, A. 2002 *e-Learning in Asia: supply and demand*, London: Observatory on Borderless Higher Education

Olsson, M. 1994 *Institutionalizing radio science in Papua New Guinea: a response to teacher demand for interactive radio instruction*, Washington DC: Education Development Center

Orivel, F. 1983 'The impact of agricultural extension services: a review of the literature' in Perraton *et al.* 1983

—— 2000 'Finance, costs and economics' in Yates and Bradley 2000

Overseas Development Administration 1984 *British aid to education in developing countries*, London: HMSO

—— 1990 *Into the nineties: an education policy for British aid*, London

Oxenham, J. 2004 *The quality of programmes and policies regarding literacy and skills development* (Background paper for 2005 EFA Monitoring Report), Paris: UNESCO

Paine, T. 1906 [1791] *The rights of man*, London: Dent

Panda, S. 1999 'Developments, networking and convergence in India' in Harry 1999

—— 2005 'Higher education and national development: Reflections on the Indian experience' *Distance education* 26 (2): 205–25

Panda, S. and Garg, S. 2003 'Distance learning in India with open schools' in Bradley 2003

Panda, S., Khan, A. and Garg, S. 1999 'Growth and development of the National Open University', in S. Panda (ed.) *Open and distance education: Policies, practices and quality concerns*, New Delhi: Aravali

Perraton, H. (ed.) 1982 *Alternative routes to formal education: distance teaching for school equivalency*, Baltimore: Johns Hopkins University Press

—— 1983a 'Mass media, basic education and agricultural extension' in Perraton *et al.* 1983

—— 1983b *The National Correspondence College of Zambia and its costs*, (mimeo) Cambridge: International Extension College

—— 1984 *Costs and effects of mass media for adult basic education: a study in comparative evaluation*, (Unpublished University of London PhD thesis)

—— 1987 'The costs of distance education' (mimeo) (Background paper for Briggs group) London: Commonwealth Secretariat

—— (ed.) 1993 *Distance education for teacher training*, London: Routledge

—— 1997 *International research in open and distance learning: report of a feasibility study*, Cambridge: International Research Foundation for Open Learning

—— 2004a 'Aims and purpose' in Perraton and Lentell 2004

—— 2004b 'Resources' in Perraton and Lentell 2004

Perraton, H. and Lentell, H. (ed.) 2004 *Policy for open and distance learning*, London: Routledge

Perraton, H. and Naidu, C. G. (ed.) 2006 'Counting the cost' in A. Hope and P. Guiton *Strategies for sustainable open and distance learning*, London: Routledge

Perraton, H., Creed, C. and Robinson, B. 2002 *Teacher education guidelines: using open and distance learning*, Paris: UNESCO

Perraton, H., Robinson, B. and Creed 2001 *Teacher education through distance learning: technology, curriculum, evaluation, cost*, Paris: UNESCO

—— (ed.) 2006 *International case studies of teacher education at a distance*, Oldenburg: BIS, University of Oldenburg

Perraton, H. *et al.* (ed.) 1983 *Basic education and agricultural extension: costs effects and alternatives* (World Bank Staff Working Paper 564), Washington DC: World Bank

Perry, W. 1997 'The Indira Gandhi National Open University' in Mugridge 1997

Pirsig, R. M. 1991 *Lila: an inquiry into morals*, London: Black Swan

Planning Commission 1992 *Eighth Five Year Plan*, New Delhi: Government of India

—— 2002 *Tenth Five Year Plan*, New Delhi: Government of India

Potashnik, M. 1996 'Chile's learning network' *Education and technology technical notes series* 1 (2)

Potter, C. 2006 'Interactive radio for supporting teachers of English as a second language, OLSET, South Africa' in Perraton, Robinson, and Creed 2006

Potter, C. and Naidoo, G. 2006 'Using interactive radio to enhance classroom learning and reach schools, classrooms, teachers and learners' *Distance education* 27 (1): 63–86

Qiang, Z.-W. and Pitt, A. 2004 *Contribution of information and communication technologies to growth* (World Bank Working Paper 24), Washington DC: World Bank

Radio Learning Project (n.d.) *Interactive radio instruction* Newton, MA: Agency for International Development/Education Development Center

Ramirez, F. O. 1997 'The nation-state, citizenship, and educational change: institutionalization and globalization' in W. K. Cummings and N. F. McGinn (ed.) *International handbook of education and development: preparing schools, students and nations for the twenty-first century*, Oxford: Pergamon

Ramirez, H. 1994 'Programs and drop-out in Universidad Estatal a Distancia (UNED) of Costa Rica' *American journal of distance education* 8 (3): 64–73

Raza, R. 2004 *Using distance education for skills development (Report to Department for International Development)*, Cambridge: International Research Foundation for Open Learning

Reddy, R. 1997 'Andhra Pradesh Open University' in Mugridge 1997

Reddy, V. 2002 'Graduates of Indira Gandhi National Open University: How are they placed?' available at http://www.col.org.pcf2/papers/reddy_v.pdf (accessed 12 January 2006)

Renwick, W., Shale, D. and Rao, C. 1992 *Distance education at the University of the West Indies*, Vancouver: Commonwealth of Learning

Robinson, B. 1993 'The Primary Teachers' Orientation Course, Allama Iqbal Open University' in Perraton 1993

—— 1997 'Distance education for primary teacher training in developing countries' in J. Lynch, C. Modgil and S. Modgil (ed.) *Education and development: tradition and innovation* volume 3 *Innovations in delivering primary education*, London: Cassell Educational Press

Rogers, E. M. with Shoemaker, F. F. 1971 *Communication of innovations*, New York: Free Press

Romain, R. I. and Armstrong, L. 1987 *Review of World Bank operations in non-formal education and training*, Washington DC: Education and Training Department, World Bank

Romiszowski, A. 2004 *A study of distance education public policy and practice in the higher education sectors of selected countries* (Background paper for CHE distance higher education study), available at http://www.che.ac.za/documents/d000070/Background_Paper1_Romiszowski.pdf (accessed 12 January 2006)

Rose, J. B. 1999 'Multipurpose Community Telecentres in support of people-centred development', in R. W'O. Okot-Uma *et al.* (ed.) *Information technology and globalisation: implications for people-centred development*, London: SFI Publishing

Rumajogee, A. R. 2003 'Le statut de l'enseignement à distance et l'apprentissage libre dans les pays francophones de l'Afrique subsaharienne', in C. Chaillot (ed.) *L'usage des réseaux pour l'éducation en Afrique*, Paris: RESAFAD-TICE

Rumble, G 1981 'The cost analysis of distance teaching. Costa Rica's Universidad Estatal a Distancia' *Higher Education* 10: 375–401

—— 1989 '"Open learning", "distance learning", and the misuse of language' *Open learning* 4 (2): 28–36

—— 1997 *The costs and economics of open and distance learning*, London: Kogan Page

—— 1999 'The Bangladesh Open University: mission and promise' in Harry 1999

—— 2001 'The costs and costing of networked learning' *Journal of asynchronous learning networks* 5 (2): 75–96

Rumble, G. and Harry, K. (ed.) 1982 *The distance teaching universities*, London: Croom Helm

Rumble, G. and Keegan, D. 1982 'The DTUs: an appraisal' in Rumble and Harry 1982

Russell, T. and McPherson, S. 2001 'Indicators of success in teacher education: a review and analysis of recent research', paper presented to Pan-Canadian Education Research Agenda Symposium on *Teacher Education/Educator Training*, Québec: Université Laval, 22–23 May

Sadiman, A. S. 1994 'The Indonesian Open Junior Secondary Schools' in Mukhopadhyay and Phillips 1994

—— 1995 'SMP Terbuka – the Indonesian Open Junior Secondary Schools: its future prospects' in National Open School 1995 *Planning and management of open schooling: report of the international study visit-cum-conference*, New Delhi

Sadiman, A. S. and Rahardjo, R. 1997 'Contribution of SMP Terbuka toward lifelong learning in Indonesia', in M. J. Hatton (ed.) *Lifelong learning: policies, practices and programs*, Toronto: School of Media Studies, Humber College

Sadiman, A. S. *et al.* 1995 *SMP Terbuka the Open Junior Secondary School: an Indonesian case study*, Paris: UNESCO

Sahoo, P. K. 2000 'Professional education for teachers through distance education', in N. K. Dash and S. B. Menon (ed.) *Training of professionals through distance education in south Asia*, New Delhi: School of Education, IGNOU

SAIDE (South African Institute for Distance Education) 1995 *Open learning and distance education in South Africa: report of an international commission, January–April 1994*, Manzini: Macmillan

Saint, W. 1999 *Tertiary distance education and technology in sub-saharan Africa*, Washington DC: ADEA Working group on higher education, World Bank

Sargant, N. *et al.* 1989 *An evaluation of Allama Iqbal Open University*, n.p. (?London: Overseas Development Administration)

Schiefelbein, E. and Simmons, J. 1981 *Determinants of school achievement: a review of research for developing countries*, Ottawa: IDRC

Schramm, W. 1977 *Big media, little media: tools and technologies for instruction*, Beverly Hills: Sage

Secretary for Education 1996 *Annual report for year ended 31 December 1994*, Harare: Government Printer

Secretary for Education and Culture 1994 *Annual report for year ended 31 December 1992*, Harare: Government Printer

Setijadi 1987 'Distance education in Indonesia' in Asian Development Bank 1987

Sewart, D. (ed.) 1995 *One world many voices: quality in open and distance learning*, (Conference proceedings, International Council for Distance Education) Oslo: ICDE and Milton Keynes: Open University

Shale, D. and Gomes, J. 1998 'Performance indicators and university distance education providers' *Journal of distance education* 13 (1): 1–20

Sharma, A. K. and Singh, S. 1996 'Computers in education: the Indian context', in T. Plomp, R. E. Anderson and G. Kontogiannopoulou-Polydorides (ed.) *Cross national policies and practices on computers in education*, Dordrecht: Kluwer

Sharma, R. C. 2005 'Open learning in India: evolution, diversification and reaching out' *Open learning* 20 (3): 227–41

Shukla, A. 1992 'Literacy through distance education: towards an educational criterion', in Asian Association of Open Universities Conference Proceedings *The role of open universities in promoting education for all*, Seoul: Korea Air and Correspondence University

Siaciwena, R. 1994 'Zambian open secondary classes' in Mukhopadhyay and Phillips 1994

—— 1996 'The management of student support services in a dual-mode university' *Open praxis* 2: 13–15

—— (ed.) 2000 *Case studies of non-formal education by distance and open learning*, Vancouver: Commonwealth of Learning

Sibalwa, D. M. 2000 'Zambia: The radio farm forum' in Siaciwena 2000

Skilbeck, M. 2000 *Global synthesis: Education for all 2000 assessment*, Paris: UNESCO

Smith, K. n.d. *Development in distance education in Asia*, n.p.: UNESCO/International Council for Distance Education

Stenhouse, L. 1975 *An introduction to curriculum research and development*, London: Heinemann

Stone, L. 1983 'Social control and intellectual excellence', in N. Phillipson (ed.) *University, society and the future*, Edinburgh: Edinburgh University Press

Stuart, J. S. and Kunje, D. 2000 *The Malawi Integrated In-service Teacher Education programme*, Brighton: Centre for International Education, University of Sussex

Sujatha, K. 2002 *Distance education at secondary level in India*, Paris: UNESCO/IIEP

Swift, D. 1997 'The Open Learning Institute of Hong Kong' in Mugridge 1997

Tate, O. 1991 *Distance education in Zambia*, Vancouver: Commonwealth of Learning

Tau, D. T. 2005 *A case study of the Botswana College of Distance and Open Learning*, available at http://www.col.org/worldreview/vol6_cases/Ch2_CS-Tau.pdf (accessed 10 February 2006)

Tawney, R. H. 1964 [1931] *Equality*, London: Allen and Unwin

Tenambergen, E., Schwartz, R. A. and Guild, S. 1997 *Evaluation of the Kenya continuing education programme SIDA supported project*, Nairobi: Development Solutions for Africa

Tilson, T. 1991 'Sustainability in four interactive radio projects: Bolivia, Honduras, Lesotho and Papua New Guinea' in Lockheed *et al.* 1991

Torres, R. M. 1996 'Without the reform of teacher education there will be no reform of education' *Prospects* 26 (3): 447–67

UNESCO 1977 *The economics of new educational media (vol. 1): Present state of research and trends*, Paris

—— 1980 *The economics of new educational media (vol. 2): Cost and effectiveness*, Paris

—— 1982 *The economics of new educational media (vol. 3): Overview and synthesis*, Paris

—— 1991 *World education report*, Paris

—— 1993 *World education report*, Paris

—— 1994 *Statistical yearbook*, Paris

—— 1995 *World education report*, Paris

—— 1997 *Open and distance learning: prospects and policy considerations*, Paris

—— 1998 *World education report*, Paris

—— 2000 *World education report*, Paris

—— 2002a *Education for all: is the world on track (EFA Global monitoring report 2002)*, Paris

—— 2002b *Open and distance learning: Trends, policy and strategy considerations*, Paris

—— 2002c *Information and communication technologies in teacher education: A planning guide*, Paris

—— 2002d *Information and communication technologies in teacher education: A curriculum for schools and programme of teacher development*, Paris

—— 2004 *Education for all: The quality imperative (EFA Global monitoring report 2005)*, Paris

—— 2005 *Education for all: Literacy for life (EFA Global monitoring report 2006)*, Paris

UNESCO IITE (Institute for Information Technologies in Education) 2000 *Distance education for the information society: Policy, pedagogy and professional development*, Moscow

UNESCO Institute for Statistics 2005 *Global education digest*, Montreal

UNESCO/OECD 2005 *Guidelines for Quality Provision in Cross-border Higher Education*, available at http://www.oecd.org/dataoecd/27/51/35779480.pdf (accessed 9 May 2006)

USAID 1998 website available at http://www.info.usaid.gov/educ_training/link.htm (accessed 10 November 1998)

—— 2006 'IT *in schools' brings the information age to Egyptian schools*, available at www.usaid-eg.org/detail.asp?id=295 (accessed 26 February 2006)

Valérien, J., Guidon, J., Wallet, J. and Brunswic, E. 2003 *Enseignement à distance et apprentissage libre en Afrique subsaharienne: Etat des lieux dans les pays francophones fin 2001*, Reduit, Mauritius: Tertiary Education Commission

Villegas-Reimers, E. and Reimers, F. 1996 'Where are the 60 million teachers?' *Prospects* 26 (3): 469–93

Warr, D. 1992 *Distance teaching in the village*, Cambridge: International Extension College

Wei Runfang 1997 *China's radio and TV universities and the British OU, a comparative perspective*, Hagen: ZIFF

Weixiang Ma and Hawkridge, D. 1995 'China's changing policy and practice in television education, 1978–93' *International journal of educational development* 15 (1): 27–36

Wells, H. G. 1934 *Experiment in autobiography*, London: Gollancz and Cresset

Wichit Srisa-an and Tong-In Wangsotorn 1985 'The management and economics of distance education: the case of Sukhothai Thammathirat Open University Thailand', paper presented at International Council for Distance Education World Conference, Melbourne, 13–20 August

Wijeyesekara, D. 1994 'Funding of open universities: the Sri Lankan context' in Mugridge 1994

Wilson, D. N. 1991 'A comparison of open universities in Thailand and Indonesia' in Lockheed, Middleton and Nettleton 1991

Wolff, L. and Futagami, S. 1982 'The Malawi Correspondence College' in Perraton 1982

Wolff, L., Castro, C. de M., Navarro, J. C. and Garcia, N. 2002 'Television for secondary education: experience of Mexico and Brazil', in W. D. Haddad and A. Draxler *Technologies for education: Potentials, parameters and prospects*, Paris: UNESCO/Washington DC: AED

Woods, B. 1993 *Communication, technology and the development of people*, London: Routledge

World Bank 1974 *Education sector working paper*, Washington DC

—— 1980 *Education sector policy paper*, Washington DC

—— 1995 *Priorities and strategies for education: a World Bank review*, Washington DC

—— 1998 *World development report: knowledge for development*, New York: Oxford University Press

—— 1999 *Education sector strategy*, Washington DC

—— 2001 *A chance to learn: Knowledge and finance for education in sub-saharan Africa*, Washington DC

—— 2002 *Constructing knowledge societies*, Washington DC

Wrightson, T. 1997 'Northern Integrated Teacher Education Project: a case study', paper presented at the World Bank colloquium *Distance education for teacher development* Toronto: 22–5 June

—— 1998 *Distance education in action: The Northern Integrated Teacher Education Project in Uganda*, Cambridge: International Extension College

Yates, C. and Bradley, J. (ed.) 2000 *Basic education at a distance*, London: Routledge

Young, M. 1962 'Is your child in the unlucky generation?' *Where* 10, 3–4

Young, M., Perraton, H., Jenkins, J. and Dodds, T. 1980 *Distance teaching for the third world: the lion and the clockwork mouse*, London: Routledge

Zaki, W. M. 1997 'Allama Iqbal Open University' in Mugridge 1997

Zeichner, K. M. 1983 'Alternative paradigms of teacher education' *Journal of teacher education* 34 (3): 3–9

Zhang, W. Y. and Niu, J 2006 'Reaching teachers through television, China' in Perraton, Robinson, and Creed 2006

Zimbabwe Central Statistical Office 1993 *Education report, March 1993*, Harare

Index